Johann Emanuel Veith

The lords prayer

Johann Emanuel Veith

The lords prayer

ISBN/EAN: 9783741190193

Manufactured in Europe, USA, Canada, Australia, Japa

Cover: Foto ©Lupo / pixelio.de

Manufactured and distributed by brebook publishing software (www.brebook.com)

Johann Emanuel Veith

The lords prayer

CONTENTS.

CHAP.
- I. Introductory
- II. Our Father who art
- III. Our Father
- IV. Our Father who art in heaven
- V. Hallowed be Thy Name
- VI. Thy kingdom come
- VII. Thy kingdom come; Thy will be done
- VIII. Thy will be done on earth as it is in heaven
- IX. Give us this day our daily bread
- X. Give us this day our daily supersubstantial bread
- XI. And forgive us our trespasses
- XII. As we forgive them that trespass against us
- XIII. And lead us not into temptation
- XIV. And lead us not into temptation; but deliver us from evil
- XV. But deliver us from evil
- XVI. But deliver us from evil
- XVII. But deliver us from evil
- XVIII. Amen
- Ave Maria

Chapter I.

Introductory.

A SKILFUL teacher, well exercised in every beautiful and useful art, has come from distant lands to display his works; and as in his hands all is done rapidly and beautifully, there are not wanting learners, who, after they have for a long time in wonder gazed, approach near, and say, 'Master, receive us into thy school; for behold, we too, for many years past, have engaged ourselves, and have laboured in things like these, but we produce nothing. With little toil thou dost produce great and noble things, and as in play thou dost bring them to perfection. Teach us, therefore, the right means, point out to us the method and way by which we should begin.'

Thus must have thought that disciple who once drew near to the Lord and Teacher of mankind, and said, "Lord, teach us how to pray. (Luke xi.) We for thousands of years have in many ways endeavoured to pray, with words and gestures, with hymns and songs, with sacrifices and dances, with joy and with self-invented sufferings; and yet all our prayer has, for the greater part, been a fruitless labour, and without profit. Thou alone canst truly teach us how to pray; from Thee alone do we expect the right teaching." What was the occasion of this great and important petition? The disciple had seen his Master whilst in prayer in distant solitude, and his spirit had been raised to high astonishment. What could he have seen that could have awakened so pleasing a wonder within him? How did he recognise in his Master the master also of prayer? What a view was that, full of enrapturing power, which called forth from his heart so wise and so pure a desire, which drew from him that suppliant petition, "Lord, teach us how to pray!"

In the history of Christian antiquity, it is told how once the blessed Francis, named the Seraphic, was upon Mount Alverno, and how his disciple Leo, the only one who dared to intrude upon his solitude, saw him standing before his cell during the moon-bright night with his eyes turned towards the heavens, and heard him frequently repeating these words: 'Who art Thou, O Lord, my God; and who am I, Thy needy and lowly servant!' And when Leo had for a long time gazed, it appeared to him as if he saw a flaming light descending upon Francis, towards which the holy man thrice raised his hand. Fixed with astonishment, the disciple stood, and, as if afraid of further intrusion, wished to retire in silence; when Francis called to him, and said, 'Leo, what dost thou wish? dost thou come to listen to me?' He then approached nearer, praying for an explanation of the things which he had seen: Francis shewed himself willing to grant his prayer. 'When,' said he, 'thou didst hear me exclaim, 'Who art Thou, O Lord, and who am I!' I found myself surrounded with light ineffable, in which I beheld the fathomless depth of the goodness of God, and of my own poverty. Therefore did I exclaim, 'Who art Thou, O Lord, the most wise, that in Thy power and in Thy mercy Thou shouldst visit me, a creature of this earth, without strength and without power!' Then there spoke to me a voice, which commanded me to make an offering to the Lord. And I answered, 'Lord, I am wholly Thine; I possess nothing but this habit, and the cord by which it is girded; even these are Thine: what, then, have I to give Thee? The heavens and the earth, fire and water, all things are Thine.' The voice then repeated, 'Put thy hand into thy bosom, and what thou shalt find there bring forth.' I found there a golden coin of inexpressible splendour; this I raised in my hand and offered. This was repeated three times. I understood that these three pieces of gold which were shewn to me emblemed humility, poverty, and purity of heart, which the Lord had given to me to preserve, that His holy name might be honoured.'

'Who art Thou, O Lord, and who am I!' These

were the words which the blessed Francis daily addressed to God,—the breathings, the pulsations of this thinking, seeking, loving soul. For what is prayer but the sighing and longing of the created to the uncreated Being, in whom alone man can find his aim, his peace, and his glory, in whom alone he can find himself! In prayer such as this Francis lived and breathed; in this holy desire his whole life was glorified, for he had dedicated himself to humility, to poverty, and to purity, which virtues he most carefully guarded; and to whom shall it appear extraordinary or strange that these virtues were figured to him under the emblems of splendid pieces of gold? for in the kingdom of the world gold is considered the most precious of metals, and is taken in exchange for every earthly possession; and in the same manner an incomparably higher value is attributed to these virtues in the kingdom of grace. The humility of the mind of man, a clear and willing acknowledgment of his dependence, insures and preserves for him an intercourse with the Divine power and dignity; purity of heart opens to him the fulness of light and of truth; poverty of spirit, or an elevation above the seeming goods of life, makes him capable of possessing a heavenly and eternal kingdom. And thus was Francis little and great, hidden and yet noble, needy and yet abounding.

But what is the servant when compared with his lord, and what is the disciple when compared with his Master, the only one to whom this name properly belongs? "You call Me," said He to His disciples, "Lord and Master; and you do well, for so I am." He was a heavenly model, and the Mediator between God and men ; and whilst full of love towards them, He walked amongst men, to heal them, to teach them, and to form them; still was His intercourse most intimate and uninterrupted with God, whom even as man He called His Father, to whom, in every moment of time, He offered His whole being; that in humility the most profound, in entire poverty, and in continued self-denial, He might perfect the great work of redemption. Although His life upon earth was, in this manner, an uninterrupted prayer, still did He learn to retire into the calmness of solitude, on the summits of mountains, to commune with His heavenly Father; and if any thing extraordinary was observed in Francis during the moments of his prayer, what must we think of Him who united in Himself an earthly and a celestial, a divine and human existence! It may, then, be easily understood why the disciple approached to Him with this earnest petition : " Lord, teach us how to pray." Had he not seen Him perform many other acts far more splendid, and which might appear more worthy of imitation? Why did he not say, " Teach us to rule the elements, teach us to heal the sick and the infirm, teach us to walk upon the waves of the sea?" Probably because he well knew that of all employments and operations which have been assigned to mortal men, there was none more exalted and dignified, none more necessary and more precious, than the exercise of prayer. 'Who will not stand astonished,' exclaims St. John Chrysostom; 'who will not admire the mild condescension of God, who permits us, even commands us, to speak to Him, and to lay open our desires before Him! He who does not seek, who does not love this discourse with God, is void of true life and of sound understanding. This is the most evident proof of a want of understanding, that man will not acknowledge the greatness of this honour, and that the neglect of prayer is the death of the soul.'

What does this golden-mouthed orator understand by true life? Certainly that intercourse of the created spirit with its Creator; for from the commerce of love all its beatitude flows. And what understanding is that which he calls 'sound?' That knowledge which the created spirit has acquired of its finitude and dependence, in which alone it can find the holy perfection of its being. But to the sacred orator there are opposed foolish men, who will not convince themselves of the high dignity and signification of prayer; and who place in this very fact the proof which they deem the most evident of their superior understanding. Of the objections and attacks with which they assail this ancient truth, which is grounded in the very soul of man, who is ignorant? 'The eternal Father,' they say, 'is not like to the great ones of this earth, of whom the proverb tells, that we must pray to them. He does not, like to them, stand in need of our petitions and narrations, by which we, senselessly enough, would assist His omniscience, as with a *Pro memoria*.'

Do not these objections seem full of strength? So let it be. Little as the Lord of the universe may be compared with the lords of the earth, He is still not only a great Lord, but a Lord to whom we must pray. Thus, at least, His apostle teaches: " Pray without ceasing; for this is the will of God in you all." (1 Thess. v.) But if human logic would persuade us that the omniscient God has no need of our narrations, the Word itself has also declared it: "When you pray, speak not much, as the heathens (who, on account of the number of their deities, ascribed to them only limited powers); for your Father knoweth what is needful for you before you ask Him." (Matt. vi. 7, 8.) Why, then, does he command us to pray, to seek, and to knock? Only, as St. Augustine teaches, that the desire of our mind, our spiritual life, which is a loving conversion to God, may be exercised and increased, and that we, by this exercise, may become more capable of those rich gifts which His benevolent infinite love has prepared for us.

Many are the forms and degrees of poverty upon this earth, but none perhaps was ever more extraordinary than that of a simple peasant in an Austrian Alpine region. This man having abandoned house and home, wandered amongst the mountains without shoes, almost without covering, and without care for himself. An ecclesiastic, who was engaged in giving catechetical instructions in these remote valleys, and whom this poor man accompanied on his journeyings, wished to make him a small present. This the indigent man declined. The priest doubled the gift, and endeavoured to compel him to accept it. 'Take this little,' he said, 'that you may procure for yourself what is necessary to cover you.' The simple man steadfastly refused, and gave as his reason, 'I can receive nothing, for I have no pocket!'[1] Was not this man poorer than poverty itself? To be deprived of every thing, and to be able to receive nothing, as he was deprived of the capability of receiving, whether this latter want

[1] This happened to the author of this work in the year 1825.

be in the ordinary signification—the want of a purse or pocket, or in the more abstract sense—capacity, is not this poverty complete?

But that which this honest peasant declared in his simplicity is not of so rare occurrence as it might, at first sight, seem. 'Great, exceedingly great,' says St. Augustine, 'is that which God would give us; but our heart is too narrow, too small for His gift.' The fulness of the goodness of God never fails; but the readiness, the capability of receiving it are often wanting. And if the inspired singer of the Psalms confess before the Lord, "I have run in the way of Thy commandments, because Thou hast enlarged my heart," the tepid and the negligent man must say, 'I have gone back in the way of Thy commandments, because my heart is narrowed, and hath no space for Thy graces.' The interior of his spirit is neglected; and the greater is his poverty, the more difficult is the remedy. The assistance of Him from whom every good gift cometh is ever ready; but the son of earth, who shuns the light and prayer, has no will to receive it, and either courteously or uncourteously declines it, in however kindly terms it may be proffered. How, then, can he think of imploring the invisible Giver for invisible gifts? And, in truth, as these spiritual gifts must be unknown, and consequently of no worth to man estranged from God, prayer for him can be no easy task; and as a sick man (to use the words of Origen) does not ask for things that are conducive to his health, but for those to which a diseased desire inclines him, so we, in the constantly occurring infirmities of this life, frequently pray for things that are not useful to us.

Wise, therefore, was the desire of that disciple who approached his Master with that ardent supplication, "Lord, teach us how to pray." Teach us to seek after light and life, that we may be able to receive the gifts of light and life; teach us, who are alone and abandoned, and who feel nought in ourselves save darkness and self-seeking,—teach us to sigh to Him who alone can beatify us; as it is written, "I have opened my mouth, and have drawn the breath *of life*, because I have desired Thy commandments." (Psalm cxviii.)

And how fully was this petition heard! To it we are indebted for that simple, exalted, celestial form of prayer, which, as it was given by the Lord, has been named the LORD'S PRAYER; and which, in the power of its effects, in the fulness of its contents, in the brevity and clearness of its expression, proves the divinity of its origin. For if we consider this prayer in its power, it displays to us the high dignity of Him who gave it. 'Let us pray,' says St. Cyprian, 'as the Divine Master has taught us, that, when we pray, the Father may hear again the words of the Son. For if we have received the promise that we shall receive all things whatsoever we ask in His name, how much more powerful will our supplication be, when we ask not only in His name, but with His words!' If we meditate upon it in the fulness of its contents, we shall find that it comprehends, without exception, all those things of which we can be worthy, and for which we should dare to pray. Yes, as St. Augustine shews, if we examine all the prayers which are scattered through the books of the sacred Scripture, we should find no more than is contained in the words of the Lord's Prayer.

When, for example, Solomon prays, "Grant, O Lord, that Thou mayst be honoured;" and when the Psalmist sings, "Blessed be the name of the Lord," what more is expressed than the petition, "Hallowed be Thy name?" When we read in the Psalm, "Shew us, O Lord, Thy face, and we shall be blessed," what do these words declare more than the second petition, "Thy kingdom come?" Again, when it is said in the Psalms, "Direct, O Lord, my steps according to the words of Thy truth; teach me to do Thy will," what is said more than "Thy will be done on earth, as it is in heaven?" When we find amongst the Proverbs, "Send me neither poverty nor riches, but grant what is sufficient for my life," is this different from the petition, "Give us this day our daily bread?" When the divine Psalmist exclaims, "O Lord, remember David, and all his meekness;" and again, "If I repay evil with evil, may I become a shame before my enemies," what signification do these words contain? The same that is expressed by the fifth petition, "Forgive us our trespasses, as we forgive them that trespass against us." When the son of Sirach prays, "Take from me the desire of sensuality, and deliver me not to the spirit of insolence and licentiousness," he says as much as, "Lead us not into temptation." And when, finally, it is said in the Psalms, "Save me, O Lord, from evil men, from the wicked and perverse deliver me," the prayer is similar to the last petition, "Deliver us from evil."

With justice, therefore, did St. Cyprian call the Lord's Prayer the Gospel abridged. And if we further consider how, by the vast riches of its contents, by its

connexion, and by its clearness, it accommodates itself
to all times and to all persons; how it is clear and
comprehensible to the unlearned, and yet contains an
inexhaustible source of thought and meditation for the
learned; and lastly, how by its simplicity, like to the
clear blue of the heavens, it contains within itself an immeasurable depth, and embraces all the regions of the
doctrines of faith and of moral truth: it is sufficiently
evident that this prayer, to be fully understood in all
its relations, requires meditation the most mature, which
is the more necessary, as it declares and regulates the
highest duties of human life.

But as the thinking and inquiring spirit seeks to
enter into its every and inmost depths, in order that
it may comprehend the whole in its parts, and these in
their unity, so does it endeavour to gain the image and
view of the whole. When the traveller has gained an
eminence, from which the splendours of a royal city
or a beautiful country are spread before his eyes, he
will desire immediately to continue his journey; but
before he enters the streets of that city, or passes
through the vales of that lovely champaign, he will
tarry for a time to gaze upon the whole, thereby to
regulate his view. The Lord's Prayer, considered from
the right point of believing and docile love, presents
to us a wide and beautiful region of thought, which extends itself into immeasurable space. Here are heights
pointing to the heavens, and veiled in part with clouds:
"Our Father, who art in heaven." Here are seen
strong and splendid castles and pinnacles: "Thy kingdom come." Here vineyards and cornfields flourish
and bloom: "Give us this day our daily bread." Here

labyrinths and furious whirlpools threaten: "Lead us not into temptation." Here dark gulfs and abysses open beneath us: "Deliver us from evil."

But if we look upon the whole, a beautiful and symmetrical order presents itself; for after we have raised the eyes of our spirit upwards to the Father of lights, from whom alone every good gift cometh, we confess before all other things, that we prefer His honour and glory to every thing else, and even to ourselves, in the unconditional petition, "Hallowed be Thy name," in which the following petitions are contained, as means to an end. For that God may be glorified in His external revelations, we pray, first, for those goods by which the above-named principal object may be obtained; and we pray that those evils may be averted which are opposed to this end. These goods are threefold, and in order and dignity they are heavenly, spiritual, and temporal. For the heavenly, the most exalted, we should pray without conditions, "Thy kingdom come;" for the spiritual, or the gifts of grace, we should pray relatively, as for gifts which conduct to the heavenly, "Thy will be done on earth as it is in heaven;" for the temporal, in a manner much more confined, inasmuch as they may be not prejudicial, but conducive to our spiritual welfare, "Give us this day our daily bread."

Opposed in hostile array to these goods is a like number of evils, for the averting of which we earnestly pray. The first and principal petition is indeed without a contrary; for the glory, the sanctity, and absolute beatitude of God can in nowise be contracted; and however creatures may conduct themselves, His name shall be for ever glorified, whether it be by His mercy or by His justice, which are both revelations of His one eternal love. We pray, therefore, only that we may be guarded from those evils which impede our own welfare. And as in the attainment of heavenly goods or beatitude, only sin opposes, we pray, "Forgive us our trespasses." And as spiritual goods, the effects of divine grace, can be frustrated or darkened by nothing so much as by the many allurements and occasions of evil, which are not less unavoidable than dangerous to the earthly pilgrim, we supplicate, "Lead us not into temptation." Finally, as temporal evils are opposed to temporal goods, and eternal evils to eternal goods, so, to be preserved from both, we pray, "Deliver us from evil." And since in this series of petitions all is marked that we, as spiritual beings, should spiritually ask and pray for, we conclude the whole with the expression of holy desire, of confidence, and of sure expectation, with that short word, "Amen," which is the closing point of all the petitions which the Lord's Prayer contains, in that number, full of signification, seven; a number which was prefigured by the seven ears of fruit which sprung from one stem, and by the seven seals of that mysterious book which no one but the Lamb could open.

Shall we now distinguish this sevenfold number according to our earthly time; the seven petitions according to the seven days of the week? If so, to the Sunday belongs the first petition, "Hallowed be Thy name." For this day, sacred to the service of God, and called by the Pagans the day of the sun (of Phœbus), was consecrated by the Church to the spiritual sun of truth, to our risen Saviour, of whom the Psalms sing,

"He hath placed His tabernacle in the sun." Monday was known in ancient times as the day of the moon; and the Scripture admonishes us, by a similitude of the ever-changing moon, of the mutability of a foolish mind, and of the instability of this earthly world, to exhort us to keep a heavenly object before our eyes in all our works and employments, which we commence anew every Monday, in order that we may be ever turned towards the kingdom of heaven; and that the first amongst the days of our labours may in truth be to us a serene Monday, corresponding to the petition, "Thy kingdom come."

Tuesday was sacred of old to Mars, the god of war; and we are thereby reminded of the words of Job, "That the life of man is a warfare upon earth." Again, as this word signifies [in German] the day of service, we are admonished of our duty to the invisible Lord and Ruler of the universe, whom we are bound to serve with willing obedience. Both significations, the spiritual warfare against evil, and the worship of God by our virtuous actions, are contained in the petition, "Thy will be done on earth as it is in heaven."

As, moreover, Wednesday, or mid-week, stands in the midst of the days of the week, and represents the present, between the past and the future, so may be applied to it the petition, "Give us this day our daily bread." Anciently it was known as the day of Mercury, the god of buyers and sellers. So this petition admonishes us, in the midst of our labours, to be content with a sufficiency which is grounded upon integrity.

Thursday, as the name declares, is the day of Jupiter, or of the northern Thor; and points out to us, in contrast to the menacing and terrible deity of the unredeemed and pagan tribes, that monument of the eternal sin-offering, the sacred banquet of Jesus, the gift of Divine love, which the hatred and perversity of men can never prevent; and incites us to the serious meditation of the petition, "Forgive us our trespasses, as we forgive them that trespass against us."

Friday was formerly the day of Venus, or of the northern goddess Freea, and was devoted to licentiousness, to false freedom, or libertinism; but it now brings to our mind the bloody sacrifice of Divine love, which liberated us from the slavery of our passions, and exalted us to spiritual freedom. Hence corresponds to it the petition which prays that we may be preserved for ever from this slavery, "Lead us not into temptation."

Saturday was, in the old law, the Sabbath, or day of rest; amongst the Pagans it was the day of Saturn, the god of all-destroying time. The tomb, in which our Redeemer on this day reposed, points out to us the entrance into true rest, the exchange of time for eternity, of appearance for the joyful reality, for which we pray in that word of conclusion—thus may it be—"Amen."

CHAPTER II.

Our Father who art.

WHEN, in any necessity, we wish to secure the favour and assistance of a powerful and influential man, what is the first thing with which we engage ourselves? Certainly to acquaint ourselves with his name, his rank, and the title which it is proper to use in our address, or in the superscription, lest we injure our cause in the very commencement: for he whose favour we seek may reasonably require of us that we should know of him two things: first, that he exists and lives; and secondly, what rank he occupies. Shall this condition hold only within the limits of this world of men, and not also when we turn ourselves to one who is infinitely above this world—to the absolute Lord of the universe? The apostle answers: "Without faith it is impossible to please God; for he who would come to God, must believe that He is, and that He is the rewarder of those who seek Him." God, on His part, does not, indeed, stand in need of our acknowledgment and adoration, but this confession of the existence of God, and this veneration, is the chief and most essential of all those things of which we stand in need. "To know Thee, and to confess to Thee," as it is said in the book of Wisdom, "is perfect justification; to acknowledge Thy justice and Thy power, is the root of immortality." More plainly did our Divine Redeemer teach the same truth, when, looking up to heaven, He said: "This is eternal life, to know Thee, the only true God, and Him whom Thou hast sent, Jesus Christ."

But in what does this knowledge consist? In two things. For he who would come to God, must first believe that He is; that is, he must believe that He exists and lives; and secondly, that He is the rewarder of those who rightly seek Him. He must therefore confess, not only the existence and essence of God, but also the manner of His relation towards us, that being turned, in the riches of His loving goodness, towards us, He is ready to impart to us of the fulness of His beatitude. This loving God, His essence, and His relation toward us, were shewn to us by our Lord, when He said: "Thus shalt thou pray: Our Father who art in heaven." Simple words, indeed; but in these few and simple words what an unmeasurable fulness of hidden truths! They are like the bud, from which, when it opens itself to our mind, is unfolded the wonderful flower of Revelation; for the inmost nature and essence of God are signified by those words—"Father who art;" His relation to us, His creatures, is expressed in the words "Our Father."

Let us first meditate upon the name, FATHER, and ask ourselves whether this be only an allegorical, figurative name, by which God is honoured as the Creator and Preserver of all things; whether God is named Father, without being so truly and essentially, and in a Divine manner; or, what is the same thing, whether we may call God our Father, without believing that He is really and truly a Father? The holy Prophet Isaias shall answer: "Thus saith the Lord, Shall not I, that make others to bring forth children, Myself bring forth? Shall I, who give generation to others, be barren? saith the Lord thy God." (Isaias lxvi. 9.) Thus answereth also the Apostle St. Paul: "I bend my knee before the Father of our Lord Jesus Christ, from whom all paternity draweth its name, in heaven and upon earth." From these words it is evident that the contrary is the truth,—that the invisible God does not bear the name of Father as if borrowed and derived from the properties of a father upon earth; but, as all which is derived from the power and essence of God is essentially grounded in His nature, and as all paternity upon earth is only conditional and mediate, God alone, the Author of all being and of life, is, in the absolute sense of the word, a Father. This divine paternity is the mystery of the Trinity, more clearly and more expressly signified by the words "who art;" for these are the words from which the most exalted of all supernatural truths are unfolded to the faithful and thinking mind.

There is here in our way a stone of scandal, thrown by ignorance, which must be either removed or passed over. 'Wherefore all this labour, all this excessive ingenuity?' exclaim those who will not think; 'wherefore all this labour of thought and of mind upon a subject in which every attempt of human reason is, if not full of danger and worthy of punishment, at least without any fruitful result? Is not the Trinity of God a mystery, an article of faith, and far above all the comprehensive powers of the human mind? Why, then, seek for knowledge in matters of pure faith?' So many questions can be met only by others. The human mind, in its present condition, is indeed not capable of discovering these truths, or rather, the Deity itself, without its Divine assistance, which is full of love. "No one knoweth the Son but the Father; and no one knoweth the Father but the Son, and to whom the Son shall reveal Him." But does faith exclude all thought? Does the Divine wisdom, by its revelation, destroy or confine the life and workings of the created understanding? Is it intended that light should illumine or darken our powers and properties? and shall the divine light of revealed truths obscure our understanding, or shall it not rather enlighten it? Were the first the case, would not the infidel be right, when he sees nothing in a faithful soul but night, or darkness in the sun? The true knowledge of the Triune God is the only fountain of light to the intelligent and moral life of man. Should we not, then, labour to arrive at some precision in this knowledge? 'Certainly,' answers St. Augustin; 'for to understand the mystery of the Trinity with a rational mind, and with a soul fearing God, should employ all the exertions of a Christian.'

Or shall the favourite objection be raised, that this mystery is too profound, too hidden, and too immeasurable, to render it prudent to venture into this vast ocean? If so, that sublime father of the Church, St. Cyril of Jerusalem, will propose another question, which was perhaps never more deserving of serious consideration than at a time when infidelity, or a half faith, adorns itself with the holy semblance of intellectual perspicuity, while the defenders of the true faith retreat behind the bulwarks of authority, which their opponents neither receive nor respect. 'Shall I,' says the holy Cyril, 'shall I, because I cannot exhaust the fountain and the stream, not draw for myself according to the measure that may be sufficient for me? And when I enter into a garden where a thousand different fruits present themselves to view, shall I retire, because I cannot consume the whole? And because I cannot contain the bright and flaming sun within my eyes, shall I on that account deny myself the light of day?' What shall we answer to this wise man? No, we ought not, and we will not: we will not, indeed, be so foolish as to gaze with bold eyes upon the Divine Sun; nor shall we on that account avoid the light of day, which it pours down upon us. This mild light shines upon us in those words, "Our Father, Thou who art."

What does this wonderful word *Thou* express, with which we address the invisible God? Every *Thou* is an *I* opposed to a *Me;* consequently, this Thou expresses a Divine I. 'My God!' exclaims the seraphic Francis, 'who art Thou, and who am I?' 'My Lord and my God!' exclaims St. Austin, 'may I know myself, may I know Thee!' For the Divine essence can be known to us only in proportion as we meditate upon our own nature. How wonderful, how enigmatical a being is this *I!* I know, I feel that I am; and this intimate knowledge and sensation, from which all my other knowledge proceeds, is my self-knowledge. But I know also that this self-knowledge has entered later; for I know that I existed before this idea was awakened within me. I know also that I see around me, or perceive by my other senses, other things that are not myself. I see my body in its outward form, but not myself; in the same manner as my eye sees all other things, but does not see itself. But what is this? I see, but I do not behold myself. It is expressed more clearly by these words, 'I cannot comprehend myself.' I cannot obtain for myself a full view of my essence. And why? 'Because I do not exist of myself.'

We will hear upon this subject a venerable man, the holy Gregory, Bishop of Tours, who had penetrated deeply into this simple but profound truth. When this learned man, to whom the kingdom of the Franks is so much indebted, had come to Rome, he was received with every mark of distinction by his great contemporary of the same name, the sainted Pope Gregory. Whilst the Pontiff was employed in shewing to him the buildings and monuments of Rome, and had conducted him into the Church of the Apostles, he could not contain within his heart his wonder, how Providence had bestowed upon this man the highest gifts of mind; for the far-famed Gregory of Tours was of low stature, and of a mean and unpromising appearance. But this small man displayed at once the power and acuteness of his mind; for he had in that moment divined the thoughts of his exalted friend and host. Smiling, he looked up to him and said, 'It is the Lord who hath made us, and not we ourselves; He is the same in the great and in the small.'

What words are these which the holy Bishop here employed! They are taken from the 99th Psalm:

"Serve ye the Lord with gladness. Come in before His presence with exceeding great joy. Know ye that the Lord He is God; He made us, and not we ourselves." By these words we are conducted to a higher degree of knowledge. They teach us that the essence of our nature, which is expressed by the word 'I,' exists not of itself, but is derived from a higher and absolute power, which we name the Godhead. But if this absolute power be the author of our existence, what is it in itself? Is it the soul, the hidden interior spring of all power and motion, blind in itself, impassible and unconscious? How can this be? It is thus that the Psalmist sings: "Shall He who planted the ear not hear? Shall He who formed the eye not see? Shall He who teacheth man wisdom be without wisdom?" That is, shall He who hath gifted us with our essence possess no essence in Himself? Shall He who hath planted and awakened within us our consciousness be Himself considered an impersonal, unconscious being?

Far from us be this extravagant, although, in this age of the idolatry of nature, too frequent error. God is the uncreated, unconditional, self-existent, and therefore the only eternal Being, the Father of light, as the apostle says; that is, of spiritual, conscious creatures, from whom, therefore, "all paternity in heaven and on earth derives its name;" that is to say, from whom every created being in the world of spirits and of men receives its origin; who, in virtue of His eternal existence, designates Himself by no other name than this: "I am who am;" and whom we invoke, in like manner, by the same name—"Our Father WHO ART."

Thus have we learnt to know the Divine essence, or

the self-consciousness in God; we have discovered, on the other hand, that we can arrive at a representation of our own essence only *mediately*, that is, through the manifestation of its powers, in thought, in will, and in sensation. Hence it will appear, that we are not in a condition to contemplate our own essence, that is, *immediately* to behold ourselves. From this will arise another question: whether the uncreated Divine essence be fully revealed to itself; or, in other words, whether God has fully beheld and comprehended Himself from all eternity? The answer to this question cannot be doubtful, for that God fully comprehends His own essence no one can doubt. And if no one can deny this, so no one who is reasonable can deny the Trinity of God.

But is not this a false, or too rapid a conclusion? Certainly not. For *how* does it happen that God fully beholds and knows Himself? Thus; that He, who by Himself is what He is, draws forth His own essence, and places it before Himself. To comprehend this we may turn our reflection back upon our own essence, the counterpart of the Divine consciousness. I see my own figure represented on a mirror, but it is only a lifeless, a shadowy form, and only the form of my corporeal substance. My real being and essence, my spiritual essence, I cannot see, because it cannot be reproduced, and I cannot, therefore, place it before me. But God beholds Himself in all His splendour; He is visible to Himself; His essence, which is named the *subject*, becomes the *object* of His contemplation; and this perfect figure of His living personal Divine essence, since it is a perfect figure, is consequently living, personal, and divine; it is His twofold second self. This other self, this eternal real essential thought of God is the Logos, or the Word; spiritual, eternal, born of the Father, of one and the same essence with Him.

Now the Father beholds Himself in the Son, and the Son in the Father. In their personality they are distinct, but in their essence they are one, as our Redeemer Himself taught: "I and the Father are one." This mutual knowledge of perfect essential unity is also a Divine thought, which proceeds from both, and which unites both, and which, therefore, possesses essence and personality. This was clearly expressed by Richard St. Victor: 'As thou canst correctly say, I love myself, and I love myself with a love which is in me towards myself; so thou wouldst express thyself rightly, if thou wert to say, God loves Himself, and with a love which is in Himself towards Himself.' And thus the Divine life manifests itself from all eternity in a threefold self, or in a threefold personality, in a unity of inseparable essence, and in this wonderful plurality and unity is founded the absolute beatitude of God.

How enrapturing for the created spirit of man must be this knowledge of his God, who, in His unity of essence possesses omnipotence, and in His Trinity of persons the plenitude of beatitude! It is related in the Greek histories of the seventh century that the emperor Constans left, at his death, three sons, of whom the eldest, Constantine Pogonatus, succeeded him on the throne. But the Greeks insisted that the two brothers Tiberius and Heracleus, should be crowned with Constantine; for, said they, as we believe in the most sacred Trinity, we will have three princes to reign over us. Pious as this desire might be, it deeply wounded, with the poisoned dart of envy, the first-born prince, who therefore caused his brothers to be maimed, and afterwards put to death. This deed was truly most cruel; but the demand of the people, which caused it, was not wise. For it is absurd to seek in a triumvirate of sovereign princes a symbol of the three absolute persons who rule the universe. In the first case there are three created beings, and three persons essentially distinct, who would contend for the sovereignty, and who would offer impediments the one to the other. In the sacred Trinity there are three distinct persons, not separated from each other, but united in one essence and in eternal love.

For the Son is distinct from the Father, and the Holy Ghost is distinct from the Father and the Son; yet the Son and the Holy Ghost are not different in nature from the Father, but are of one essence with Him; so that the Father is entire in the Son, the Son in the Father, and the Holy Ghost in both. Hence, we Christians know and confess one God, who possesses beatitude in Himself, and whose essence is mutual love. What a celestial light is that which faith pours down upon the thinking mind! What a delight for the man to whom it is given to profess this supreme mystery in love! We are told in the legends of the blessed Ida, that when she was kneeling and praying in solitude, she was once seen illumined by a glowing light as of three brilliant suns. If this be understood spiritually, we may say that every Christian who knows, and in love professes, the mystery of the Trinity, will be, as often as he raises his mind to the Divine omnipresence, enlightened with a threefold sun, or rather with one brilliant sun of truth; and that no one can utter these words, "Our Father who art," in spirit and truth, without directing them to the one indivisible Trinity.

As of this there can be no doubt, why are we not rather taught to say: 'God three in one, who art in heaven?' Why simply "Our Father?" First, because in the name of Father, the sacred Trinity is fully designated; for the Father is the origin and source of all things, and owes His being to no other origin. The Son, also, is a source of all things, and His origin is from the Father. The Holy Ghost has its source in the Father and in the Son, but is not Himself a source, but the perfection and plenitude. Secondly, because the name of Father is a name of love, of kindness, and of sweet care, and marks those divinely good things which are externally imparted to us. This love, which thus externally displays itself, and which we must attribute to all the three Divine persons, is an external revelation of God, and is expressed by the words, "Our Father."

We have hitherto endeavoured to consider the Divine being and essence as it is in itself; but these words conduct us to the other side of that knowledge which we should have of God—to His relation towards us. They tell us of the revelation of God to such beings which are distinct from Him, and which consequently are not God, and are not divine, which would not exist if they had not been by Him created, but which have been created and called into being, that He might impart to them some portion of that splendour and beatitude which He possesses in Himself. But what creatures are above all others capable of this participation? We may learn from the conversation which is recorded in the life of the poet Torquato Tasso. Charles IX. king of France, once asked him, whom he considered the most happy? Tasso did not long consider, but answered, God! 'We know this,' said the king; 'and the question could not, therefore, have referred to God. Who, then, out of God, and after God, is the most happy?' 'He,' answered Tasso, 'who is the most like to God.' For, as there can exist no absolute being and life, and no beatitude, which is not in God and from God, a participation of this beatitude necessarily constitutes a likeness to God. But only those creatures on whom this likeness has been impressed are capable of this participation, and to these only is God, in the real signification of the word, truly a Father. Have stones, trees, animals, the planets, has the sun, any pretensions to this relation with God? Or, what is the same thing, can we call God the Father of these things? Or, as the modern phrase will have it, can we call Him the Father of nature?

Many a pious mind indeed has endeavoured to trace in the forms and movements of nature the seal of the Trinity, and the impression of the Master and Lord of all things in the number three. These endeavours may, perhaps, be well intended, but can never lead to the light of true knowledge. Thus, some two hundred years ago, there lived at Rome a man named Francesco Foliano, who dedicated his entire life to the adoration of this high mystery, and endeavoured to direct all his actions and omissions symbolically to it. The room in which he dwelt was built of three walls, in the form of a triangle, his bed was composed of three boards, and his table rested on three legs. When he read in a book, he paused after every third page; when he ate, he divided his bread into three parts; and when walking, he described triangles with his steps. This triangular mode of thinking is neither to be proposed or imitated. We must, nevertheless, if we wish truly to estimate the signification of the Divine paternity towards us, and of our relation to it, endeavour to understand the three lines of a great immeasurable triangle, without which knowledge we shall never be able to comprehend our own self in its essence and personality, and consequently in its relation to God: 'If I may know myself,' exclaims St. Austin, 'I shall know Thee, O Lord.'

But what are the three sides, to a knowledge of which it is fitting that we arrive? They are the three orders or principal classes of things in the creation, the free spirit, the material substance, and, finally, the compound resulting from the union of both—human nature. For let us again descend into the depths of our self-consciousness, and ask, 'Who am I?' We shall receive for answer: 'In me there is a twofold substance, and I am myself a third, the result of the union of the two. If I consider myself in regard to my body, I am like the plants and beasts of the field, unfree, and subjected, even against my own will, to the laws of nature. For this corporeal being is not my entire self, for this self is also spiritual and free. I can elect and act, or, at least, can wish as I will. I am, therefore, on one side an organic being, living, increasing, feeling, like the trees and the beasts; but I am, at the same time, a spiritual being, infinitely different, by my inward freedom, from mere nature, and raised high above it. There is, therefore, in me a twofold being and life—a life of nature, and a spiritual life, and yet there is but one entire self, which is, at the same time, corporeal and spiritual, free and unfree, which thinks and feels, but so that in this personality the life of the spirit predominates.' But who is He who has united in us two substances so distinct? Certainly He who created the world of nature and the spiritual world, and who placed man as a harmony and union of the two, in order that in him the life of nature might enter into a spiritual consciousness, and might attain the object of all creation, which is beatitude. This is, therefore, the impression of the Divine paternity in us, that we should represent the fulness and the perfection of the collected world of creation, and the perfect external revelation of God; that in us spirit and nature, by their living union, might be made capable of the beatitude of God.

But since man (as will be shewn in the course of these considerations under different petitions of the Lord's prayer) forfeited, by the abuse of his freedom, his claim to this participation, this impression of the Divine paternity, if not destroyed, was made less perceptible. In his fallen state, opposed as he was to the Divine love, he saw, in terror, the omnipotence and the justice of God; and hence in the writings of the Old Testament, God is named less frequently, Father, but generally, Lord, Omnipotent, Sovereign, King, patient yet terrible in His chastisements. For in this fallen state all men, as the Apostle says, were slaves; subject to the elements of this world, to temptations, to the inclinations of passion, to half-consciousness, and to the natural life. But He who is our Father, and who had decreed from eternity to be so, sent a remedy to this misery of the human race. "As a father hath compassion on his children, so hath the Lord compassion on them that fear Him. For according to the height of the heavens above the earth, He hath strengthened His mercy towards them that fear Him." (Psalm cii.)

For, as the Apostle teaches, "When the fulness of time was come, God sent His Son, made of a woman, made under the law, to redeem those who were under the law, that we might receive the adoption of sons; and because you are sons, God has sent the Spirit of His Son in your hearts, crying, Abba, Father; we are not any more servants but sons." This is the great mystery which we proclaim and confess, when we say to God, "Our Father." For with these words we call to mind the incarnation of His only-begotten eternal Son, who, by this assumption of human nature, raised us to the dignity of children of His Father, "who gave to all who received Him power to be made the sons of God, who were born not of the flesh, but of God." To pass now in review all that we have hitherto said, what do we say, what do we confess, as often as we repeat these words, "Our Father who art?" We confess, first, the mystery of the Trinity, which, to the thinking mind illumined by faith, so truly and essentially displays itself, that it cannot possibly think of any but a Triune God. We confess also the love of God to us, and our similitude to Him, which is the seal of this love. But in what does this similitude consist? That in God there is an uncreated absolute self-consciousness, but in us a consciousness created and conditional, in which the world of nature and of spirit are united; so that man stands in contrast with his Creator, as an integrating number of the university of creation. For in God, as He exists by Himself, one inseparable essence developes itself in three persons; but in man a twofold life converges into one point of personality, that in him and by him creation might be perfected and glorified in the Divine love.

But man, in the great moment of his self-perfection, turned away from this love by his own free-will; he frustrated the designs of this love in his regard, and, inasmuch as in him lay, he renounced his dignity. He did not, however, frustrate for ever the work of the Divine love, which revealed again all its splendour. When, therefore, we call God "Our Father," what do we thereby confess? We confess, in the third place, that this Father, who is rich in love, sent His only-begotten Son to restore again the bond of union; and how was this effected? The divine Logos united, by His incarnation, a twofold essence in one person—the divine and human; or rather a threefold essence—the divine, the corporeal, and the spiritual; for the eternal Word espoused the created life of nature and of spirit, that He might become the new and celestial Adam, the first-born amongst His brethren. "Behold!" exclaims St. John, "what love the Father has shewn us, that we should be called, and should be the sons of God," that God should not only be called, but should in reality be our Father! But, as St. Ambrose says, God is our Father if we do well, our Judge if we commit sin! 'Ah, what anxiety fills my soul,' exclaims St. Augustin, 'lest while I call Him Father, I should do any thing unworthy of such a parent.' Well have we reason often to cry out, as an enlightened German virgin, the holy Gertrude, was wont to pray: 'Receive us, O eternal Father, into Thy loving paternity, that we may come to Thee by the obedience of free-will. Receive us, O Divine Son, into Thy heavenly brotherhood of love, that Thou mayest be our friend, our teacher, and our guide. Receive us, O God the Holy Ghost, into Thy merciful love, that Thou mayest enlighten and strengthen our spirits. Receive us, O Triune God, into Thy infinite mercy, that Thy holy will may be done in us and by us.'

CHAPTER III.

Our Father.

THAT disciple, when he approached his Divine Master to present to Him his petition, did not say, Lord, teach *me* to pray, but teach *us* how to pray. The Spirit that inspired him to utter these words was not a spirit of selfishness, but the Spirit of truth and of love. Hence his petition was granted in the same form in which it was presented: " Thus shall *you* pray, Our Father who art in heaven."

Nowhere are the motives which impel us to repeat this prayer more powerfully rehearsed than in that introduction or preface which the Church prefixes to it during the holy sacrifice of the Mass; " Being instructed in Thy saving precepts, and following Thy Divine directions, we *presume* to say ' Our Father who art in heaven.' " By these words we confess, that of ourselves and through our own fault, we possess not the right to call God our Father, and that we have regained this right only through Christ, by whose command we dare to declare it. For, as the Apostle teaches, " We have not again received the spirit of servitude in fear, but the spirit of adoption as children, by which we cry, Abba, Father"—the spirit of love, which proceeds from God to unite us with Him. What, then, do we owe to such a Father? Honour, gratitude, obedience, and, before all, love.

For, in ordinary life, there are many benefits and services which cannot be remunerated by similar services, but by other means. With love it is not so. Love must be repaid by love; and Divine love, which surpasseth all understanding, must be repaid by a mutual love which is not narrow-hearted, and which does not on every occasion complain, saying, This burden is too heavy; this trial is too severe; this labour too much. What is too much? That which exceeds moderation. "When," says St. Paul, "we were dead by sin, God hath made us living in Christ, by His exceeding great love;" that is, which surpasses all measure. Is not the *too much*, therefore, on the side of God? The *too little* is on our side.

In the old German chronicles it is related, that in the battle which was fought between Maurice of Saxony and Albert of Brandenburg, the two sons of the Duke of Braunschweig fell beneath the sword. It was endeavoured to convey this melancholy intelligence to the Duke in as mild a manner as possible. The messenger, therefore, first spoke to him thus, 'Your younger son has been slain.' The Duke, a man firm as a rock, betrayed no commotion, but concealed his grief behind a kind of sportiveness. 'Who can help it?' he exclaimed. But now the second Job's messenger appeared, and told him that his eldest son, a youth of excellent promise, had also been left upon the field of battle. The man of iron frame could no longer command himself; tears streamed from his eyes, and he burst forth into this exclamation of anguish, 'Ah, this is too much!' We, too, have heard of many a combat and battle that have been fought, both by the wicked and the virtuous, upon this earth, each with their peculiar arms: the one party with hatred and with lies; the other with truth and with love. When we hear how many an excellent and high-minded hero, who fought for light and right, has fallen a victim to wickedness; as when, for example, the *holy* seer, who was slain by the sword, and the philosophic seer, who drank-in death with poison, because they both opposed lies and idolatry; we perhaps lament the fate of these heroes, or rather of their miserable enemies; but we perhaps add the remark, How heavy was their burden! But it will be said that even the God-Man, in whom the plenitude of the Divine beauty and goodness displayed itself, and who alone is worthy of our adoration and love, fell in this fight—the just for the unjust. Those words will be repeated to us, "God so loved the world, that He gave His only-begotten Son;" and what shall we reply? Truly, we exclaim, this is too much; and tears stream from our eyes, tears of gratitude for such boundless love. We hear that the Divine Word became Man, and closed a life of poverty and labour with a death of sorrows, to heal our deep misery. Truly, this is all too much; and whatever we can do in return would be all too little.

But St. Paul has said of some believers, "All do not believe the Gospel." This he said first of those who boast of their faith, of pure reason. But all do not believe reason! For these cold half-thinkers blunt the arrow that would enter their hearts, or turn it aside, and exclaim, 'Truly, this is too much,' but in a sense opposed to that above mentioned. 'How,' they continue, with an apparently holy zeal, 'did the infinite God, the Lord of the universe, become man?' and immediately they intone their song of jubilee and their much-praised hymn, which is comprised in two strophes. In the first, they exclaim: 'How diminutively small is the planet upon which we dwell, and how much smaller still, in comparison with the universe, are we; and we therefore consider it an absurdity to suppose that the infinite God should have descended into this small angle of the world!' In this first strophe they humble (if they do not debase) themselves, they annihilate themselves; they make of themselves microscopic objects, and give the greatest honour to God; in the second strophe they ascend a degree higher, they give laws to God, and declare the mystery of the incarnation to be incomprehensible and impossible. An innumerable body of people, from every tribe and condition, sing with them the concluding chorus, an imaginary grave-song for deceased Christianity.

He, therefore, who would preserve internal light and life, and would guard himself against the darkness of error, must before all other things labour to attain clearness and certainty of intention. Should we raise our eyes, like these men, towards the measureless world of nature, and contemplate the diminutiveness of this earth and of its inhabitants, we shall find that thousands of years have passed away since the inspired Singer of the Psalms did the same, and exclaimed, "I see Thy heavens, the work of Thy hands, the moon and the stars, which Thou hast founded." He contemplates the nightly heavens, which open to our wondering eyes so mysterious and so boundless a view, and what does he add? He exclaims, as did the seraphic St. Francis, 'Who art Thou, O Lord, Creator of all, and who am I?' "What is man, that Thou art mindful of him, and the Son of man, that Thou dost visit him? Thou hast made him little less than the angels; Thou hast crowned him with glory and honour, and placed him over the works of Thy hands."

Behold here a new turn in the discourse; for, in truth, what is man? We have already seen that he is the living union of the spiritual and natural life, and that consequently he comprises in his nature the whole of creation, the harmony (*concentus*) of the grand cause of the world. In him is perfected the contrast of the creature with the Creator, and nature is exalted into consciousness. But is he who has arrived to personality or spiritual freedom, to be esteemed great or small in a mechanical manner? Can we say that an elephant, a mountain, or a celestial body, is greater than man, because it occupies a greater degree of space? We have heard the words by which St. Gregory of Tours revealed the secret thought of his friend; and who now requires to be told, that in the estimation of spiritual greatness, the appearance of the body cannot be taken into consideration? A Christian, a wise man of antiquity, indeed, found such instruction necessary. Alypiana, daughter of St. Gorgonia, and niece of the great doctor of the Church, St. Gregory Nazianzen, was married to a certain Nicobulus, who treated her with contempt, on account of her small and somewhat deformed figure. The letter which St. Gregory wrote to him has been preserved. 'You despise,' he writes, 'you despise your spouse, Alypiana, and you contemn her, because she is small and unworthy of your high descent, O great and large man, giant in size as well as in strength! Exult in your magnitude and high birth, shew the world that you yield in nothing to the giants of old! You sport with your horse, and you hunt the wild beasts; and your spouse can undertake nothing that is honourable, but sits at home with her spindle and distaff. What does this mean? But she prays, she is employed always with God; and if you will condescend to observe her, you will find that she understands well how to be silent at proper times, and when to speak words of prudence; how serious she is, and how strong-minded; what advantage she brings into your house, and how faithfully she loves her consort. When you have observed all this, confess with the wise man of Greece, 'truly the mind is not to be measured by the size of the body, and the outward man must direct his eyes to the interior.''

These words, 'the mind is not to be measured,' prove the dignity of human nature in its full signification and position in the universe; and, at the same time, the nothingness of the first objection. But how shall we meet the second, which denies the possibility of the union of the Divine and human natures? This objection is vaunted forth, and it would seem that those who appeal to their so-called pure reason could never sufficiently laud it. But it is, and for the same reasons, not inferior to the first in weakness. They imagine that it is incomprehensible, and even impossible, that two natures, the Divine and human, so opposed to each other, should form a living union. But whilst they in general deny the union of two different natures, they deny themselves, or their own essence. For is not our essence corporeal and spiritual; free, and at the same time not free; and still, does it not form but one consciousness, only one I? But we all say, and say with justice, 'I eat; I am cold; I am warm;' although our spirit, as such, cannot experience these sensations: we say also, 'I am ill; I die;' although our spirit cannot suffer infirmity or die. We say, on the other hand, 'I think; I understand; I judge;' although our body can neither think, nor perform any operation of the spirit. Yet these expressions are not faults or incorrect, but true and just, because in our nature the corporeal as well as the spiritual life have their parts, and both are most intimately connected.

If, therefore, it cannot be denied, that spirit and matter may be united in the same man, the union of the Divinity with the humanity cannot be denied in one and the same Christ, in whom a Divine and human consciousness were placed in living union; or in whom a human consciousness was raised to a union with the Divine consciousness of the eternal Word. What do they do, who will not acknowledge this twofold essence in one and the same Christ? Wonderful zealots, who preach a pure faith in Christ, but who know nothing, and who will learn nothing of a true knowledge of Christ? To that great question which He once addressed to the ancient Pharisees, "What think you of Christ, whose son is He?" these, their modern disciples, answer, 'He is indeed the Son of God, in the highest and most noble (the tropical) sense, the chosen One of God, the beloved of God, the ideal of human nature!' They cease not to repeat that He Himself oftentimes names Himself the Son of man, and make but little account that He has often, and in the most solemn manner, called Himself the Son of God (for example, John v.). But why do they take only certain passages of the Gospel, and give to them this spiritless, this vague interpretation? How can they, in that profound, almost enthusiastic reverence, which they profess to feel, reconcile those apparently harsh contradictions which occur so often in His own discourses?

For once He taught, "As the Father hath life in Himself, so hath He given to the Son to have life in Himself." He here gives to Himself an eternal and divine essence, in the manner as it is possessed by the eternal Father; and in the same sense He said also, "I am the resurrection and the life." And yet, on another occasion, He predicated the contrary of Himself, for He confessed and did not deny "My soul is sorrowful even unto death." And in the last hour of His conflict He exclaimed, "My God, my God, why hast Thou forsaken Me!" Again He taught, "I and the Father are one;" but how can it be reconciled with this unity of essence, if at another time He says, "The day and the hour no man knoweth, not even the Son, but only the Father?" He once said to His opponents, "Before Abraham was, I AM;" but they, remarking the apparent contradiction contained in these words, "took up stones to cast at Him; for," they exclaimed, "Thou art not yet fifty years old." Again, when warning His disciples against presumption, which had begun to manifest itself amongst them, He said, "I verily have seen Satan fall like lightning from heaven." How could the man Jesus Christ have given evidence of an event which took place before the creation of the human race?

These many apparent contradictions and enigmas, which are found in the Gospels, are to be explained in the same manner in which we reconcile so many others which we have constantly in our mouth; as when we say, 'I eat; I think; I am mortal; I am immortal; I have sensations; I have ideas;' as often as we speak of our body as being our possession and our property, even without an idea of its organisation (my body, my eyes, my hand); as often as we say of ourselves, 'I walk; I breathe; I digest,' without thinking of the organs, or of their actions, which are thereby put in operation. Our corporeal life enters into our spiritual essence, and, distinct as it essentially is from the spirit, it is in our idea of man's creation necessarily connected with it. For the essence of man is the union of his spiritual and corporeal life. Nature, in its efforts and agonies for consciousness, can attain its end by no other means than by being received into the life of the spirit; the spirit receives its fulness of life only in God, and this union with God is the end and object of its endeavours.

This unity with God is that which was enjoyed really and essentially by the man Jesus Christ, in the Divine Word, for He was the first-born among many brethren, whom He was to redeem and to exalt to a reunion with God. Hence He speaks of Himself sometimes as God, sometimes as man, for His human consciousness has been received into the Divine consciousness of the Word, and both are united in one person.

Not figuratively, therefore, not merely by excellence,

and consequently not by comparison, but essentially and truly, is Christ the Son of God, the only-begotten of the Father; and therefore not only in His uncreated essence as the Divine Word is He the Son of God, but also in His created human nature; for this was a new creation, but without terrestrial paternity. Other men attain to this dignity only by grace, by means of adoption. The only-begotten is but one; the adopted are many. Hence our Lord, as often as He speaks of His eternal Father in reference to Himself, says, "My Father;" but when speaking of Him in reference to others, He says, "Your Father"—"I ascend to My Father and to your Father." He, then, alone has power to call the eternal Father His Father; as when He says in the prophetic Psalm (the 88th), "He shall call upon Me, Thou art My Father." But we, who are many, may not use this expression, "You are brethren; and one is your Father, who is in heaven." We are, therefore, taught to call upon Him, saying, "*Our Father.*" By this expression, our attention is directed to all and to each one, who have the same right to God as ourselves, as the same Divine essence lovingly reveals and imparts itself to one as to another. What, then, do these words of invocation, "Our Father," contain? They contain the two greatest commandments, "Thou shalt love the Lord thy God with thy whole heart, and thy neighbour as thyself;" they contain, moreover, the living cause, which closely connects these two commandments, "thou shalt love the Lord thy God with thy whole heart," because He is a Father; "thou shalt love thy neighbour as thyself," because God is thy Father and his Father,—because He is OUR Father.

It was not, therefore, without reason that the holy Dorotheus represented this twofold precept under the figure of a circle; in which from one centre equal rays are drawn to all points of the circumference, or return from these points to the same centre. The point or centre of our spiritual life is in God and in His law; and to all who stand around, the like object is proposed, to find in God their essential and beatifying THOU; for as they are directed to one and the same centre, they are mutually neighbours to each other; and therefore should preserve towards each other harmony and love. When a man separates himself in hatred from his neighbour, when he exalts himself above him, or servilely or idolatrously subjects himself to him, he departs from his point in the circumference; he belongs no more to it, and has lost his centre. He, therefore, who is torn away by ambition, by avarice, or by sensuality, cannot, without speaking falsely, utter these words, "Our Father;" for he has departed from that living circle, which is designated by this word, OUR.

If we come to speak of the particular irregularities, by which this beautiful word OUR is destroyed, we shall speak, first, of those words *mine* and *thine*, which St. John Chrysostom names the 'cold words mine and thine,' because they are opposed to holy love, and are the causes of contentions innumerable. The golden-mouthed orator relates a contest of another kind, which its extraordinary nature renders remarkable. 'A peasant,' he tells us, 'sold a field, without knowing that a treasure lay therein concealed. The purchaser, in cultivating the field, discovered the riches, and hastened immediately to the peasant, and obliged him to take back what he had sold; 'for,' said he, 'I purchased the field, not the treasure which it contained.' The other refused, declaring that he had no further right to the land which he had sold. They thus contested for a long time, until at length an arbitrator, whom they selected, said, laughing, 'I will decide your dispute; but I will take, as my reward, that which neither of you will receive.'

Is this, indeed, a true history? Many will certainly receive it only as a fable; because the mine and thine are now more common than the OUR. The first Christian communities would have seen nothing fabulous in this narration; for they had but one heart and one soul; and neither had avarice, nor envy, nor pride disturbed their holy life. It is, indeed, necessary that a distinction of rank and station should be observed upon this earth; and this distinction is of divine institution; but the very knowledge of this institution should exclude all pride. There was once written on the window of an hotel at Innspruck the ancient German legend:[1]

> When Adam delved and Evè span,
> Who was then the gentleman?

But a celebrated Austrian duke wrote another rhyme underneath:[2]

> I am as ev'ry other man;
> But God made me a gentleman.

That is, I am in essence a man like others, but God hath granted to me to possess a higher rank than many

---

[1] Al Adam hackt' und Eva spann,
Wo war alsda ein Edelmann?

[2] Ich bin ein Mann, wie ein andrer Mann;
Jedoch mir Got der Ehren gann.

others. For the dignity which is enjoyed by individuals in their place in society, is one thing; but the pride, by which men lose their position, is another.

"And now, O Lord," exclaims the Seer, "Thou art our Father, we are but dust; Thou art our Maker, and we are all the work of Thy hands." By creation, we are all of one essence, and members of one family; and we have been united more closely together in a new life by the work of redemption; "for," as the Apostle says, "in Christ Jesus you are all one, you are all children of God, by faith in Christ." (Gal. iii.) In Him, who as a new centre, as the head and heart of the human race, entered into the midst of us, was united the twofold precept of the love of God and our neighbour; for He was our God; and by His human nature He became our brother, to unite us among ourselves and to our Father.

CHAPTER IV.

Our Father who art in Heaven.

AS in the porticoes and colonnades which form the approach to a temple or palace, there is to be seen much that is noble and worthy of observation; to gaze upon which we would willingly for a time delay; so the introduction to the seven petitions, which form the Lord's Prayer, is rich in knowledge, sublime, which it is not permitted to us to pass by without attention. For, as in the words of this preface, "Our Father who art," the essence of God in a threefold personality, and our single personality, in a twofold relative essence, are clearly shewn; so the words, "Our Father," proclaim the paternity of God towards us in its full external revelation, and also our relation to Him and to our neighbour.

But we are especially commanded to pray thus, "Our Father who art in heaven;" and as this command is neither unessential nor unnecessary, we find ourselves placed upon an exalted region, which may be to us a labyrinth, from which thought and imagination cannot free us; unless a series of profound considerations should spin for us an Ariadnian clue.[1] Of an earthly monarch it must be evident, that, even should he be an Attila, he must possess a residence, from which his power goes forth; and that he ennobles his residence, and his residence him: he ennobles his dwelling-place, because he raises the city in which he dwells to be the metropolis of his kingdom: his residence ennobles him, because the magnificence of the buildings, the brilliancy of his court and of his guards, are signs of his power and grandeur. But can we imagine or say, even in figure, any thing like this of the dwelling-place of the Almighty? Whatever we might say would appear childish, rather than childly (*vielmehr kindisch als kindlich*), and would contradict the ideas which we have of His infinitude. "The heavens," exclaimed Solomon, "and the heaven of heavens, cannot contain Thee." Shall we be led away by the error that God occupies space, or that He needs a place for His residence? No, says the idea of His infinite being; God is not within space.

Where, then, is God? Everywhere. He fills, as the Scriptures tell us, heaven and earth; and no one can flee from His presence. Where, then, shall we find Him? Shall it be in heaven, or upon earth? Nowhere, answers the thinking mind; for God is not within space. Let fall, then, thy wings, thou God-seeking soul; thou seekest and knowest not where;

---

[1] An allusion to the fable which tells us that Ariadne delivered Theseus from the labyrinth at Crete by spinning for him a clue of thread.

thou seekest Him in every place, and dost find Him not; and thou dost fall at length in despair, amidst those Pantheists, whose deity, the soul of the world, that all and one, that hidden life of things, is everywhere and nowhere; everywhere as a power, nowhere as an absolute personality! And yet we read in so many places of the Scripture, "To Thee, O Lord, have I raised my eyes; to Thee, who dwellest in heaven." "You shall not swear by the heaven, for it is the throne of God," said our Divine Redeemer, who, as often as He prayed or blessed His followers, raised His eyes to heaven; who so often said, "My Father and your Father, who is in heaven;" and who prescribed this invocation, "Our Father who art in heaven." If God be not in heaven, and if the heaven be not His dwelling-place, wherefore these words?

Thus it is with two important questions, which are dependent the one upon the other. First, how we are to understand, in its true and proper signification, the expression, "Who art in heaven;" secondly, for what purpose has it been prescribed, and what we are taught by it? The first of these questions leads us up to heaven itself, and to the understanding of what heaven is. But who shall give us this understanding? "Who hath ascended into heaven, and given us information thereof?"

From the hand of the huntsman, according to the ancient usage of the chase, the noble falcon raised itself, and ascending with rapid and powerful wing into the air, it seized its prey in its flight. But scarcely did it return, before the huntsman took the prey from its talons, covered its eyes with the hood, and fastened down its feet on the perch. How did the falcon then labour to free itself from these bands! In vain did it endeavour to tear them with its beak; in vain to free its eyes from the veil that was before them; in vain did it endeavour with its wings to soar again on high. That which it seized in its flight, it was not permitted to possess. Like to such a falcon was that exalted and highly-favoured man, to whom it was once given to be borne away on the wings of his soul, to enter into the ethereal Paradise, and to draw from the source of all holiness. But scarcely had he been raised thereto, when he was doomed to return to earth again; his eyes were again veiled, the sweet taste of heavenly delights was withdrawn, and his feet were again fastened down; that is, his spirit was again chained to his mortal, grief-laden body, to the labours of his earthly calling. What he had seen in the clear fulness of reality, he now saw only as in a glass and in enigma, and could reveal nothing. But his desire of heavenly things had become stronger; so that more frequently than before his soul sighed for its flight to heaven, as he himself declared, when he said: "Christ is my life, and to die is gain: I desire to be dissolved, and to be with Christ." But we will listen to himself: "I know a man in Christ (whether in the body or out of the body, I know not, God knows,) who was rapt to the third heaven in Paradise; and heard secret words, which it is not granted to man to utter." (2 Cor. xii.) If, then, it were not given to him, the Apostle of the Gentiles, to speak and to teach those things which he had seen, who will dare to attempt an explanation of them?

But as the *how* is a different question from the

what, and as faith and reasoning give us an answer to other questions, so let it be sufficient for us that the Apostle speaks of a "third heaven," as also in the Psalms, in the Prophets, and Gospels, not unfrequently is mention made of heavens, in the plural number. But three heavens are distinguished before all others: one, created and visible; another, created and invisible; and the third, uncreated and invisible. What we are to understand by that which, in ordinary language, is named the created and visible heaven, is clear enough; for it is not necessary that we should now say that by this word we designate, not only the atmosphere, in which this our world is suspended, but also that boundless space wherein the planets of the solar system are unceasingly circling, and in which those countless stars are seen shining; which, whether they be considered as millions of worlds and solar systems, or whatever else they may be thought, still display to us the glory of Him by whom they were created; for, as the Psalmist sings, "The heavens shew forth the glory of God, and the firmament proclaims the work of His hands." Is this heaven, are these systems or heavens, as they have been named by astronomers, the dwelling-place of which we speak when we say, "Our Father, who art in heaven?" With this error the people of ancient Paganism contented themselves, when they assigned to their Jupiter, their Juno, and their Apollo, a residence in these regions. Thus also Cosroes, famous, or rather infamous in history, king of Persia, and the most formidable of the enemies of the Eastern Roman empire, went so far in his folly to be honoured as a god, that he formed for himself a species of atmospheric heaven. This was a high tower, covered with silver, and adorned with precious stones; upon the interior vault of which the sun, the moon, and the stars, of elaborate workmanship, shone in golden splendour. He sat in the midst of the tower upon a high throne, he had a glittering sun above his head, and beneath his feet a skilfully-formed machine, by means of which he produced a noise like thunder, and poured out streams of water like rain.

To what purpose does this machine-god serve us in our present inquiry—this Cosroes, who was humbled by the Romans, and hurled from his heaven sooner than he had foreseen? But, foolish as he was, he at least thundered whenever he wished; and is, therefore, more to be honoured than that interior soul of the world which is everywhere and nowhere; which lightens in the clouds, blooms on the trees, creeps in reptiles, swims in fishes, and thinks in man, without possessing consciousness or free-will in itself. In what is this error of modern times, which would make God the soul of nature, and nature the body of God, superior to that of ancient Paganism? In nothing more, than that ancient error gave room to the imagination, which personified and dramatised all the powers and forms of nature. The principle is the same in the modern and in the Pagan error, which considers the essence of God as the central essence of the universe, and does not view God as exterior to the world, but interior to it.

But those who, with simple and sincere minds, not only contemplate in the visible creation its Divine Author, but also honour Him as such, find in the created world only works of the free Divine will, and testimonies or revelations of His omnipotence. "The heavens shew forth the glory of God, and the firmament proclaims the work of His hands." "The firmament on high is His beauty; the beauty of heaven with its glorious show. The sun, when he appeareth, shewing forth at his rising (an admirable instrument) the work of the Most High." (Ecclus. xliii. 1, 2). The boundless space of heaven, which, as in love, embraces all nature, and which forms and retains, by its mysterious powers, corporeal light and life, as it is a symbol of the bounty and splendour of God, so it is also of that essentially different, incorporeal, and spiritual heaven, which is named in the Scripture 'the heaven of heavens.' For that higher order and portion of the created world, and to which nature is subject, is formed of those spiritual creatures, whose essence is in the light of self-consciousness and of freedom, and who are frequently compared in the Scriptures to the stars. (Job xxxviii. 7.)

If it be asked, whether the dwelling of God be in this heaven, which is impenetrable to the ken of human eye, we may, in a certain sense, answer that it is; for thus writes the seraphic Francis in his paraphrase of the Lord's Prayer, "Our Father, who art in heaven, in the angels, and in holy souls." As upon the waters of a clear fount the sun is mirrored from on high, so every pure spiritual creature which is lovingly turned towards God will be enlightened by the light of His splendour. In this sense also spoke the holy Teresa: 'Where the king is, there is his court; where God is, there is heaven.' The soul therefore finds not God in external things, but spiritually within itself; and for this it has the word of the Lord: " If any one shall keep My words, My Father will love him, and We will come to him, and make Our abode with him." In truth, the soul in which God thus dwells may be named a heaven. Shall we, then, in consequence of this truth, pray to Him thus: 'Our Father, who art in our souls?' This would be a dangerous and a deceptive speech; for this form of prayer is used by those who adore the God within them, or rather who adore themselves. They might give this kind of adoration to their own reason, which they call an emanation from the vast ocean of the light of God, or a pure, absolute, and divine reason; or they might adore in a more harsh pantheistic manner that spirit of the world, which, continually striving, is incorporated in nature until it arrives at a higher development in man. If, indeed, these devout persons should pay high honours to Christ, calling Him divine, and profess themselves His adorers, they will confess Him to be no more than that man in whom the divine and all-animating Spirit arrived at its greatest splendour and dignity.

How can it be of any real advantage in an age in which self-adoration and the idolatry of reason prevails, to explain the mystery of heaven as the habitation of God in this mysterious and mystic sense? It is true and certain that, if God dwell within our souls by His grace and by the illumination of His Spirit, these souls may be called a heaven; but, alas! there are too many souls in which God does not dwell. It is indeed true, that for the existence of God there was need neither of our souls, nor of pure spirits, nor of this world of creation. All these might not have been, and God would have existed; for the world cannot be imagined without God; but without the world we may imagine

God, for He is independent, and has His being both within and from Himself.

In what consists the world and its creation? In the idea of God and His divine will. As God, in virtue of His independence (existing by Himself), knows from all eternity His own nature, He knows also whether there be or can be any thing which He is not. That which proceeds from His being and essence is divine and eternal. Hence the Son and the Holy Ghost are uncreated, and of one and the same essence with the Father. But the creation comes not from the essence of God as a procession or emanation, for God is not the world, neither is the world God; consequently it is not of the divine essence. God is independent, that is, He is of Himself what He is and what He thinks; but the world is dependent, both as to the thought that produced it and as to the incorporation of this thought, by the love and omnipotence of God; for every thought which has been carried into effect in the creation of the world is an idea of God, of something which is not Himself; and as God can create only that which is not Himself, we say that He created this world from nothing, for He carried into effect by creation His idea of that which is not Himself.

Whether, therefore, this world had or had not been, whether the visible heaven with its planets, whether the invisible heaven with its spiritual creatures, whether the universe of creation, in its threefold kingdom of spirit, nature, and mankind, be or be not, still God exists; and *where?* In heaven, as our Lord and Saviour commanded us to say? or " in light inaccessible," as the Apostle expresses himself? " in His holy temple," as the Psalmist sings? "on the throne of His Majesty," as St. John and the holy prophet Daniel beheld Him? What do these figures signify? That God dwells, and lives, and exists from eternity in Himself, in His threefold essence. What, then, is heaven, in the strict and proper sense of the word? The absolute being and existence of God in Himself and by Himself. And where else shall we seek Him but in His own essence? Should this appear difficult to our understanding, we must remember that the Apostle has even now told us that He dwells "in light inaccessible;" and St. John the Baptist says, " No one (of mortals) has ever seen God: the only-begotten Son, who is in the bosom of the Father, He hath declared Him." Whence did the Son of God come? From heaven. From the heaven of the stars? How from heaven? Because from all eternity He was in the bosom of His Father, that is, in the essence of God.

When, therefore, we call upon God, and say, "Our Father, who art in heaven," what do we express by these latter words? The expression "who art" is a designation of time; the expression "who art in heaven" is a designation of place. Hence St. John Damascene sublimely and simply teaches, 'God is space to Himself;' that is, He dwells and reposes within Himself. What do we understand by time and space? Time or succession is shewn in the development or progress of our life, space in the actual existence of any thing. Both these are the foundations of a created being; but in God can we imagine either time or space?

The words "who art" designate the divine eternity, which knows neither yesterday nor to-morrow, but is one continued to-day, a true and essential present; whilst our present time is no more than a fugitive moment, of which we can scarcely form the idea before it has passed away. Again, these words, " who art in heaven," teach us that God exists and reposes in Himself, in His sacred, triple personality and infinity; that He is not, therefore, the interior animating soul of the world; for creation is a work of His free power, a manifestation of His ideas, springing not from necessity, but from the fulness of His free and loving will. And when, according to the powers which have been given to us mortal men, we shall have raised ourselves, with St. Paul, to the third heaven, that is, to God Himself, that we may meditate upon those words, " Our Father, who art in heaven," let us return to ourselves again on earth, and ask what moral instruction and knowledge are contained in these words; and here, again, we shall have the blessed Apostle for our guide: " Seek the things that are above," he says; " not the things that are upon the earth." He therefore exhorts us to turn away the eyes of our spirit from earthly and corporeal things, and to raise them towards God; but God is not within the sphere of this world, but above the world. We must, therefore, when we turn to God and raise ourselves to Him, raise our eyes to heaven, that is, above.

Hence man, amongst all earthly creatures, is the only one who, by his admirable or rather wonderful organisation, stands erect, and turns himself towards heaven, to shew that he is created for God and for heaven; and indeed, as in man there is a natural and a spiritual life, the living union of which he represents, he has a father upon earth from whom he receives his corporeal life, but infinitely above is his Father who is in heaven, the Father of lights, who is the immediate Creator of his spiritual life. In this sense the seraphic Francis spoke, when, having been unjustly disinherited and abandoned by his earthly father, he uttered those well-known words: 'Now I can truly say, Our Father, who art in heaven;' that is, I can now wholly, and without reserve, turn myself to that Father who is above this earth.

But even by this heavenly Father man was once abandoned, or, to speak more truly, man, by his own force and proud act, tore himself from the paternity of God; and the broken band could be again united only by God, when He gave to fallen man a divine Mediator and Redeemer, who, in His sublime personality, united for ever the divine and human natures. And as, by this wonderful personality, human nature was, in Christ, placed at the right hand of the Father; that is, as it was exalted in His power and glory; we have in heaven, in the very sanctuary of God, not only a Father, but a Brother also in our human created nature, who is our Mediator and Intercessor with the Father. To Him how fervently and how steadfastly should our eyes, our heart, and our affections be turned!

It is related of the blessed Christina, who was called the Wonderful, that she once entered into a church, in which one of the nobles of Belgium, Lewis Vanloen, was kneeling at the entrance, surrounded with many of his warriors. Christina, who knew him, wished to pass beyond the troop, but suddenly stopped, as if she had something to say to him, and bent down towards him. The Count looked up to her, and she, with sweet fervour, said to him, 'O Lord, how beautiful art Thou!' The soldiers, who heard her words, were diverted, and exclaimed, 'Lord, did you hear how the Saint has praised you?' But he answered, 'Cease; you understand her not: I know well whom she would praise. She did not mean me, but the heavenly and immortal Lord, who is more beautiful than all, and from whom all beauty comes.' 'Thou hast answered well,' said Christina; 'and if that be true, why dost thou not love Him?' The blessed Christina might address the same question to us; and what could we reply? That we love Him not, because we do not see Him. And why do we not see Him? Because He is in heaven, and we are upon the earth, veiled round by a corporeal world. But it is for this very reason that the Apostle admonishes us to consider rather the invisible than the visible. "That which is visible is temporal, that which is invisible is eternal." But how shall we contemplate that which is invisible? This is the power and the object of faith, which comes to the aid of man, a creature composed of spirit and of nature, and who is by the spirit raised above nature, and by nature removed from the spirit; it is faith which establishes his dignity and his virtue. "For we walk now," says the Apostle, "in faith, not in vision." As often, therefore, as we pray, "Our Father, who art in heaven," we make profession of our faith,—of our faith in a true, eternal Father, who has revealed Himself to us, and made Himself visible through His only-begotten Son. We confess Him to be the all-seeing Observer, Rewarder, and Judge of all that which, by the power of our free-will, we think or do against or according to His law;

we confess Him to be a most loving Father, who forgets none of His children, but who is careful of all as of one, and of one as of all, and who will conduct all to the end and object of their being. As He is the object of our faith, so He is also of our entire hope. Or shall we fear that He can forget individuals because they are many, as it might happen in a numerous family, where individual members might be neglected through the want, in their earthly father, of means or of time for their care?

It is told of the blessed Vincent of Paul, that, notwithstanding his many and great labours in the propagation of religion, in his institutions for the care of the sick, for the education and improvement of children in ecclesiastical seminaries, in the relief of provinces which had been laid waste by pestilence and famine, he still found time to attend to a commission which he received from a virtuous tailor, who requested him, in a letter from the country, to purchase for him in Paris some needles, and to send them to him. St. Vincent, in the midst of his many and laborious occupations, did not neglect even this trifling request; for he might have remembered those words of our Lord, "Be ye perfect, as your heavenly Father is perfect;" and who, as the Psalmist says, is highly exalted, and who turns His view to lowly things. God alone is exalted in His absolute being and essence; and He therefore looks down with pleasure upon those who, in humility, confess His grandeur and His absolute essence; whilst, in contrast with Him, they find themselves in their full dependence upon, and subject themselves to, Him in the obedience of love.

The higher the sun shines in the heaven, and the nearer it approaches to the zenith, the more powerful are the effects of its light and heat; the deeper towards the horizon, the more weak are the effects of both. The higher the grandeur and the sanctity of God ascend above our spiritual circle of sight, or, what is the same thing, the more humbly we confess ourselves to be dependent beings and in our true relations to God, the more powerful will be in us the light of faith and the fervour of love. And we shall look to our Father, who is in heaven, as to the eternal spiritual Sun, who beholds all, regulates all, and imparts to all light and happiness. But should doubts arise, like dark clouds and mists, to obscure this warm and consoling faith,— for trouble and sorrow are everywhere natives of this earth, and now with the power of a tempest, and now with slow and heavy pace, effect their dominion over us,—and the Divine assistance does not come, as by miracle, to aid us, let us look up, even on that account, the more, and exclaim, 'Our Father, who art in heaven, deliver us from evil; Thou art in heaven, and we are upon earth; Thou art in Thy eternal existence, and we are in time; Thou art in Thy absolute power, and we are in a state of change and of probation. To whom shall we cry, we who are upon earth, if not to Thee, our Father, who art in heaven?'

Yes, in all the trials, dangers, and pains of this ever-changing life, let us turn to our Father in heaven, and say, 'Nothing of all these things that have happened occurs without Thy knowledge, without Thy ordinance, without Thy permission, without Thy guidance, and without Thy providence; because Thou art our Father, and because Thou art in heaven. Because Thou art in heaven, not in the world, not in nature, but over and above. Thou art the Lord of the natural, of the spiritual, and human world, and dost preserve all things within their limits, which they may not pass over. Because Thou art a Father, Thou dost shew Thyself as the friend and guardian of those whom Thou hast created, that they may know and find themselves and Thee; and Thou art their friend and guardian, even then, when Thou dost visit them with afflictions, that Thou mayest lead them into a true knowledge of themselves, and mayest teach them to purify their own hearts. For to what end are we afflicted with sorrows in this world? That, with that faithless son in the Gospel, we may arrive at a true knowledge of ourselves, and say, "I will arise and go to my Father, and confess, Father, I have sinned against heaven and before Thee." "Against heaven and before Thee;" for Thou art in heaven, and Thou Thyself art heaven, splendid and wonderful in Thy grandeur and infinitude, but known, and glorified, and praised in the created heaven, in Thy glorious angels, and in the beatified spirits. "But who," says the holy Job, "who will give to me, that I may know Thee, find Thee, and stand before Thy throne?" What an immeasurable abyss is there between earth and heaven! What an impenetrable mystery in the formation of the creature from the uncreated thought! What an endless distance between the creature and the Creator!

But this same Creator is Father also; and the creatures whom He has ennobled with intelligence are His children. And if ever it should happen that a miserable, forgotten son should stand before his beloved father, who, being surrounded by noble lords arrayed in their most splendid robes, is seated upon his throne, will not he, the son, not being able to approach or to ascend the steps of that throne to embrace his beloved father, weep in his anguish, in his poverty and abandonment? The father shall see his tears, and his paternal heart shall be moved; he will descend from his throne to embrace the sorrowing one, to comfort him, and to place him at his side. Such is the condition of a soul that has wandered, but which now returns and seeks its God, and the merciful, celestial, paternal love which is expressed in these words, "Thus saith the Lord, The heaven is My throne, and the earth the footstool of My feet; upon whom shall I look, if not upon the poor who is of contrite heart, and who fears My words?" Hence we say, 'Our Father, who art in heaven; Thou dost dwell on high and in light inaccessible. We know not the way to Thee, but Thou hast a way to us. Thy kingdom come. May Thy heaven descend to us, and may Thy splendour shine upon our souls.'

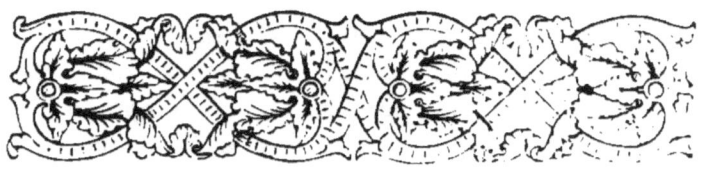

CHAPTER V.

Hallowed be Thy Name.

IF we inhabit or journey through a country in which a barbaric, rude, and vulgar mode of speech prevails, which, although it displeases us, we are nevertheless compelled to use; and if, at the same time, we are certain that, sooner or later, we shall enter another region, which is our true home, and where honour and happiness await us, where no other than an elegant, pure, and noble language is spoken,—we should undoubtedly labour to acquire that speech, which will be the only one that we shall be hereafter able to use, and without which we shall not obtain entrance into that happy country. We now dwell and wander upon this earthly world, which is our first home, but a desolate one; and the language that is spoken here is earthly, obscure, often selfish, impure, and without truth, betraying the elements of which it is composed; for, as the Baptist said, "He that is of this earth, of the earth he is, and of the earth he speaketh." Our future and true home is heaven, and the language that we shall speak 'there is heavenly. But where shall we learn this language, if not upon this earth? and how shall we be made citizens of this heavenly kingdom, unless we take with us the principles at least of this spiritual human language?

Hence, as St. Dominic teaches, the Lord Himself was our instructor in this heavenly language, when He taught us the first of the seven petitions, "Hallowed be Thy name." In this prayer we pray for the language of the angels, which is ever employed in praising and glorifying God, as it is expressed in the introduction to the Canon of the Mass: 'It is truly meet and just, right, and available to salvation, that we always, and in all places, should give thanks to Thee, O holy God, Father almighty, eternal Lord, whom the angels and archangels praise, the cherubim and seraphim, with whom we beseech Thee that we may be permitted to join our voices, saying, Holy, holy, holy, Lord God of Sabaoth, the heavens and the earth are full of Thy glory.' But does it not appear that we say one thing in this song of praise, 'Holy is the Lord,' and another in the prayer, "Hallowed be Thy name?" As God is essentially holy, how can we pray that His name may be sanctified? What, then, is the signification of this petition, so exalted in its expression; and why does it precede all others? We will first examine how we should endeavour to understand it. Having in the introduction turned ourselves to our heavenly Father, and invoked His holy name, we now look forward to that great end towards which all our other petitions are directed. For do we pray that His kingdom may come, that His will may be done, that He would give us this day our daily bread, with only our own interest in view? Certainly not; for this were too little, and unworthy of the Divine love. We should have in our prayers the honour and glory of God as our object; for it is the duty of good children that they should have in view, not so much their own happiness, as that of their beloved parent. And, in truth, to love God purely for God's sake, and not for our own advantage; to wish that God may receive the highest and supreme honour, seems much like a sublime thought. But, viewing this subject in a nearer light, does it appear as if, in this sense, we prayed *for* God? We can pray for ourselves and our neighbour; but dare we to pray for God? Are not the honour and the happiness of God perfect and eternal?

The answer to this question must be as follows: It is certain, and beyond all doubt, that the beatitude of God can in itself receive no addition, and can suffer no loss. But externally He can receive glory; and this is only that honour which He expects and requires from creatures whom He has created for His honour. For thus it is said by the prophet: "Every one who shall call upon My name, I have created him for My honour." (Isaias xliii.) It has been attempted to illustrate this proposition by different examples. As an architect or sculptor produces his work not for himself, but for the use and pleasure of others, and looks for honour as his principal reward; so God produced the works of creation for the benefit and pleasure of man, but proposed, as the last end of creation and of His providence towards man, His own glory and honour. For should we, on the other hand, suppose that the chief end for which He called creatures into existence was the felicity of these same creatures, we should be compelled to confess that, as all are not happy, this end would frequently be not attained. But as the design which God proposes to Himself can never be frustrated, we must seek this in His own honour, which maintains itself, and will ever remain, whether creatures be happy or not. In this last case, the justice of God will be glorified. When, therefore, we pray, "Hallowed be Thy name," let our earnest desire be, that God may receive from all rational creatures that honour and homage which are His due, and which, as such, are an external good and possession of God.

But, strictly speaking, whither does this, perhaps improper, interpretation conduct us? It has happened to many a traveller, placing himself too securely in his chariot to proceed on his journey, that, instead of going forwards, he has gone backwards in his course, his guide having taken wrong ways amidst the darkness of the night. The same may happen to us on our way of interpreting this first petition, proceeding onwards as we have begun, incautiously and too securely. For on this path, where we are surrounded by the obscurity of inadequate expression, we may arrive at an end very different from that which we first proposed. For if the honour and homage which the creature can present to the Creator be not essentially an internal, but an external good, and which the Creator may exact as a tribute to Himself, which He can exact from the creature whom He has brought into existence to pay Him this honour; the omission of this act, or the refusal of it, must be an external (accidental) evil, which He must necessarily hate and punish. To deny Him this external good, is to offer to Him dishonour, injury, and contempt; and He would be deprived of that honour which we thus withhold from Him.

The more these troubled views and half thoughts are pursued into their consequences, the greater will be the obscurity introduced into the service of God. But how differently are we taught by the Psalmist, when he says, "Preserve me, O Lord, for I have put my trust in Thee: I have said to the Lord, Thou art my God, for Thou hast no need of my goods," &c. (Psalm xv.) That is, I hope in Thee, I adore Thee, I praise Thee as my God; for I, on my part, am entirely dependent on Thee, and Thou hast need neither of me nor mine; because Thou art happy and glorious in Thyself, and no creature can add to Thee or take away from Thee, either within or without. How beautifully does the book of Wisdom teach us, in the words of its very commencement: "Think of the Lord in goodness, and seek Him in simplicity of heart." And how profoundly did those Dalmatian Bishops profess this, when, from the Council of Chalcedon, they wrote to the Emperor Leo: 'The full perfection of Christian Catholic faith is contained in these words, "Think of the Lord in goodness;" that is, in truth, and in a manner which becomes the Divinity; "and seek Him in simplicity of heart."' "Think of the Lord in goodness;" 'For what,' asks St. Bernard, 'is God, but the almighty will, the immutable wisdom, the highest philosophy and supreme power?' "Praise the Lord, sing to Him with psalms; for He is good, and His mercy endureth for ever." Yes; when our divine Redeemer was honoured with the name of good Master, He declined this appellation, which was given to Him not as to the God-Man, but as to a simple man. "Why dost thou call Me good?" He said; "no one is (essentially) good but God alone." And, as St. Gregory Nazianzen says, 'No other is good but God.'

But what is the essential, true, and pure good? Benevolent love, without any admixture of self-interest. And should we endeavour to escape from this truth by the assertion, that God did indeed create all men that He might beatify them; but that His chief object was, the honour which, as an external good (*ad extus*), He receives from them, we are in danger of wandering, by a twofold path, away from sacred truth.

First, we form a false idea of the holy omnipotence of God, and we place Him in a kind of dependence upon creatures, who possess free-will to give or to refuse this external honour; for He has indeed full power to punish those who withhold this tribute of adoration from Him, but He is deprived of this external honour by the disobedience of His creatures. Secondly, we form a no less erroneous idea of the Divine love; for we mingle with it a purely human motive of self-interest, which robs it of its purity. And from this, what follows? A numerous party of men, who have renounced their Christian faith, but who, notwithstanding this darkening of their intellect, possess enough of natural acuteness to gather from certain, not ecclesiastical but mere human school ideas, inconsequent and perverse doctrines; they take to themselves the honour due to God; and although their followers do not admit, in a truly orthodox sense, the mystery of the Trinity, the redemption of man, and the divinity of Jesus

Christ, they exclaim, with a holy enthusiasm, "Hallowed be Thy name." They give their own signification to this sacred prayer; for they ask, 'Does God need the bending of our knees? does He require our acts of piety? will He be injured, will He be indignant, will He be rejoiced, or made more happy, if we refuse or offer to Him this homage of reverence and adoration? Is this to hallow the name of God, to imagine that such things can cause in Him indignation or pleasure? Is this to confess the dignity, the loveliness, and the love of God, to believe and to assert that He imputes to all mankind the personal sin of Adam — that He will punish, with the eternal fire of hell, the momentary offence of a man who has been led away by sudden impulse? Verily,' they exclaim, 'this is a crying sin against God; it is to tread beneath our feet the Divine honour, and to desecrate the name of God, as well as the dignity of our own divine reason.'

In an ancient chronicle of the year 1580, compiled by Gabriel Prateolus, we may read the following history. Two hardened drunkards entered together into a tavern, and after they had taken their places and filled their bowls, they pledged themselves, amidst great laughter, in many a dissolute health or toast. At length one raised his cup on high, and asked, 'To whom shall I now drink?' 'Stupid man!' answered his companion, 'drink to God; and you shall hear how He will answer you.' The other continued, 'Of which wine shall I drink — of the old, or of the new?' 'As you please,' replied the companion. 'Here, then,' exclaimed the debauchee, 'I will drink this health in . . year's wine; for although it is but wretched drink, it is good enough for Him.' He then raised the filled cup, and said, 'To Thy health, Lord God! Tell me; for I wonder whether it will please Thee: if Thou hadst given better wine this year, Thy drink would have been better.' And thus far his words; but what happened? This may be read in the work of Prateolus; but he tells us, amongst other things, that the drunkard, stiffening through his whole body, stood powerless and as if turned into stone; and that his companion, seized with anguish, ran from this scene of blasphemy.

What will be said or thought of this narration? Those who have not been imbued with modern ideas— men of every rank, of education, of opinion, and faith— will, without doubt, assent to it; but our modern believers will not so easily give their belief to Prateolus; and should they even allow the truth of his history, they will attribute the extraordinary issue which we have here recounted, partly to natural causes, and partly to superstition. They will, in their indignation, exclaim, 'Why relate to us, men of cultivated minds, histories such as this?' And why should we not relate them? Because they are not consonant to the prevailing ideas, according to which we cannot provoke the indignation of God, or excite Him, like an exasperated man, to revenge by such miserable blasphemies. God is indeed above all human excess and error; for He is wisdom and love. In what anguish is that man, who, borne about by the foaming and overwhelming waves, seizes a plank, or a piece of broken ice, fearing lest every moment this last means of escape may be torn from him! Upon such a support, and in the midst of furious waves, without knowing whither it may be carried, is the human mind, which is made the prey of a tempest of doubts. The corporeal life of man is not indeed thereby endangered; but the peril to his soul, to his salvation, which is founded on sacred truth, upon faith, is the greater. And what is this peril? That the ideas and opinions upon the most important interests of our life, and which are opposed to each other, may err, and may take away from under our feet every firm ground of support; for the one party exclaims, 'Give to God the honour that is due, or He will punish you;' the other also exclaims, 'Give honour to God, and confess that He needs not thy adoration, otherwise thou art not a thinking man, but an unintellectual darkling.' 'Tremble before God,' says the former, 'and live before Him in awe and in fear; for He is most holy and terrible in His justice, for of this hell presents us an evident testimony.' 'Be not a fool,' says the latter; 'cast behind thee saddening cares and scruples, make thyself happy during life, and enjoy whatever presents itself to thee; for thou hast in heaven a merciful and a holy Father, who will condemn none of His creatures; for, as the poet says,

' All sins shall be forgiven,
And hell no more shall be.'

Thus are we placed in straits between these two systems, both of which importunely press us to follow their principles. Which of the two shall we adopt as the true one? Neither. Fear them not, O Christian, but place thyself in the saving bark of prayer, and exclaim with the Psalmist, " Preserve me, O God, in the right way, for in Thee have I hoped: I have said to Thee, Thou art my God, *because* Thou hast not need of my goods." Truly this *because* contains the entire mystery, and clears from our path all danger of error. For if the question be repeated, Did God create *this* world,—this world of spirit, of nature, and of man,—for His own honour? Certainly He did; and the answer is confirmed on every page of the sacred Scriptures. " I am the Lord; I will not give My glory to another: every one who shall call upon My name, I have created and formed for My glory." That is, the honour of existence and being of Himself belongs to God alone; and every creature is thereby commanded to acknowledge its Creator, and to subject itself with reverential honour to His will. But the new and peculiar question which now rises is this, What is the glory of God, and in what does it consist? The answer to this question shall lead us through whirlpools and clouds, and place us on a lovely and firm land.

The glory of God is the bright splendour, the revelation of the sanctity of God; the sanctity of God, as St. Thomas of Aquin and all the Fathers teach, is the purity of His love. The manner and the means by which this purity of His love reveals itself is twofold. For the first revelation is purely internal, namely, the eternal love of the Father and of the Son in the Holy Ghost. The other, or external revelation of the Divine love, displayed itself, first in the work of creation, and again more fully in the creative work of redemption. Of both our blessed Redeemer spoke before the completion of this latter work: " I have glorified Thee upon earth; and now, O Father, glorify Me with that glory which I had with Thee before the world was." But the Divine, and in itself pure and holy love, proceeded forth out from itself, and placed upon this world beings in themselves free and conscious, that He might reveal Himself to them, and impart to them that life and beatitude as soon as they should make themselves, by their own free choice, worthy of so great a blessing. We first perceive the sanctity of God, or the purity of His love, when we see that God, neither by the creation of the world, nor by the love and adoration which creatures present to Him, can add any thing to His holiness, as He could lose nothing should they, of their own free will, turn away from Him. " If thou sin," said Eliu to Job, " if thou sin, what shalt thou hurt Him? and if thy iniquities be multiplied, what shalt thou do against Him? and if thou do justly, what shalt thou give Him, or what shall He receive of thy hand?" (Job xxxv.) We must, then, acknowledge that our love towards God is an exercise of our free will, but is essentially necessary for our happiness; for in God, and with God, we gain ourselves in all things, and lose nothing; whilst, on the contrary, in us, and with us, God neither gains nor loses: His love towards us is, therefore, most pure. This knowledge of the sanctity of God,—that is, of the entire purity of His love,—is the honour of God; and we pray that this knowledge may be universally extended, when we say, " Hallowed be Thy name;" as if we said, may Thy wonderful, pure, and exhaustless love, the perfection and purity of Thy will, be gratefully acknowledged, comprehended, praised, and glorified by all rational creatures, that all may partake of immortal life and of eternal happiness in Thee, that Thou mayst be over them as a bright sun, to draw them to Thyself: may they in Thee find their end and their happiness; but iniquity and darkness shall surround them, if they turn themselves from Thee.

To whom is unknown the ancient fable of the young Narcissus, from whom a flower still derives its name? Being enamoured of his own beauty, he approached so near to the mirror of a fountain, that he fell in, and in his mirror found his grave. What did Narcissus do? He wished to behold *himself;* he loved and he lost himself in considering this self. Like to Narcissus is every Christian who wishes to find his repose and happiness in himself or in any other created being; he falls into and is lost in the depths of his own poverty. Hence it is said, "He who loves his soul shall lose it." If the creature turn its thoughts upon itself, it shall perish in itself; for only in the infinite Divine life, in the union with God, can it find its holy perfection: and that it may find it, that it may be capable of such a perfection, it was endowed with freedom of will. And what a gift was this! What a present of peerless worth, which gives evidence of the purity of the Divine love! For, that God might endow His creature with this freedom, He, in a manner, despoiled Himself of it; He gave that which was peculiarly His own, and in favour of His creature He seemed to renounce His omnipotence; giving to His creature a freedom of will and of acting which excludes all co-action. God does not destroy this liberty, which forms the essence of the creature; for He would then, in contradiction with Himself, take away the essence of the creatures which He had formed. But if the creature, of its own free election, should seek itself, and depart from its God, it will become unholy, and must not dare to cast the blame on God; for although God alone be the fulness of life and of being, He cannot prevent a separation from Him from terminating in woful misery. Thus justice is not excluded from the Divine love, or rather this justice of God (as we will shew later) is the seal of the holiness of His love, as the fault which exists in every sin is made evident by this knowledge. Hence it is written in the sacred Scriptures, "The Lord of Hosts shall be exalted in judgment, the holy God shall be hallowed in justice;" that is, even in His severest judgments, even in the awful manifestations of His chastising justice, the holiness of God and the purity of His love to men shall be made known.

But is this manifestation of justice the object of our prayer when we say, "Hallowed be Thy name?" Not exclusively; for by this petition we ask rather that God would grant to all men His divine grace, His love, and a participation in His glory. But is not this the object of the following petition: "Thy kingdom come?" and if so, what is the peculiar intent of this first petition? That we should pray for the propagation of the knowledge of Divine love, not so much in relation to men and to their spiritual welfare, for we shall consider this in the following petition, but rather in love to God Himself, and in the fervour of a pure love, as far as the creature can exercise this love towards his Creator. It may be that an apparently trifling example may make this more evident. For, in comparison with this sublime doctrine, every earthly similitude must appear but trifling. When a traveller, passing through the American or African deserts, beholds a majestic tree, the far-spreading crown of which is adorned with brilliant and sweet-smelling blossoms, he will know that this noble tree possesses all its grand beauties, whether man behold it and repose beneath its shade or not. He will immediately desire that other men should see this glorious sight. Thus it is in every thing that rejoices us or excites our admiration. We wish that all whom we love should take part in our admiration and joy. So it is with those whom we love and honour on account of their spiritual excellence; and the greater the number of those who have learned to prize this merit, the greater is our joy. But to what a height must this arise, when, by a perversity of the world, the object of our admiration and of our love is our own foolish self!

When, with a truly animated fervour, we have confessed that to God alone essentially belong power, beauty, and goodness, we shall, as a consequence, desire that He should be loved, sought, praised, and adored by all rational creatures; and we shall desire this from a pure love of Him, and from a joy in His attributes. In this fervour of love we shall mutually exhort each other to praise God; yes, like the inspired Psalmist (Ps. cxlviii.), we shall call upon all creatures, without exception, to join in this chorus of praise. He calls first upon the heavens, the angels, and celestial spirits; then upon the firmament, the sun, and the stars. He next descends to the elements, the meteors, and to the feathered inhabitants of the air; next to the earth, to its mountains, abysses, trees, and beasts. He then directs his discourse to the rational inhabitants of the earth, to its kings and princes, to young men, to virgins, and to the aged, to all, that they should praise the exalted name of God. After he has thus passed, in beautifully designed order, through the entire series of created beings, from angels to things inanimate, and to men, he concludes, returning again to rational creatures, with this general invitation : "Let every spirit praise the Lord" (Ps. cl.); let every creature endowed with reason dedicate its life, and exert every effort, that the name of God may be hallowed on earth as it is in heaven. Such also is the theme of the canticle of the three children at Babylon : "All ye works of the Lord," thus invoking the whole of creation, their hymn begins : "All ye works of the Lord, bless the Lord, praise and exalt Him for ever." It turns then to the creatures of the spiritual world : "Ye angels of the Lord, bless the Lord; all ye heavens, bless the Lord." It then passes to nature in all its forms, great and small, in all its developments of physical and organic life; thence, again, to beings of natural and spiritual life, which represent creation in its fulness and collectiveness, and which it arranges before us in order the most beautiful. It invites to the praise of God the sun and the stars, rain and snow, whirlwinds and fire, clouds and lightning, the earth and its fountains, the beasts of the earth, the sons of men, the servants of the Lord, the souls of the just, the holy, and all that are humble of heart. To this canticle the Church has added her tribute of praise, saying, 'Let us bless the Father, the Son, and the Holy Ghost; let us praise Him and exalt Him for ever!' 'For verily,' as St. Ambrose says, 'this is a great canticle, and nothing can be more sublime than this song of praise, 'Glory be to the Father, and to the Son, and to the Holy Ghost.'' For what can be more powerful and more exalted in the mouth and heart of man than this joyful profession of his faith in the divine Trinity! What was the chief object proposed by our blessed Redeemer to Himself during His sojourn on this earth? The hallowing of the name of God, the new and perfect revelation of the essence, truth, and love of God. What impelled the Apostles, so that, without fear and without terror, they threw themselves into the midst of ferocious people, like defenceless sheep amongst ravenous wolves? The burning desire to spread amongst all nations the knowledge of the love of the eternal Father, and of the glory of His eternal Son. This holy desire, that all men may know and love God, and by this obedience honour Him, we also express as often as we pray: "Hallowed be Thy name." We express it in general terms, as the fulfilment of it by all men is not within our power; but in this general form of expression we include ourselves, praying to God that His name may be sanctified by us. And as this depends partly on the power and assistance of God, and partly on our own will and work, it is evident that this petition should not be a mere empty desire, a powerless wish, but a serious and earnest resolve, accompanied with that exertion which is required on our part. To this belongs the true and living knowledge and adoration of the Triune Godhead. For this knowledge raises man to a supernatural state, but cannot be preserved without some sacrifice, and without a persevering fidelity; for it is to the Christian the foundation of all other merit, even the motive of his pardon and reconciliation. So, at least, it is expressed in that prayer which the Church offers for those who are combating with death, and who are already standing at the gates of eternity: 'Remember not, O Lord, his former sins and excesses, which the fervour of evil desires has caused in him. For although he has sinned, he hath not denied the Father, Son, and Holy Ghost, but has believed.'

It is recorded in the ancient martyrologies that a noble Roman lady, named Sophia, had three daughters, whose names were Fides, Spes, and Charitas. These three virgins suffered, one after another, cruel torments and death for the Christian faith. During their sufferings their mother exclaimed with joy: 'How happy am I that I have been made worthy to honour the sacred Trinity in my daughters!' Although this narration should not be generally received as an historical truth, but as a species of parable, as Sophia signifies wisdom, and the names of the three daughters signify faith, hope, and charity, it nevertheless is valuable, even when thus spiritually understood. For when the Divine wisdom imparted itself to man, it formed in him those three heavenly virtues, in the active exercise of which consists the true adoration of God. The name of God is sanctified by faith, which speaks to us of the eternal and external revelation of God; it is sanctified by hope, which grounds itself upon the pure love and goodness of God; it is sanctified by charity, which is ever striving towards God, and which bears evidence to us that God is the end and sanctification of all creatures. But all three bear the martyr's palm; since, being of heavenly descent, they are strangers upon earth, and have to endure many a severe conflict. But the more faithful the Christian is in these conflicts, the more will the name of God be sanctified in him. What a rude combat had not Job, the prince of sufferers, to endure, when poverty, pain, and scorn provoked him to speak against God, and to blaspheme! When, however, the long ordeal had passed, and happiness had turned once more to his house, there were born to him seven sons and three daughters: the names of the sons, contrary to the oriental custom, are not recorded; but we have the names of the daughters, who are praised in the Scriptures as miracles of beauty. The first of these Job named Day; the second Cassia, which signifies a perfume or spice; and to the third he gave a name, the import of which is, the horn of abundance, or the horn of Amalthea.

These extraordinary names were given to his daughters by the great prophet not without cause, nor have they been handed down without cause to posterity, for they contain a high and spiritual sense. The Day signifies faith, which illumines the soul; the spicy Cassia signifies hope, which preserves immortality in the corruptible body of man; the horn of abundance is emblematical of holy love or charity, from which the perfection of all true virtue, of all spiritual gifts proceeds: "The fulness of wisdom," we are told by the son of Sirach, "is the fear of God; she shall fill all her house with her increase, and the storehouses with her treasures, with holy peace and the fruits of salvation." For this confession and this meditation of the sanctity of God, in which the fear of God reposes, contains within itself all spiritual good; and who shall convince himself or others that he hallows the sacred name of God, if he does not fear His infinite majesty?

God, indeed, does not stand in need of our adorations for the increase of His happiness; but we require every moment His assisting and sanctifying grace: "We have all sinned," says St. Paul, "and need the glory of God." The sanctity of God and the purity of His loving will shall always triumph, whether He hath pity on His creature or whether He reject him, for the fault is always and only in the creature: nor is there any consolation for us in this; but our care to walk in fear in the presence of this sanctity and this truth must be more earnest and persevering;—to walk in fear, which is between the extremes of thoughtlessness and of servile cowardice: "Ye who fear the Lord, believe Him, and your reward shall not be lost; ye who fear the Lord, obey Him, and His mercy shall rejoice you; ye who fear the Lord, love Him, and your hearts shall be enlightened." How does this reverence manifest itself, and what are its fruits? "They that fear the Lord will not be incredulous to His word; and they that love Him will keep His way: they that fear the Lord will prepare their hearts, and in His sight will sanctify their souls; they that fear the Lord keep His commandments, and will have patience, even until His visitation." (Ecclus. ii.) "For He is just in all His ways, and holy in all His works. The Lord is nigh to all them that call upon Him; to all who call upon Him in truth. My mouth shall praise the Lord; and let all flesh bless His holy name." (Ps. cxliv.)

CHAPTER VI.

Thy Kingdom come.

THE teachers of Christian antiquity were accustomed to liken prayer to a golden chain which hung suspended from heaven to earth, to raise the minds of men from earthly to heavenly things. But with no prayer was this figure more just than when applied in particular to the Lord's Prayer. From the height of heaven this prayer commences, "Our Father, who art in heaven," and to the lowest depths it descends, "Deliver us from evil." But the seven petitions of this prayer, in their mutual relation with each other, may be compared to the seven links of a chain, which depend one on another, and which are with each other closely interwoven.

The principal or highest of these links is the first petition, "Hallowed be Thy name." But how shall this sublime end be attained? How shall this wish be effected before all things and above all things? This we are taught by the second petition, "Thy kingdom come."

And how does this kingdom of God obtain dominion upon the earth? By this means, that the will of God become the law of man, to which he willingly gives obedience. And this is made manifest in the third petition, "Thy will be done on earth, as it is in heaven." But what are the means, and what the auxiliaries, which enable us to obey the will of God during our life upon this earth? The dispensing of those natural and spiritual gifts which strengthen and support man in his present state of existence in his corporeal and spiritual essence. And in this sense succeeds the fourth petition, "Give us this day our daily bread." But as this nourishment and support of the entire man cannot be effected without the cure of that infirmity which, as a stain, and as the forerunner of death upon the soul, prevents every increase and spiritual perfection, we pray, in the fifth petition, "Forgive us our trespasses." And when this petition has been granted, there necessarily arises the desire that we should be defended and guarded by the Divine protection from every danger, that we may not lose what we have received, and fall into new sins; and hence we repeat this petition, "Lead us not into temptation." But what is the immediate cause and occasion of the many temptations which surround us, and in the midst of the confusion of which we are compelled to live? Principally the manifold evils, partly visible and partly invisible, in the world of nature and of spirit, which spring originally from temptations which have been but weakly resisted; and which evils, having once arisen, and being multiplied, become so many roots of temptation. For this reason we conclude with the petition, "Deliver us from evil."

If we now return upon this chain in an ascending order (which can indeed be done only when the last three petitions have been considered and fully understood), we shall have that first most sublime and universal petition which is expressed in the words of the introduction of the profession of our faith in the divine Trinity, and upon which we have already meditated, "Our Father, who art in heaven." *Father* in Thine own essence; eternally considering Thyself, beholding Thyself, and loving Thyself, in Thy only-begotten Son, through the Holy Ghost; reposing in Thyself, and ever sufficient of Thyself; but *our* Father, whilst, in pure love to us, and in Thy omnipotence, Thou didst create us, in order to give us Thyself for our beatitude; grant that the sanctity of Thy essence and of Thy love may be known, loved, and adored by all Thy spiritual creatures; and above all by men, for Thou alone art worthy of love and of adoration! "Hallowed be Thy Name." Extend Thy dominion over us! may the revelation of Thy love shine in all its splendour upon us, that Thy creatures may know and love Thee with all their powers, and arrive, by means of this knowledge and obedient love, to that end which has been proposed to them! "Thy kingdom come;" and may it extend its power upon earth, as through the spiritual heavens; upon earthly men, as it does upon heavenly spirits! For this must be evident to every man, whatever may be his faith, that God, as Creator and only Author of all things, possesses absolute dominion, and that every one is subject to His omnipotence, whether he know it and wish it or not. "Lord, almighty King," it is said in the Scripture, "in Thy power all things are placed, and there is no one who can resist Thy strength!" The sacred Scripture speaks here in particular of the dominion of the Divine love over those creatures whom He has made capable of His revelations, that they may seek Him and find Him with a loving will. These creatures are the purely spiritual essences, but more especially men. Upon what, then, do we think, and whither do our thoughts arise, when we pray to our eternal Father that " His kingdom may come?" We cannot speak of *His* kingdom, unless there were other kingdoms, in opposition to which our Saviour said, "My kingdom is not of this world." How these kingdoms stand in regard to each other can be learned only from the internal and external relations of man to God, to nature, and to human society.

For as every one knows that the mountain or hill which is within the horizon of his home is always the same, whether it shine beneath the sun, or be veiled by clouds, whether it be covered with hail or snow, or whether blooming verdure adorn it; so we all know and experience that our essence is always one, simple and imperishable, whether we be in joy or in sorrow, in health or in sickness, in prosperity or adversity, in life or in death, in this place or in that, in happiness or in misery. We know also that our essence is so different from all external things, that, whereas they increase, come and go, and disappear, our consciousness ever remains the same. The younger we are, the more innocent we must be; in more advanced age, the more we are inclined to sense and to vanity, the deeper is our consciousness sunk in the life of nature, and darkened by its unclean and unfree elements: the older we become and the more mature, the more do tribulations, wounds, and bitter experience increase; and, above all, the more the light of truth enlightens us in conscience, in faith, and in grace, the more clear will appear to us the severe contrast between our interior spiritual being, and the world of appearances; it teaches us that, in this world of appearances, nothing can make us happy; that all passes away except conscience, and the merit or demerit which is marked therein. Thus is the human spirit subjected to different general laws and powers, which strive for the mastery or dominion over him; that is, over his will. For, as man belongs to two kingdoms, of which he represents the living unity, the higher elements hold the dominion over the lower, that the spirit may rule over nature. But as man, in that important moment when he decided upon his liberty, abandoned the eminence of his spiritual position,—when he turned away from the beatifying end of his being, and exiled himself from the kingdom of Divine love, then (as shall be shewn in its proper place[1]) nature, opposed to the spirit, began to assert its blind dominion; and man, instead of ruling the kingdom of nature, mourned under the weight of its laws, dependent on its elements and power, and was in continual strife with the hostility of external or collective nature, against the blind impulses of his own individual nature, and was thus subjected to corruption and death. Moreover, as man — as he is not only spiritual, but also a natural essence—by his nature represents a whole or a race, from which individuals proceed from generation to generation; so each one belongs to the whole body, and more particularly to his contem-

[1] In the exposition of the sixth and seventh petitions.

porary men upon earth; to society, which is called the world, and which divides itself into the various kingdoms of the world; inasmuch as this society of men is held together and is governed by lawful superiors, and by the observance of mutual duties. As in this relation every individual is a citizen of the world, and subject also to an earthly kingdom, so each one has his great or his small private kingdom, in which he is, or ought to be, lord; whether this kingdom consist of extensive possessions, or of a mere angle of land; whether it be over cities and territories, or only over a cot or a shed. And who is not pleased with this, his kingdom? who does not find pleasure in ruling and in governing, in possessing and enjoying? Still each one must feel, let him endeavour to conceal it or not, how untenable is his edifice, and how loose the rock upon which it is built. The famed Dionysius, who had made himself master of Sicily, had prepared a mighty fleet of four hundred ships, and a most powerful army; he had fortified the city of Syracuse with strong walls, and had compelled his rivals to retire. Did he not think that his kingdom was imperishable? But, whilst with a portion of his fleet he had sailed towards Italy, Dion proceeded against Syracuse to make himself master of that city. A message was immediately despatched to Dionysius; but the courier placed in the same leathern pocket in which were his letters some cooked flesh; and, whilst he slept on the way, a wolf approached and carried away his bag. The messenger dared not present himself without his letters before the king, who, as Dion thus gained time, lost all his acquired power, and was compelled to pass the remainder of his days in the poor occupation of a schoolmaster. What a trivial circumstance was here sufficient to effect the ruin of a mighty kingdom! But there is nothing upon this earth which can promise to man undisturbed possession, or which can truly make man happy; nothing which can fill his spiritual life with the fulness of peace and of joy, that can be found only in absolute life, in God. That courtier who was standing near Alphonsus, king of Arragon, whilst a sum of several thousand golden pieces was presented to him, could not conceal his desire to become the master of so much wealth: 'And ah!' he exclaimed, 'if this were mine, how happy should I be!' 'Be it so,' said the king; 'take it, and be happy.' Who does not see the irony of these words with which the gift was accompanied? Every one who is deluded by the error that happiness is to be found in the goods of this earth is governed by the kingdom of this world; a kingdom in that sense in which Christ said, "The world hateth Me, and I the world;" for, in this sense, by the word 'kingdom of this world,' nothing else is understood than the earthly dominion of error, of lies, and of folly; and in this sense he is designated as "Prince of this world" who was a liar and deceiver from the beginning.

When the human spirit, by its own free act, had turned from God into the path of perversity, and had come into opposition with nature, the pride of sensual life, in union with the blindness and avarice of spirit, and with the wiles of the old tempter, whom sin had made prince of this world, called up every bad passion, which turned away more and more the efforts of man towards his heavenly end, and held him captive in error and in moral degradation. Error and spiritual blindness displayed itself in the monstrous doctrines and fables of Paganism; moral degradation, in a violent inclination to sensual gratification, and to all the bad passions which spring from man's self-love.

Still the Divine mercy did not entirely abandon men, but, introducing and preparing the work of their redemption, it spoke to them by the revelation of the voice of conscience. They, however, in disobedience to this voice, and borne away by the impulse of nature, fell into new crimes, the consequence of which was a more heavy darkness of spiritual knowledge. Thus, by degrees, the spirit lost its clear knowledge of itself, as something essentially different from unfree nature; and in proportion as the spirit of man lost itself in nature, nature exalted him to the dignity of the Godhead; and thus the religious and moral life of man was buried in the awful night of infidelity, of idolatry, and of false knowledge. Thus did the pagan world become a kingdom of darkness and of lies; and the corrupt spirit, which at first despised the love of God, and placed its happiness in unholy hostility against Him, now raised itself into contempt against the Deity, and looked upon the perverted world as its kingdom. For this reason, as St. John teaches, the Son of God appeared, that He might destroy the work of Satan. "As long as a strong man armed keepeth his court, those things are in peace which he possesseth; but if a stronger than he come upon him, and overcome him, he will take away all his armour in which he trusted, and will distribute his spoils." (Luke xi.) As long, that is, as the old stain of sin, and the consequent punishment of the separation from the sanctity and the love of God, lay upon mankind, the human race was bound in the bonds of sin, in ignorance, and in mental captivity, exposed to the wiles of the tempter, and sunk more deeply in its own misery. But when, in the fulness of time, in the period of the most complete corruption, the same Divine Word which had revealed itself in the voice of conscience appeared amongst men as the Son of God and of man, and by His voluntary obedience expiated sin, and effected a reconciliation of man with God; then were the arms of the strong one broken, darkness fled before the new splendours of revelation, wickedness before the new life of love; and a new kingdom of infinite power and dignity was founded upon earth, which, from its founder and ruler, is called the kingdom of God—the kingdom of heaven: the kingdom of God, because it extends the renewed dominion of God's love over mankind; the kingdom of heaven, because it effects their spiritual regeneration by the new and heavenly Adam. But as this kingdom rules over creatures, and unites within itself the visible and invisible spirit and nature, it is, therefore, itself visible and invisible, external and internal. It is an internal kingdom, inasmuch as it is spiritual; and hence our Saviour says, "The kingdom of God comes not with tumult and with power, and it shall not be said, Lo, it is here or there! for behold, it is within your souls." But as, in the nature of man, spirit and body cannot be so separated, as if they were halves of his being, so the kingdom of God cannot rule the souls of men, without, at the same time, laying its foundations in their corporeal visible nature; and hence this kingdom was compared by our Redeemer to a city built upon a mountain, and which cannot, therefore, be concealed.

Our Redeemer came as a man amongst men, that He might belong to all men, and that all might belong to Him; and as the entire human race exists through Him, so it is necessary that He be continually present amongst mankind, so that each one who shall desire it may partake of the fruits of redemption. This continued and real presence of the redeeming humanity of Christ, and the consequent continuance of the work of redemption, is the kingdom of God upon earth—the Church. The Church is, therefore, not merely an assemblage of the faithful, nor a certain invisible spiritual bond between men seeking God, but it is the ever continuing, living intercourse between Christ and men, by which He extends to all His merits; and this by means of a visible living form, which being an organic whole reposes upon unity. For as we men are capable of redemption, and possess a Redeemer only as we are members of a specific race or of one great whole; so the Church, which is the continual redemption, must be organically formed, and the continued office of the mediatorship or priesthood of Christ must be continued by earthly servants and representatives, who, ranging themselves around a visible head, as did the Apostles once around St. Peter, form the ecclesiastical hierarchy. Only by means of this divine institution was it and is it possible that the sanctification which was gained by Christ for man could be applied to all those who seek it in a spirit of voluntary obedience. This sanctification is twofold. It consists, first, in the merits of the sacrifice of Christ, which should be applied, not only to all men in general, but to each one in particular; so that Christ may appear before His Father in each one, and in each one in Christ. This is effected in the unbloody sacrifice in which our blessed Saviour daily offers Himself and is offered to His eternal Father as the property of mankind. But not only this merit of the Lord, but the fruit also of this merit is the property of the Church—the imparting of the divine Spirit and the reconciliation of man with God. This imparting of the divine Spirit, considering the nature of man, is effected also in a visible manner, partly under the guidance of the teaching Church, by which it is preserved in the constant possession of the uncorrupted truths of salvation, and partly in those gifts and graces which are adapted to all the wants and epochs of human life, and which, under the name of sacraments, are intended either to reconcile with God, through Jesus Christ, those who have been separated from Him, or to strengthen and to arm those who are united with Him. Now, as there is but one human nature, and, consequently, only one Christ, and only one way of life and of holiness through Him, how can there be more than one true Church? And this one true Church, how can it be otherwise named than that which alone sanctifies us, as there is but one Sanctifier, who is present in it, and in it imparts His gifts?

When, therefore, we repeat the petition, "Thy kingdom come," we pray, not so much for the institution of the kingdom of grace, for this was founded more than eighteen centuries ago, as for the extension of the same over the whole human race in every region of the habitable globe; that our Saviour, who belongs to the human race, may belong to every individual, and that the continued work of the redemption in the Church may be applied to all men. Should it, then, surprise us that this great work of God has made but slow advances over the earth, that so great and extensive territories are still veiled in the darkness of Paganism, that the rude Deism and fatalism of the monstrous Alcoran should dominate in those countries where once the Church in all its glory flourished? The answer to this is found on the first page of the Gospel, "The Light shone in darkness, and the darkness did not comprehend it; He came unto His own, and His own did not receive Him." The second answer was given by the Apostle, that mighty conqueror in the service of Christ, who, with untiring zeal, and with a sacrifice at which we can never sufficiently wonder, travelled over Europe and Asia to bear the kingdom of God to men, when he said, "How shall they call upon Him in whom they do not believe; and how shall they believe in Him of whom they have not heard; and how shall they hear, if no one announce Him?" We pray, therefore, in the second petition, that the Lord would arm with the spirit of His love, patience, and self-devotion, new heralds and bearers of His salvation, who, like the Apostles of India, Cochin China, and Japan, of Peru and Canada in the last centuries, may go forth to drive the errors of Paganism from the earth, and to open the way of the liberty of the children of God to the slaves of error and of sin. And, that our petition may not consist in mere empty words, but may be an invocation of the Divine assistance and blessing upon our undertakings, a not less easy than joyful opportunity for effectual co-operation has been offered to zealous Catholics by the institutions of modern times.[1]

Instead of the ancient superstitious idolatry, we have now, in the west, south, and east, the new or modern idolatry, which, in the midst of the primitive doctrines of Christianity, rears its proud head and displays itself, in part theoretically, as pantheistical wisdom, and in part practically, in its apostacy from Christ, and consequently from the Church, as an idolatry of sensuality, and an abandonment of all the laws of morality. We must, therefore, when we repeat this petition, "Thy kingdom come," pray for the multitudes of those who contemn Christ, who belong to the Church in name only, but are not nourished from its source of life. They shall not, indeed, destroy this kingdom, to which has been given the promise, that "the gates of hell shall not prevail against it;" but they do destroy the kingdom of God within their own souls, and stand therefore in great need of the prayers of their brethren.

But let those who earnestly endeavour to remain within this kingdom look up with confidence to Him whom it secures to them as a Father. "Behold," —thus they are instructed in the hundred and thirty-third Psalm—"behold, now, bless ye the Lord, all ye servants of the Lord, who stand in the house of the

---

[1] Namely, the Leopoldine Institution, a flourishing union for the Catholic missions in North America; and the Society for the Propagation of the Faith, founded at Lyons; in support of which the smallest assistance must be of even greater value than the two mites which the poor widow cast into the treasury of the Temple, and which our Saviour, estimating them by the charity of the donor, declared to be of more worth than the rich presents of others.

Lord, in the courts of the house of God. In the nights lift up your hands in the holy places, and bless ye the Lord. May the Lord out of Sion bless you, He that made heaven and earth." "The house of God is the Church of the living God, the pillar and the ground of truth" (1 Tim. iii.); the court of the house of God is the Church militant, the entrance to the Church triumphant in heaven. From the Church militant, in the night of this earthly life, we raise our hands to the holy places, namely, to the Triune God; and He who made heaven and earth, and who, by the Church, has founded a kingdom of heaven upon earth, blesses His people from Sion,—that is, in the Church and through the Church; for thus was it promised by the ancient Seer, " The law shall go forth from Sion, and the word of the Lord from Jerusalem."

CHAPTER VII.

Thy kingdom come; Thy will be done.

HILST the kingdom of God upon earth, as the visible militant Church, effects the intercourse of man with God, and strengthens the spiritually regenerated gifts of grace, that he may be able to withstand his earthly trials, there is another kingdom of God—the heavenly kingdom above this earth, in which faith is exchanged for vision, grace for the fulness of happiness; in which no trial can find entrance; until, at length, when this earthly time shall have closed, the eternal and perfect kingdom of God shall be founded, in which the entire man shall be admitted to glory and beatitude. " For until now we groan within ourselves, waiting for the adoption of the sons of God, the redemption of our body." (Rom. viii.) Of this kingdom of glory we are taught to think when we pray to our eternal Father, that His kingdom may come; for " if we be sons, we are heirs also."

We must therefore consider with what feelings we

repeat this prayer, and whether our desires correspond to its signification. For there are two classes of men from whose hearts this prayer could not proceed. To the first class belong those obstinate unbelievers who systematically defend themselves in their perversities; to the second, those imperfect Christians, who, although not untrue to the Divine law, are still attached with greater love to the life of this earth. Can the former desire the coming of the kingdom of God? The petition, "Thy kingdom come," would, in their mouths, bear an awful signification. It would be as if they said, 'May Thy justice descend upon us; may Thy immutable sanctity and truth reveal themselves to us; may Thy chastising omnipotence seize us, and bear us away to that place where we shall never more abuse our liberty—that divine gift which came from Thee.' And how can imperfect and lukewarm Christians, who are enamoured with worldly pleasures, seriously pray, "Thy kingdom come," whilst they look upon the gates of death, which lead to this kingdom, with terror, and whilst they would willingly remain for centuries upon this earth?

We are told of a rich man in Belgium, who, when his physicians had lost all hopes of his recovery, caused himself to be taken into his pleasure-grounds, where, looking with tearful eyes upon the beautiful scene before him, he uttered in his anguish these foolish words: 'Why should I depart from this place; I have never sought my heaven away from thee; why canst thou not give me this earth?' How far was this unhappy man from understanding the second petition of the Lord's Prayer! But the Divine love, which will not leave us in so baneful an error, and which therefore shews itself as a strong love, has provided that we should open our eyes to the truth; and that nature and the world should exhibit themselves in such varying scenes of frailty and corruption, that it is impossible, even for the most thoughtless, not to behold this changing and fleeting nature of all worldly things.

In the chronicles of the fifteenth century, a princess is mentioned who possessed all the endowments that could make her shine in the kingdom of this world; and who nevertheless freely resigned all these pretensions. Johanna of Portugal, daughter of King Alphonsus, was called a miracle of beauty; but who might be named the despair of painters, for so many of them were sent to paint her portrait, and all confessed that no power of art could imitate such beauty. It is related of Louis XI., a man whose superstitious devotion is well known, that, when he beheld her portrait (which, however, was far inferior to the original), he threw himself upon his knees, and fanatically thanked God, who had condescended to permit him to look upon such a reflection of heavenly beauty. If ever there were princess upon this earth who could lay claim to the grandeur of this world, was it not Johanna? But within her soul there lay a deep and melancholy seriousness, which despised all thoughts of marriage, and which must be considered as a presentiment of future events. In vain did the Dauphin of France (afterwards Charles VIII.) and Maximilian, son of the Emperor Frederic, endeavour to gain her hand. But scarcely had Charles ascended his throne, when he sent an embassy to Lisbon, through which he not only renewed his suit, but accompanied it with threats of vengeance. John, king of Portugal, enraged against his sister, compelled her to listen to his prayer. The princess asked for a short time, in which she might deliberate. She passed some hours in prayer, and then declared to her brother, that she was willing to give her hand to the king, if he were alive to accept it. The prince was surprised by this speech; but, after a few days, the intelligence arrived that the young king was dead. It was not long before an embassy arrived on a similar purpose from Richard III., king of England. Again Johanna requested time for thought; she deferred her answer for some days, she prayed and wept much; but at length approached her brother with calmness, and declared that she was ready to sail that hour for England, if he to whom she was to be betrothed was still alive. 'If he be dead,' she added, 'grant me this boon, the only one I ask, that you will no more compel me to listen to like propositions; for you must see that they are contrary to the will of God.' The king, struck with the composure and firmness of her manner, believed, by anticipation, that which, during the week, was announced by messengers of grief. What followed is learned from the sequel of this history. This wonder of beauty, this Christian Turandot, retired into a monastery. There followed an event which, although not impossible, nor to be classed amongst ancient legends, is yet most wonderful. The princess formed her little garden in the court of the cloister, in which she planted with her own hand orange and lemon-trees, roses and lilies. But she soon died; and when her corpse was borne through the cloister, all her trees and flowers languished, and never raised their drooping leaves again. For, as the Seer exclaimed, "All flesh is grass, and its glory like the flower of the field; the grass is withered, and the flower is fallen: the word of the Lord remaineth for ever." This great thought had taken possession of the heart of this princess, whose life upon this earth was like that of the flower; and, with the Psalmist, she thought, "What have I in heaven? and besides Thee, what do I desire upon earth? My flesh and my heart have fainted away; Thou art the God of my heart, and the God that is my portion for ever. For behold, they that go far from Thee shall perish; Thou hast destroyed all them that are disloyal to Thee." (Psalm lxxii.)

Against this idea, which is painful to the world and to a life of worldly pleasure, many an objection may be urged. For it may be said, Where is the man who can devote himself entirely to God, who can seek Him alone, and live upon this earth a superterrestrial life? The answer is easy: That man may be found every where, and each one is that man. For let any one be found in difficulties, in occupations, in cares, labours, and troubles, he then stands, in regard to God, in the relation of a creature and child to his Creator and Father; each one is united in a strict bond of union with a God-Man, his Redeemer, by means of, and in, the Church; each one is engaged in one duty, which surpasses all others, namely, his spiritual warfare; each one is burdened with one important care; let him not fail in zeal and fidelity in this great duty.

Let us now seat ourselves on some extreme height of danger, abandonment, and want; let us represent to ourselves a wanderer, who, journeying amidst Alpine ice and snow, like that noble German prince of whom history tells, comes at last to the edge of an awful precipice of rock, where, full of anguish, and in want of every help, he clings to the stone, waiting with horror, until, weakened by hunger, he shall fall into the fathomless abyss;—let us imagine a man awakened from his sleep by the roar of waters and the crash of ice, borne away, together with his little cabin, clinging to a beam, or perhaps to a tree. Covered with snow and rain, stiff with fear, he looks through the horrid night, and sees the ice approaching nearer and nearer, and the waters rising higher and higher, and his watery grave opening beneath him. What is, and what should be, his last and only thought? 'Lord, omnipotent God, inscrutable in wonder, the kingdom of this world now passeth away from me, and Thine is approaching; remember not, O Lord, the follies and sins of which I have been guilty against Thy truth, Thy sanctity, and love; have mercy on me, Thy creature, whom Thou hast redeemed.' Truly he is happy whose life being thus perilled, within whom glows the light of this thought; and thrice happy he, if he bear with him the testimony of a good conscience. But where should he who has not this testimony in his favour look for help in the time of danger? A Polish king, Sigismund II., was called, in derision, the King of the East, because he was accustomed to defer even the most important affairs to the rising of the morning sun, and hence he seldom brought any thing to a successful result. But he who has learnt to seek his kingdom, his riches, and possessions, not exclusively in this world, will guard himself from such folly, and will exert every effort to preserve or to recover his portion in that kingdom which is subject to no change.

We are commanded, as St. Augustin remarks, to pray thus: "Thy kingdom come," not, 'Let us come into Thy kingdom;' because we must aspire to the joys of a future life by means of a distaste of this earthly life, and we must, therefore, wait and persevere until that life should come. For as the kingdom of God is made one with that blessed life for which we hope, and at which we can arrive only through the gate of death, we are taught by the parables of the wise and foolish virgins, and of the servants who continued to watch through the night for their master, that we must persevere in watchfulness and in patience until the unknown hour shall come. Still are we not allowed to wish for death; for death is a punishment of the sin with which the whole human race is stained. But if we speak of that eternal kingdom of God which shall commence with the resurrection of the dead, the coming of this kingdom to men is solemnly announced, when men shall live in glorified love upon a new or glorified earth. (Apoc. xxi.) Finally, if we speak of the kingdom of God as it should be within ourselves, we arrive at this, not so much by our entrance into the kingdom of God, as by its approach towards us, as it is declared by the words: "Do penance; for the kingdom of heaven is at hand." The approach of this kingdom, and its establishment in our souls, are effected when God establishes His full empire within us and over us, when we submit to this empire by a willing and loving obedience to His will.

When, therefore, we utter this petition, of which of the significations contained therein must we principally think? Our Saviour taught us, when He said: "Not every one that saith to Me, Lord, Lord, shall enter into the kingdom of heaven; (not every one who speaks of the kingdom and dominion of God has, on that account, a part in this kingdom;) but he that doth the will of My Father." Hence this petition, "Thy kingdom come," is necessarily and immediately followed by the third petition, "Thy will be done."

For, from a superficial consideration, there might arise the question, Why is this third petition necessary? God spoke, "Let there be light, and there was light; He commanded, and all things were created." What, then, has this word of man, "Thy will be done," to do with the Divine omnipotence? The will of God is necessarily all-powerful; nature and the elements are subject to Him; His will is deed: "Fire, hail, snow, and stormy winds fulfil His word." (Psalm cxlviii.) And if the whole universe be subject to Him, has He not power to lead irresistibly the hearts of men, that they should will what He wills, and should act according to the commands of His wisdom? But the contradiction which lies in this question is made manifest, as soon as we fully comprehend our own nature. Our personal existence and being is, on the one side, corporeal and unfree; on the other, spiritual, and consequently free. Our corporeal life is subject to the laws of nature, and therefore God is its sovereign Lord, as He is of all nature. But the spirit is not like the body, circumscribed by natural life; it is not, as many vain systems have taught, a spark from the ocean of the light of God—an emanation from God; but it was created immediately by God, and was gifted by its Creator with the dignity and privileges of freedom; so that, of its own free choice, it can obey or contradict the will of God: a great and inestimable gift! When Diogenes, a man who sought renown by his contempt of all human grandeur, was asked what was, without exception, the choicest and best of things given to mortal man, 'Freedom,' he answered from his tub. If this answer be taken in its true, that is, in its spiritual sense, nothing can be more important. By my free-will, I am what I am. I possess this personal being, indeed, originally from God; I am not the creator of my being, but I am the co-creator of my existence, inasmuch as by my own free-will I can determine and act; for, as a great teacher said, 'He who created me without myself (when I was not), will not save me without myself (without my free co-operation).'

What a high mystery! Have I a free-will at the cost of the Divine freedom? Has the Divine Omnipotence imparted to me a power which places bounds to this same Omnipotence? In externals, and in a certain sense, this is true; for, when God created free creatures, spirits and men, He deprived Himself in part of His unconditional dominion over them; He surrendered His freedom; and this in the holiness of His will, in the purity of His love, to bestow upon them the fulness of His essential holiness; of which, without a likeness of God, that is, without freedom, they can have no part. This freedom, then, the highest and the noblest of my endowments, a gift entirely divine, I can employ for the accomplishment of that end for which it was given to me by God, for the perfection and sanctification of my being, when I obey the Divine will. It is in my power also to employ it in my ruin; when, in opposition to God, I estrange myself from His love, and I can continue so eternally, but in existence of lies and of misery, which is wretched, unhappy, and nothing, without being annihilated. 'Joy to the will,' says St. Augustin, 'when it is good; woe to the will when it is evil; but whether it be good or evil, it is still a will.' What is this evil will? An unholy, self-destroying freedom. 'An evil will,' as St. Anthony of Padua expresses himself, 'is an evil tree, the roots of which are passion—the trunk, obstinacy—the branches, sinful actions—the leaves, lying and vain words—and the fruit, eternal death.' That is, an eternal life in an eternal separation from God; an eternal existence without light and love; an eternal effort and agony without effect. This tree struck its roots even in Paradise, whilst man was in his primitive innocence; widely and more widely it stretched forth its branches; it became the wood of the cross on which the Restorer of good will to men suffered the death of reconciliation.

For in what consists the first cause of the perversity of our will? In a rude, self-condemning delusion. The Divine will is the absolute law to which the human will should bend; but, conscious of its freedom, it will assert it, and does so by acts of disobedience. Disobedience conducts inevitably to a separation from God, thence to the powerless, miserable state of a perpetual lie; whilst obedience sweetly conducts to God, and consequently to the intended end for which freedom was given.

But the man who opposes the contempt of disobedience to the Divine law, not only alienates himself from the paternal love of God, but follows also into the slavery of nature, over which he can hold spiritual dominion only by his fidelity to the Divine law. On two grounds, therefore, he changes the relation of God to himself; for it can no longer be considered as the relation of a father to his child, but as that of a sovereign lord to a rebellious slave. Hence the perfection of the obedience of the new and heavenly Man, who came in the form of a servant to redeem those who were in slavery. "I came down from heaven, not to do My own will, but the will of My Father, who sent Me;—in the head of the book it is written of Me, that I should do Thy will, O Lord: I have declared Thy justice in a great church; I have declared Thy truth and Thy salvation." (Psalm xxxix.) The Divine will, which spoke only in command to the conscience, and as a law to enslaved man, our divine Redeemer revealed as the law of love. He also brought with Him grace, or heavenly strength, to enable us to obey this law: by the sanctity of His life, and by the entire subjection of His human will to all the Divine precepts, He shines as a living example before us. When, therefore, He taught us thus to pray, "Thy will be done," He intended that will, which is made known to us by a triple revelation, in conscience, in the law, and in the Church, as a Divine precept; and also as a hidden command of God, which is then first made manifest when it proceeds to action. In its full signification, this petition would run thus: 'May Thy will be done, O Father, in us (by us) and towards us.' In us, or by us, that we may fulfil the Divine will revealed to us in the Divine law, which we resist by our disobedience. Towards us, inasmuch as the Divine will is made manifest to us in those ordinances which we cannot withstand, but against which we may rebel. "Remember this," says the Prophet; "remember the former age; for I am God, and there is no God beside, neither is there the like to Me; who shew from the beginning the things that shall be at last, and from ancient times the things that as yet are not done; saying, My counsel shall stand, and all My will shall be done." (Isaias xlvi.) To this will of God we should conform by a joyful obedience. When, therefore, we meditate upon this Divine will, which is revealed to us as a law, we pray, in the third petition, for the assistance of Divine grace, which may lighten and strengthen our will, that we may do that which is pleasing to God. Of this kind of prayer, there is contained in the Psalms a rich abundance. "Direct, O Lord, my way, that I may observe Thy commands; direct my steps according to Thy words, that no injustice may rule over me; give me understanding, that I may know Thy commands; teach me to do Thy will, for Thou art my God." In the same manner wrote St. Paul to one of the first Christian Churches: "I pray daily for you, that you may be filled with the knowledge of the will of God, in all wisdom and spiritual understanding: that you may walk worthy of God, in all things pleasing, fruitful in good works." (Col. i.) As much, therefore, as we contemplate this Divine will, which reveals itself in the dispensations of His providence, we look upon our model, Jesus Christ, who prayed to His eternal Father, "Not as I will, but as Thou wilt;" and who taught us to meditate upon this *as*, when He taught us this prayer: "Thy will be done on earth *as* it is in heaven."

In records of antiquity worthy of credibility, it is related, that Epictetus, a priest of the oriental Church, whom Latronianus, duke of the Almaridians, cast into prison on account of his religion, held this discourse with Astion, a layman, and a companion in his sufferings. 'When we shall be called to-morrow to the interrogatory, let us answer nothing but these words: We are Christians; this is our name, our family, and our country! But should God decree that we should be visited by tortures, our only words shall be: O Lord, Thy will be done.' True to their resolve, they answered every useless question that was put to them with these words: 'We are Christians; we adore Christ, and despise your idols.' In the midst of their tortures, and as often as a new pang was added to their sufferings, they exclaimed, 'Thy will be done, O Lord, in us.' Unconquered, they were carried back to prison; but Vigilantius, who had assisted at the trial, could not banish these words from his memory; and frequently, and almost against his will, he found them on his lips. Whether he considered them as words of magic, by which, as the pagans believed, all power of torture was broken, or whether a higher interpretation of them were given to him, he appeared on the fourth day publicly before Latronianus, and said, 'I am a Christian; the will of God be done in us.' He was cast into prison with Astion and Epictetus, who instructed him and baptised him. On the thirtieth day they were conducted to execution, and met their death with songs of praise: 'Blessed be the name of the Lord; for His will has been fully accomplished in us.' Was there indeed a Divine power in those words, so that their repetition and meditation upon them could convert a persecutor of Christians into a martyr? Certainly; and who can deny it? They are of Divine origin; and he who would experience their power, need only repeat them frequently and fervently to impress them living upon his heart; as we read in the thirty-ninth Psalm: "My God, I have desired it, and Thy law in the midst of my heart; Thy will I desire to obey, for it is the law and will of my will."

CHAPTER VIII.

Thy Will be done on Earth as it is in Heaven.

IF we compare the expressions of which the first three petitions of the Lord's Prayer are composed, we shall find in them all the same general and impersonal form. Why do we not utter these petitions with greater precision, thus: 'Hallow Thy name in us; may Thy kingdom come to us; fulfil Thy holy will in us?' Or in this other form: 'We will hallow Thy name; we will enter into Thy kingdom; we will fulfil Thy will?' The reason is clear enough; for if these petitions were expressed in the first form, it would seem that we intended and desired that God alone, without our co-operation, should accomplish all these things. In the second form they would assume a tone of presumption, as if we lived in the rash confidence that we could attain to so great an end by our own private powers, and without assistance from on high. We have already seen that, although God be the sole Creator of man, man is nevertheless the co-creator of his ultimate existence. For although all being and existence, and all good things, come from God, yet they come in such a manner that God works no good in us, who are free creatures, without our consent and co-operation; and as we, on the other hand, to attain to good, must employ our will and our desire, it is in such a manner that all our efforts would be fruitless and vain, without the assistance of Divine grace. "He who remaineth in Me, and I in him, the same bringeth forth much fruit; for without Me you can do nothing." (John xv.)

This, therefore, is the cause of the general and impersonal form of these three petitions; and thus we do not say, 'Fulfil and perfect Thy will in us,' nor, 'We are ready and prepared to do Thy will;' but we say, 'Thy will be done, by Thee and by us; and as this Thy will in the uncreated heaven, in the sanctuary of Thy triune essence, exists as an eternal idea, and goeth forth from Thee as law, so shall it be obeyed, through love and reverence to Thee, by us Thy spiritual creatures on earth. May Thy will live and reign, as in Thee, so in us; as in heaven, so upon this earth.' And as also in the created heaven of spirits the Divine will is fulfilled, as we read in the Psalm, "Praise ye the Lord, all His angels, who do His will;" we pray that the same may be done with the same alacrity and joy by us on earth. And as in Christ, the God-Man and Mediator, His human will was ever and entirely subject and conformable to the Divine will, in the pure accordance of love, we pray also for the grace of a like conformity, which may unite us here upon earth with God; for "he who is joined to the Lord is one spirit with Him."

And as the Prophet foretold of Christ, "The will of God shall be prosperous in His hand" (Isaiah liii.), so was the Church instituted by Him, the office of which is to teach and to preserve the will of God. "Her Just One shall come forth from Sion as brightness, and her Saviour shall be lighted up as a lamp; but Jerusalem (the Church) shall be called by a new name; she shall be a crown of glory in the hand of the Lord, and the will of God shall be in her"—she shall be the guardian of the Divine will. (Isaiah lxii.) But in what consists this Divine will, which, by means of the holy Church, is to be fulfilled in us? "This is the will of the Father, who hath sent Me," says Christ, "that every one that believeth in Me may not perish, but have everlasting life." This will of God is already fulfilled in the holy angels, and in the glorified souls of holy men; but in us not yet; and therefore we pray, "Thy will be done," as in those who have reached their happy destiny, so also in us, who are still wanderers here below, "on earth as it is in heaven." The former, in whom the Divine will is perfected, fulfil on their parts, in the most perfect manner, this holy will; for, without prejudice to their freedom, they can no more be separated, in the splendour of the Divine light, either from truth or from love; whilst, on the contrary, in us mortal men, nothing is more common than the blinding of our intelligence and the perversion of our will, and generally because nature or passion is permitted to rule over the spirit.

As the full dignity of man can be attained only when the corporeal or animal life of nature is exalted to the spirit, and is fully governed and penetrated by the spirit, when the spirit is raised up to God, and united with

Him, we may, according to the expression of St. Cyprian and of St. Gregory Nazianzen, with full justice, call the spirit of man a heaven, and his body earth. The spirit is a heaven by its heavenly offspring, by being an immediate creature of God, and by its capability of divine revelation; the body, on the contrary, is earth, because it is formed of earth, the most noble and the highest formation of created nature. "The spirit is willing," as our Saviour tells us, "but the flesh is weak." On the part of his spiritual and heavenly life, man is inclined to bend to the Divine will; not so on the part of his earthly life, which follows the weight of earthly nature. Hence, in this signification, we pray, "Thy will be done on earth as it is in heaven;" that is, as our spirit knows Thy will, and desires to obey it, so may nature also obey it, without being led away by its inclination to contradict this spirit, so that the entire man may be sanctified by grace: "Thy will be done," by our nature, as by our spirit. For this is the express teaching of the Apostle, "This is the will of God, your sanctification." And in what does this our sanctification consist? We have seen that the sanctity of God is no more than the purity of His will, of His disinterested, infinite, creative, sanctifying love. If the creature is bound to aim at sanctity (to a likeness with God), in what must this consist, if not in his turning to God in the most pure and spiritual love? Hence the Apostl carefully places the sanctification of man before every thing that might contaminate or frustrate the endeavours of his spiritual nature, which might degrade his life to a mere animal existence, in which nature, with its inclinations, reigns triumphant. "This is the will of

God, your sanctification; that you should abstain from fornication, and that every one of you should know how to possess his vessel in sanctification, not in the passion of lust, like the Gentiles, who know not God. For God has not called us unto uncleanness, but unto sanctification." (1 Thess. iv.) When, therefore, we say, "Thy will be done on earth as it is in heaven," this petition signifies, in a fuller extension, that, "as in heaven" the inclinations of nature shall no longer rule over us, but only Thy holy love; and as Thou hast promised, that after the resurrection men shall be as the angels, free from the slavery of the body, so may Thy pure and spiritual love rule over us upon earth, that by it we may overcome the impurity of our sensual inclinations, and may live worthily of Thee.

Gregory of Nazianzen, surnamed the Theologian, was yet a youth at Athens, whither he had gone to devote himself to study, when, being once engaged with his books, he fell into a slumber; and suddenly, in clear vision, there stood on his right and left hand two virgins of celestial beauty. Astonished, he asked them what was their wish; but they kindly answered, 'Trouble not thyself, for we are well known to thee, and we are named Wisdom and Chastity; we have been sent from heaven to take possession of the abode which thou hast prepared for us in thy heart; unite thy spirit with us, and we will exalt thee to the full light of the sacred Trinity.' Wisdom and purity are inseparable sisters; and he who is faithful to one will not be a stranger to the other. "The luxurious man hath heard a wise word, which shall displease him, and he shall cast it behind his back." (Ecclus. xxi.) How can the carnal man, whose life, and thoughts, and ideas are in the life of nature, have any thought or capacity for spiritual truth? His spiritual free being is under the yoke of his unfree nature; and as the whole life of nature continually strives for existence, the slave of nature is continually governed by its passions, which he, as a spiritual being, ought rather to rule; and, to his shame, he seeks delight in those things which ought to appear to him terrible, as they are the mystery of his origin. Great, or rather terrible, must we call this mystery, for it threw heaven and earth into commotion. For as man is the living unity of two contrary substances, his existence has a twofold source. As by his life of nature he belongs to one species, he has been brought into existence, as to his body, by the power of nature.

Amidst the general corruption which reigns amongst men, the Christian must frequently and seriously ponder on the exhortation of the Apostle: "Be not conformed to this world, but be reformed in the newness of your mind;" be not borne away by prevailing opinions, but examine all by the spirit of the Gospel; "that you may prove what is the *good*, and the *acceptable*, and the *perfect* will of God." (Rom. xii.) Wherefore this triple designation? Because the acts of men that are agreeable to the will of God are of a threefold rank: some are good, others better, and some perfect. Not to hate our enemy is good; to love him is better; but to benefit him is perfect. In all our works, therefore, we should act in this manner; we should endeavour to direct all our actions, not only according to the good and acceptable, but perfect will of God; and hence we do not pray only that the will of God may be done, but that it may be done on earth as perfectly as it is done in heaven. It was this desire that dictated the well-known vow of St. Teresa—always to choose the better of two good works, whenever she could make the choice. But, to act up to so exalted a vow, we should stand in need of a high degree of heavenly light and heavenly understanding; for we are as often wanting in understanding to distinguish the better and the best, as in strength to perform it. "For who among men is he that can know the counsel of God? or who can think what is the will of God? For the thoughts of mortal men are fearful, and our counsels uncertain. For the corruptible body is a load upon the soul; and the earthly habitation presseth down the mind that museth upon many things. And hardly do we guess aright at things that are upon earth, and with labour do we find the things that are before us; but the things that are in heaven, who shall search out? . . . . . For if one be perfect among the children of men; yet, if Thy wisdom be not with him, he shall be nothing regarded. . . . . Send, therefore, O Lord, Thy wisdom out of Thy holy heaven, and from the throne of Thy majesty, that she may be with me, and labour with me, that I may know what is acceptable with Thee." (Wisdom ix.)

As often, therefore, as we have to choose and to act, the guide of our choice should be no other than the Divine will, which, for most occasions, has been manifested to us as the Divine law; but, in time of anxiety and doubt, patient expectation and fervent prayer must be called to our assistance. "As we know not what to do,"—thus did the holy king Josophat once pray on an occasion of anxious doubt—"As we know not what to do, we can only turn our eyes to Thee, O Lord." But when we have no choice, when we find ourselves in the midst of events which are destined by the providence of God, and come suddenly upon us, we must exercise our will in that obedience which is called resignation and conformity to the Divine will. This, however, does not consist in a sluggish, passive, indolent repose ; else those peasants would have been right, when they saw their cottages in flames, and stood by sighing, ' It has happened by the will of God ;' but in a resignation which, with a peaceful, cheerful activity, leaves the consequence to God. It was thus that the hero of the Macchabees resigned himself when he led out his little and ill-armed band against the overpowering armies of Gorgias and Lysias. "It is better," he said to his followers, "for us to die in battle, than to see the evil of our nation and of our holies. Nevertheless, as it shall be the will of God in heaven, so be it done."

Of this active, peaceful resignation to the providence of God, which is the fairest flower in the life of a Christian, a noble princess[1] has given an example in our own times. ' A review of my past life,' she confessed, ' proves clearly to me, that all that my imagination had painted to me for the future has not happened as it promised, but far otherwise; all that it represented to me as intolerable has proved, in the event, not only tolerable, but the greatest good ; and all that I counted the greatest good, and therefore desired, has been happily denied to me. Therefore do I feel myself impelled to unconditional resignation to the

[1] The Princess Gallitzin.

will of God, and I resign myself to His providence, as does the child to the arms of its mother.'

An illustrious example of this resignation has been preserved in the life of St. Remigius, Archbishop of Rheims. Foreseeing that a year of famine was approaching, he made ample provision for the poor of his flock. But there was found a company of worthless men, who, sitting over their tankards, spoke of his watchfulness as drunkards are wont to speak. 'What can this old man mean?' they said; 'he is approaching his eightieth year. Is he going to build a new city? Is he going to carry on trade, and become a corn-dealer?' Incited by envy and insolent wickedness, they ran out and threw fire into the granaries. The news was quickly carried to the Saint, who, mounting on horseback, hastened to make preparations for saving the corn; but the fire had gained such power, that he soon saw that his attempts were too late. What did he, who was so afflicted at the sight, then do? Did he raise his voice in lamentations, and call down the vengeance of God on the malefactors? No. He dismounted from his horse, and (it was winter) he approached the fire, as one who would warm himself. 'To an old man,' he said, 'a fireplace is always acceptable.' These trials may come from the elements, from other irrational creatures, or from wicked men; but the Christian, who fears God, will receive them from the hands of His providence: and, as no reasonable man would think of accusing the lightning, or hail, or water, so neither will he be troubled against the persons of those whose wickedness God does not prevent, that He may prove and purify those whom He has chosen as His own. For if there be joy and happiness, in a word, a heaven upon earth, it is enjoyed only by those whose virtue is founded on a conformity with the Divine will. But how far is this conformity to extend? Can we be counselled, or even commanded, to wish and to desire that which may be contradictory or painful?

When St. Anselm, Archbishop of Canterbury, after many persecutions, was at length driven from his bishopric and from the country, and was already on shipboard, the winds were so unfavourable to his voyage, that the sailors were compelled to turn and steer again for the coast of England. With grief the Saint received this intelligence; for it told him that he was to return to the scene of all his troubles. 'But if,' he said, ' it should so please God, that, instead of going where I desired to go, I should be thrown again into the midst of bitter sufferings, may His holy will be done. I am ready to obey His holy will; for I am not my own, but His.' Thus he spoke, and tears filled his eyes, when suddenly there arose a favourable wind, and the sailors, who had despaired of their voyage, hastened to continue it. It appeared, therefore, that his resignation to the will of God was speedily rewarded; for, as it is said in the Psalm, "The Lord is nigh to all those who call upon Him in truth. He will do the will of those who serve Him with fear, and will hear their cry." But what is there great in resignation which is accompanied with tears and complaint? Is that perfect resignation to the will of God which is not shewn without opposition?

The same St. Anselm shall give us further instruction on this subject. He says, in his writings, 'that we are not always to wish what God may wish; but we must always wish the reason for which God wishes it.' What do these apparently enigmatical words signify? They take us back to the consideration, that the will of God is to be done, both in us and towards us. The will of God, which is to be done in us, or by us, is declared to us; and here it behoves us at all times to wish that which, according to this law, we are bound to wish, namely, that which is good, right, and true. The Divine will, on the other hand, which is done towards us, and is first made known by its effects in time, would oftentimes be so trying for us, that we should not always be bound to pray that it may be done. Who would, for example, be bound to pray that fire may destroy his house, or that death might come upon himself or family? But when such an event does take place, we are bound to resign ourselves truly to the will of God.

Thus spoke St. Chrysostom, when, immediately before his banishment, he addressed his last homily to his flock, 'Christ is with me, whom, then, shall I fear? If the whole of the entire ocean were raging against me, it would appear to me as nothing; for my words shall always be, O Lord, Thy will be done. Not what this or that man may will, but what Thou willest; Thy will is my strength, my rock, and my staff.' Whence did he derive this tranquillity of mind? Only from the grace which Christ imparts. He who shall often express the wish that Christ would prove him and strengthen him by His grace, gives (as the holy St. Gertrude teaches) to Him the keys of his interior, and will never drive Him away. This key of our innermost dwelling, namely, our own will, we give to Him, as to our Lord and Master, as often as we sincerely pray, "Thy will be done on earth as it is in heaven."

CHAPTER IX.

Give us this day our daily Bread.

IF we contemplate the beauty presented by the Lord's Prayer in the perfect symmetry of its parts, it may well be likened to a temple raised on a twofold order of pillars, whose portal and lordly vestibule pierce the clouds, and ascend above them; whilst its interior and hidden halls, resting on their lowly columns, cast a gloomy shade, and spread around a holy sadness. We need but compare, with Alphonsus Tostus, the first three with the following petitions, and we shall see a marked distinction both in their import and in their expression.

For whilst the first relate solely to the majesty and sovereignty of God, to His holy will, and His eternal law, and are therefore expressed in general and impersonal forms, as wishes and fervent aspirations—("hallowed be Thy name—Thy kingdom come—Thy will be done;") the last are confined to our wants, our frailties, and necessities, and consequently are expressed in our names: " give *us* this day our daily bread—forgive *us* our trespasses—lead *us* not into temptation—deliver *us* from evil."

A second great distinction is also observable; for whereas the perfect accomplishment of the first three petitions is only attainable in a future world, that of the last three is to be fulfilled on this earth. For should we hallow God's name in this earthly world, by acknowledging in faith and in spirit His Trinity, His truth, and His goodness, and by paying Him our homage both in word and in action, yet are we unable to honour Him with the whole power of our being, whilst yet surrounded by the darksome elements which conceal His majesty from our eyes, and which will not be removed until we enter into another life, in which "we shall behold Him as He is." (1 John iii.) And although the kingdom of God is even now founded on earth, and our citizenship therein assured on condition of fidelity, yet no one is to be esteemed happy, until he shall have entered into the regions of brightness. As, in fine, whilst struggling with the opposition that in us reigns of the earthly with the heavenly man, we cannot maintain a perfect harmony with the will of God; so the third petition cannot be entirely accomplished, until the free and thoughtful mind is released from the dominion of error, and is no longer subject to a faithless will.

Of the last four petitions, on the contrary, we need only a passing consideration to perceive that their fulfilment is to be obtained exclusively on this earth. For this daily bread, in whatever sense it be understood, can be required only in our state of growth and mortality, and not in a future life, wherein no change is known. It is in this life that we must implore the remission of our sins, since this grace is bestowed only on mortal man,—on man abiding still in the region of natural and earthly life; for, freed from this his bondage, no longer can he share in the satisfying merits of his Saviour. And again, support against temptation on earth alone can be required, since the soul, when released, is freed from all trial and from all temptation, as the patient Job has in these words expressed: "On earth man's life is a perpetual warfare" (contest or temptation). For deliverance, in fine, from evil, we can pray only in this life; since with the blessed no evil is further possible, and for the damned no redemption can exist.

Thus from the last petition of the first class do we descend to the first of the second, as to earth from heavenly heights, to the vale of tears from blissful gladness. For when, in the third petition, we have expressed our desire that the Divine will should be accomplished on earth as it is in heaven, among us mortal men as with the spirits above; we then, in the fourth petition, proceed to acknowledge, if not utterly dejected, with a sense at least of our poverty, that we are far below the glorified spirits; that not heaven but earth is yet our home; that our spiritual being is in closest union with the natural, the sinful life; and that hence, in this mortal world, we can neither be, nor think, nor act, nor fulfil the will of God, unless our material life, with its constant changes, receive that external support and aid which are necessary for its preservation. The petition, "Thy will be done," is therefore necessarily and immediately followed by this: "Give us this day our daily bread."

With humility do we pronounce this prayer, as in it are we minded of our fallen state. For when nature, which had been created to serve, revolted from its subjection to the spirit, and arose in lordlike opposition, the life of man became a chain of sorrow and of hard necessity, which retained it in perpetual dependance upon the powers and elements of external nature, and in one constant conflict with its hostile and destructive attacks. Thus many things designated both in the east and in the west by the common term of bread, such as home, employment, and clothing, are included in this petition. But not so the many, the numberless inventions of human avarice and luxury; for hearken to St. Gregory of Nyssa: 'We pray, Give us bread; but not luxurious extravagance and ornaments of gold and shining stones, not wide possessions and brilliant honours, not fine silken veils, not diversions of pleasure, or any thing whereby the soul is withdrawn from real and heavenly things: our prayer is solely, Give us bread.'

These are certainly hard words; this bread is indeed dry, and very bitter! "The necessaries of human life," says the son of Sirach, "are water, fire, iron, salt, milk, white-bread, honey, the grape of the vine, oil, and clothing." (Ecclus. xxxix.) Thus, the wise son of Sirach has opened for us a wider region, and has allowed us inhabitants of the west to interpret this bread of the east in conformity with their interpretation; but let us first hearken to another and a most enlightened man, whose views of these things claim earnest attention.

Journeying towards Rome in company with his companion Masseo, already was the seraphic St. Francis wearied and sinking beneath the mid-day sun, when he perceived a fresh and pure stream gushing from beneath an aged rock. Here they both sat down, and placing on a level stone a few pieces of black and hard bread which they had received on their journey, they commenced their frugal meal. St. Francis was much elated, and could not restrain the joy of his heart. 'Brother Masseo,' he exclaimed, 'rejoice and exult with me, and give thanks to the Lord for the great treasure He has bestowed.' Masseo, much amazed, asked to what treasure he alluded; for he could see nothing but the want of the greatest necessaries—a dinner without table, without chairs, without wine, without even the most ordinary dishes. 'O Masseo,' replied the much-contemned but joyful pattern of self-denial, 'behold an inestimable goodness. God's providence has supplied all which here seems to be wanting; for see, He has sent us this bread from friendly hands, this stream He has called forth for the refreshment of our thirst; and, moreover, in these well-formed stones He has prepared for us a table and seats. O blessed poverty! O greatest of all treasures! This was the companion of Christ on the cross; it was buried with Him in the grave; it ascended with Him into heaven!'

Thus did he speak, who, in his simplicity, would at one time call voluntary poverty his sister, at another his mistress. And who should not envy him? But by whom is he envied? Not by the rich; still less by the unwilling poor. Behold, on one side, this rippling stream; on the other, seated on his stone, the poor St. Francis, with his childlike sublimity, and his sublime and childlike joyfulness: in bitter contrast, behold the crowds of the children of men, lusting for power, sorrowful in poverty, refined and refining, adorned and adorning, oppressed by numberless wants, for which no systematic foresight is sufficiently comprehensive, no encyclopædia sufficiently voluminous; whilst the gales and tradewinds of fashion howl through their lounges and huge bazaars, levelling all, both new and ancient, in one confused destruction.

Where shall we find another Comenius, to exhibit to man once more a picture of the world adorned with innumerable woodcuts of the various implements of art, of industry, and of fortune? For if we but glance at the well-nigh countless multiplicity of objects by which the activity of hands and of machines, the industry of men and of beasts, trades, commerce, labourers, spend-thrifts, and scholars, are maintained in one constant employment; and if we then reflect, that in all this none save a few families are concerned, we shall be truly amazed how, in the midst of this activity and turmoil, we can devote one single hour to the necessities of the immortal soul.

But, what is still more embarrassing, who shall remedy this evil? The progress of refinement, we are told, continually increasing the common happiness (rather, perhaps, misery), brings these necessary consequences; luxury, against which the Roman censors were no less zealous than the solitaries of the Theban deserts, is an unavoidable evil, and therefore a true good, creating perpetually fresh sources of industry; and if, with the Christians of ancient times, we still petition for our daily bread, yet are these words more frequently uttered than considered. He who enters into the particulars of their contents will be involved in a labyrinth of ways and passages which lead through kitchens, cellars, barns, wood-markets, manufactories, granaries, gardens, farms, stables, and countless other places; and if, in addition, he be accompanied by wife and children, he would almost lose his senses on the way.

But, it will be asked, must these two words be necessarily multiplied and expanded into so dense a labyrinth as is presented through the convex-glass of earthly views? 'It is but little,' says St. Gregory of Nyssa, 'that you owe to nature and to her preservation; wherefore do you increase your own tribute?' 'My lord and king,' exclaimed a poor man to Alphonsus, king of Arragon, ' I am miserable; oppressed with debts which I have inherited from my parents. My creditor is most pitiless and avaricious; he is a stranger to all humane consideration, and his daily uncontrolled oppressions bow me to the earth.' The king, on hearing this complaint, declared, in great anger, that the inhuman creditor should not remain unpunished, and inquired his name. 'Ah, my sovereign,' replied the extraordinary man, ' you know him well; nor is his name unknown to you; for you yourself are subjected to his tyranny, only are you better provided with tribute and daily offerings; and it is on this account that your generosity may succour my necessity. To speak openly, O glorious lord and king! it is my own stomach that is this merciless creditor.' Alphonsus smiled, and considered the petition reasonable, as it was confined to the cravings of strict necessity. Similar complaints are, nevertheless, frequently uttered by those who by no means restrict themselves to the banquet of the seraphic Francis, and who yet feel themselves unhappy; for their desires have been so vitiated, that frugality has ceased to gratify.

And truly, if we consider all the artificial, and more than artificial, luxuries which load the table under the form of refreshments, luncheons, and collations; at one time warm and smoking, at another cooled by ice, seasoned, garnished, foaming in glasses, dishes, and tureens; under all shapes and colours, from clefts of rocks, from the seashore, from the Ganges and the Mississippi; and if, after this, we reflect on the petition, "Give us this day our daily bread," we may justly say, that we have reason for shame. What value or import can this petition have for him who revels in excess; who, as Seneca has well expressed it, 'makes his body an insatiate grave, which lives by the death of other creatures?'

The folly of the Duke of Clarence, who, when required to select by what death he would atone for his treason, chose to be drowned in a butt of Malmsey wine, is more frequently repeated than we generally imagine. It is in some manner repeated by all those who bury in luxury not only their corporeal but their spiritual existence, and who, abounding in common necessaries, permit themselves to be racked by insatiable desires, which hurry them from crime to crime.

Thus did it happen with the celebrated Roman Apicius, who, according to the narrations of Dion and Martial, having well-nigh squandered in his extravagance a million and a half of gold, and finding that, of this immense sum, he now possessed but one hundred thousand, became apprehensive that this would not suffice for his subsistence, and in his despair swallowed poison. True, indeed, this Apicius was a heathen; he had never heard this petition for our daily bread. But is he not followed by many who bear the

Christian name, who are not to be satisfied with little, or with moderation? These, indeed, have heard the Word, but have not embraced it. Such as truly comprehend it would not easily pray for superfluities, even though assured that they were unaccompanied by danger; neither would they petition for want and for poverty, well knowing that great riches of virtue are necessary to support great poverty; but rather would they supplicate in the words of the Wise Man: "Send me neither poverty nor riches; give me only the necessaries of life." (Proverbs xxx.)

And this is what we call our bread; and such it truly is, when acquired by rightful means — by labour and just inheritance; for unto the industry of the peaceful and laborious has been promised the blessing of Heaven. Thus, when once asked to what class of men salvation is most secure, the renowned Bellarmin made no hesitation in replying, 'Those who earn their bread by daily labour.' 'These men,' said he, 'from the earliest dawn commence their work, nor do they cease till evening has closed; thus they have no opportunity for idleness, and are furnished with occasion for the exercise of every virtue; and their pittance of bread, or rather of poverty, wherewith they nourish themselves and families, is the sweetest, the most delightful of possessions.' And is not this testimony supported by our Saviour? For His foster-father He selected a poor artisan, in whose occupation, during His years of concealment, He Himself took part. And was it not by the labour of their hands that the Apostles gained their subsistence?

Such were the sublime models which the celebrated

Ægidius, one among the first of the disciples of St. Francis, had constantly before his eyes; so that he could never be induced to allow one work-day to pass without engaging in some manual labour. The Cardinal of Tusculan, one of his most intimate friends and his warmest admirer, succeeded, after much persuasion, in engaging him to remain for some days at his palace. Ægidius, however, refused to partake of the table of his noble guest, and insisted on being allowed to earn his meals by daily labour. On one occasion the rain was so violent, that no one, not even those who, like Ægidius, had no costly dresses to save, dared to venture abroad. The Cardinal was much elated, and said to his friend, 'At length have I succeeded; to day, at least, you must dine at my table.' Ægidius listened with great composure; but, without making any reply, he went hastily to the kitchen, and seeing there great uncleanliness and disorder, began to chide the cook upon the confusion which he permitted to exist in his department. The servant received the rebuke with great submission, merely alleging, in extenuation, that there was no one from whom he could seek assistance. Such was the reply which Ægidius expected; he immediately offered his services; and, having restored all things to order, received in reward two pieces of bread, with which, as the price of his labour, he appeared at the dinner-table, refusing to taste of any thing else. The following day the rain continued with unabated violence, and all the servants refusing, in obedience to their master, to give Ægidius any employment, the Cardinal, in great joy, said to his friend, 'Now, certainly, you will be compelled to dine at my table.' Ægidius immediately proceeded to examine every apartment in the with little, and, after much search, he discovered at length two rusty knives. These he scoured and polished; and, having again received for his labour two pieces of bread, he came with them to the table of the Cardinal.

Those to whom this conduct may appear too singular and extravagant, although in Ægidius it proceeded from sincere simplicity, may compare the masters and models of Christian perfection, and such as the Church acknowledges as saints, to those players on the violin who lead the orchestra, and, on this account, have their strings toned an octave above the rest. Yet did not St. Paul declare, in presence of the faithful at Ephesus, "I have not coveted any man's silver, gold, nor apparel, as you yourselves know. For such things as were needful for me and them that are with me, these hands have furnished." (Acts xx.)

What an example! one against which no objection can be raised. The instructor of nations, the teacher of all divine wisdom, the benefactor of mankind, the light of Europe; he of whom, by excellence, it might be said, 'The labourer is worthy of his hire;' this illustrious Apostle would receive no other food, nor be clothed with other garments, than such as he had earned by the labour of his hands. What a lesson for such as live in affluence! What a condemnation of those who would, moreover, appropriate that which is not their bread, but which belongs unto their neighbour! If the idler has scarcely a right to call that his own which falls to him by the laws of society—for no one is born merely to consume the fruits of the earth—how much less has he this right, who, in his too great industry, has recourse

Ægidius to usury, and to the various other arts connected with Proteus-like avarice! "Give us this day our daily bread." Can they join in this petition who, like crows, invade the field of harvest, or, like worming moles, gnaw the roots entrusted by the farmer to the earth?

St. Bernadine relates an anecdote of an Italian peasant who went to a money-changer to receive, in smaller coin, the value of some silver. The changer counted in his presence the small coin, making use, however, in place of the first numbers, of certain words and syllables; for thus was he accustomed to secure his own profit in his exchanges. He commenced, then, with these words: 'In the name of God and of His Saints, six, seven, eight, nine.' The peasant perceived the profane fraud concealed beneath these clouds of godliness; he recounted the money, and discovered that five pieces were missing. He instantly threw back the money, exclaiming, 'Count again.' The well-practised hypocrite complied, still observing the same system; but the peasant, unwilling to be further imposed upon, exclaimed, 'Not so, my friend; count once more, and leave out God and the Saints.'

Such is the good advice which should be given to all those who, whilst they pretend great esteem for Christian practices and prayer, wind their way through a land of lies. Count, reckon, and speculate; but cease to profane the just and true God. Wherefore do you cry to Him, with the words of love, "Our Father?" Wherefore petition, "Give us this day our daily bread?" Such was the bitter reproach made by our Saviour to the Pharisees, "Your father is the devil, the spirit of lies." In like manner, your bread is not your own, but the bread of lies. And what is the voice of Scripture? "The bread of lies is sweet to a man; but afterwards his mouth is filled with a stone." (Prov. xx.) Unrighteous gain, the fruit of deceit and of lies, may at first bestow a flattering gratification; but it will finally be converted into anguish and punishment. But to lawful labour it is promised, "Thou shalt eat the labour of thine hands; blessed art thou, and it shall be well with thee." (Psalm cxxvii.)

If it be so, what consolation then remains for the needy and weak—for those who, animated by the best will, can yet gain nothing? Where is the bread which they can call their own? The prayer of our Lord is not of that egotistical form to allow any one to pray, 'Give *me* my daily bread;' but as the words of the petition are expressly, 'Give us our daily bread;' so no one should be seduced by the too natural delusion, that his possessions and acquisitions are so exclusively his own, as to allow him to apply or to squander them solely for himself. 'The Lord,' says St. Augustine, 'desires to bless the rich through the poor, and to prove the fidelity of His steward. He leaves the poor in poverty for their greater trial; he establishes the rich to prove them by the poor.' How deeply was holy Job convinced of this truth: "If I have denied to the poor what they desired, and have made the eyes of the widow wait; if I have eaten my morsel alone, and the fatherless hath not eaten thereof; if the poor man hath not been warmed with the fleece of my sheep; let God have no share in me." (Job xxxi.) What an awful judgment! What a cloud of darkness does it not cast over the heads of the hard-hearted and avaricious! We are informed by Plutarch that the inhabitants of the ancient state of Œnea had been warned by an oracle not to bestow in alms the least of their property, lest they should endanger their country, their homes, and their entire possessions. And to judge from the conduct of the self-seeker, would he not appear to have been cautioned by the same oracular voice? Every sacrifice that he makes to the welfare of his neighbour causes him no less alarm than if his whole property were in peril.

Want of charity is, however, fortunately, not in the spirit of our times; at least, of that charity which manifests itself in active assistance, and which feels the import of these words in the mouth of the poor, "Give us this day our daily bread." For their petition to their Father is not, 'Give us bread,' but 'Give us *our* bread, which Thou wilt bestow upon us through those to whom Thou hast entrusted it for us, in rich abundance.' It is, indeed, sufficiently obvious, that the poor must supplicate for that which, although destined and prepared for them by God, they do not as yet enjoy. But if the rich, and those who are in possession of a certain inheritance, are to repeat the same daily prayer, why are they to pray that God would give them what they already possess? Because, without the Divine blessing, all our labours would be fruitless, all our hopes deceitful. For "neither he that planteth is any thing, nor he that watereth, but God, who giveth the increase."

Thus do we pray the Giver of all good to bless the work of our hands, acknowledging that all is in His power, and that neither to accident nor to blind chance, neither to our skill nor to our wisdom, but to Him alone do we ascribe all things. For he who would consider any other as the God of what he possesses is guilty of the lie of Satan, who, in his usurped dignity of prince of this world, shewed to the Redeemer the kingdoms of the earth, boldly declaring, "All these are mine, and I give them to whom I will." In opposition to the old deceiver, and in obedience to the command of Christ, do the rich petition for their daily bread, lest they should be deprived of that which already they possess; and that they may be mindful of the precept of the Apostle, not to think highly of themselves, nor to trust in perishable possessions, but in the living God. (1 Tim. vi.)

In fine, whether rich or poor, we all petition for our daily brea for the present day, lest we should ever lose sight of the frail and transitory nature of our existence on earth. For, as it is only by reason of our earthly captivity, which is comprised in a series of years and of days, that we stand in need of our daily bread; so by the word 'bread' we are reminded of death, and are cautioned not to anticipate Providence by imitating the rich man in the parable, who filled his barns for an immeasurable futurity; yet more forcibly are we warned by the little word 'this day' to banish all those anxious and painful solicitudes which spring from a diffidence in the goodness of God. A reasonable and well-ordered prudence is, indeed, not forbidden by Divine wisdom. It tells us rather to go to the ant, and learn from her to make, in reasonable time, provision for the future. By it also are we sent to the birds of the air, which neither sow nor reap, but, as St. Augustine says, fly and flutter about in search of their food. That which in these creatures is but the impulse of nature, is in man perfected by reason and experience. They may in this life attain to their end; but to man is proposed a far more exalted end—his perfection and felicity through God. And whereas the brute creation dream away their existence without one reflection on the Author of all life and existence; in us this knowledge is essentially grounded in the very depth of our spiritual consciousness, from which, if duly cherished, the sacred duty of gratitude will spontaneously spring. "What," exclaims the Psalmist, "shall I render the Lord for all that He has given to me? I will take the chalice of salvation, and call upon the name of the Lord."

It is recorded of Albert duke of Belgium, that he sent daily to an aged nobleman, who had become impoverished by war, dishes of the most costly viands from his own table. The person employed in conveying these presents did not belong to the ducal court, and was moreover strictly cautioned not to give the least intimation of the bountiful benefactor. The first time the messenger arrived, the poor man appeared wholly astonished; but when, during the ensuing days, and months, and years that he yet lived, the same kindness was continued regularly and without intermission, his eagerness to know his beneficent friend daily increased; and in his anxiety he would often say, 'My only fear is, that death will arrive before I shall be able to testify my gratitude.' What manifold gifts do we not receive from our invisible Benefactor each day, each hour, each moment of our lives! What gifts, both spiritual and temporal; what necessaries, without which our existence would instantly cease; what other countless benefits which gladden our minds and our senses! And wherefore, instead of receiving them with indifference, as though they came of necessity, are we not daily awakened to fresh gratitude towards the continuous goodness of our Benefactor? For to whom is the Giver unknown? And what should we more apprehend than to depart this life without having expressed our thankfulness to Him? 'Nothing,' says St. Augustine, 'is more shortly expressed, more joyful to hear, more sweet to understand, or more useful to perform, than what is expressed in these three words: Thank the Lord.' "Bless the Lord, O my soul, and all that is within me bless His holy name. Bless the Lord, O my soul, and never forget all that He has done for thee. Bless the Lord, all His works, in all the places of His dominion; my soul, bless thou the Lord." (Ps. cii.)

CHAPTER X.

𝕲𝖎𝖛𝖊 𝖚𝖘 𝖙𝖍𝖎𝖘 𝖉𝖆𝖞 𝖔𝖚𝖗 𝖉𝖆𝖎𝖑𝖞 𝖘𝖚𝖕𝖊𝖗𝖘𝖚𝖇𝖘𝖙𝖆𝖓𝖙𝖎𝖆𝖑 𝕭𝖗𝖊𝖆𝖉.

IT would be difficult to find a text of Scripture more variously expressed and translated, than this of the fourth petition, "Give us this day our daily bread." In the Syriac version it is rendered, 'Give us this day the bread of our necessity;' in the works of St. Euthemius it is called, our 'sufficient bread.' In some Greek Bibles we read, our 'future bread;' in others, our 'excellent and chosen bread.' By St. Luke, and after him by St. Cyprian and other ancient Fathers, it is termed our 'daily bread;' whilst in St. Matthew, and in the translation by St. Jerome, it is styled our 'supersubstantial bread.'

Amidst so many versions and interpretations, it will be asked, Which is correct? Without doubt they are all correct; for essentially they are all of one signification. For whether we petition for the bread of our necessity, or for our future and excellent bread, or for our sufficient and daily bread, we equally signify all those objects of which we ever stand in need, so long as the hallowing of God's name, the obtaining of His kingdom, and the fulfilment of His will, are duties incumbent upon us in this mortal body, and during our earthly pilgrimage.

That, however, independent of our other necessities, the food which sustains our life ought more particularly to be termed our bread, our excellent, our substantial, our supersubstantial bread, and how it is entitled to all these appellations, will be the more easily manifest, the nearer we approach to Him who stands in no need of this bread. "With Thee," says the Psalmist, "is the fountain of life; and in Thy light we shall behold the light." For it is the Uncreated alone who lives in Himself and by Himself; for in His being He contains the fountain and perfection of life; but, on the contrary, all creatures that exist and have being, exist through God; as far, at least, as existence proceeds from Him; that is, through His all-powerful will, which has brought into actual existence His thoughts, His eternal ideas of creatures. And thus, in the name of rational, as well as irrational creation, did the Psalmist sing, "To Thee do all creatures look, that in due season Thou wouldst give them food. Thou pourest out, and they collect; Thou openest Thy hand, and with Thy bounty all things are filled. Thou turnest aside Thy countenance, and they perish. Thou withdrawest Thy spirit, and they wither and return to dust."

All created life is comprised in three classes: the spiritual, as in the pure spirits; the natural, as in stones, and plants, and beasts; and the human, or spiritual and natural life, as in mankind. The pure spirits, who have not fallen from their first and noble end, find the happiness of their life in and from God; and in this sense it was that Raphael spoke to the two Tobiases of the bread unseen wherewith he was nourished. Plants and beasts, the representation of the entire natural existence, are, in their being, increase, and decay, in one perpetual communication with the powers and elements of universal nature, on which they are ever dependent. In man, however, these relations and connexions extend to an order wholly different. For though the human body, by its construction and its vital functions, be included in the highest order of animal organisation, and represent the perfection of natural existence, yet is it, as we before observed, elevated far above the bounds of nature. It is, indeed, in man that nature attains to that personality and consciousness, which, in her own captive state, she never could acquire; but she attains it by her connexion and intimate union with the spiritual life, in whose dominion she herself is lost. Thus, by its personal union with the spirit, is the body exalted; and is, or originally was, subject to the spirit; and thus, by the life of the immortal spirit, it is raised above the mutability of nature; and, in the human person, secure of that which is the property of the spirit—eternal existence.

An import somewhat different must in consequence be given to our petition, when we pray to our eternal Father, "Give us this day our daily bread." Earthly though we be, by our mortal bodies, and thus of earthly nourishment in constant need, yet, as we have a heavenly Father, our food must all be considered differently from that of the brute creation. Their bodies return to their original dust, or rather are converted into the elements of universal nature; but as our bodies are subservient to a life of far-surpassing dignity, we rightly pray for our chosen, our supersubstantial bread; for this food, by becoming the nourishment of the body, which is an ingredient of our twofold being, is converted into our, that is, into human nature.

Should any one, in his moderation—extreme, rather than well-regulated—consider these views as extravagant, he must argue with the boundless love of God; he must complain of the exalted dignity and pre-eminence to which, even in his human nature, he has been exalted. For, to the thoughtless and frivolous man, what can be less acceptable than this dignity of his humanity? These words, however, of St. Matthew, "Give us this day our supersubstantial bread," are not so much extravagant, as uncommon and elevated words, which we may with confidence employ as a foundation whereon to raise an edifice, by which we shall be conducted to yet higher comprehension; for the tower of our faith, resting upon the temple of the teaching Church, is not a Babylonish tower, which is lost in the clouds, but one which pierces far above them.

If, then, the foundation of this building be secure—if this daily bread, this nourishment of our bodies, be a supersubstantial bread; for it is raised above itself, and elevated into the higher region of our corporeal being, which, to the spirit, is an instrument for its action, and for the attainment of felicity, and shall be eternally espoused to it; it follows—and here is the first story of the building—that man should not eat his bread, unless it be blessed by the hand of God, and without referring it to His Divine Honour, according to the admonition of St. Paul: "Whether you eat, or whether you drink, or whatever else you do, do all for the glory of God." (1 Cor. x.)

What, eat and drink for the glory of God! What relation can these actions bear to the Divine glory? We may well reply, in the words of an old proverb—a proverb not yet so trite, as not to contain much fruitful subject for reflection—and which justly says, 'By eating and drinking the soul and body are held together.' This union of the soul and body in one personality is the condition, the being of human nature, though its true, its highest object is, to know and to honour God. As, then, this union, this mortal existence of man, is dependent on the nourishment of the body, so may this duty, though not immediately, be subservient to the glory of God; and therefore, as St. Cyprian observes, we not only petition for our necessary food, but also that we may receive this food from the hand of God, that it may be blessed by Him, and that, by conducing to the health of the body, it may render it more vigorous in the service of its God.

Such were the sentiments of so many holy anchorites, who made use of meat and drink for no other end, and who are worthy that we should here make mention of them. It is narrated by the holy Abbot Pastor, that, in the time of the Emperor Theodosius the Great, a recluse dwelt on a spot not far distant from Constantinople, and whither the Emperor was accustomed sometimes to resort. Having heard the hermit highly extolled as a man entirely detached from the world, and who never quitted his retreat, Theodosius resolved to visit him. Without attendants, unaccompanied by any signs of his dignity, and clothed in but mean apparel, he approached the sainted man, and thus accosted him: 'My father, I would dine with you to-day.' The hermit replied, 'With all willingness; but first let us join in prayer.' Having prayed for some time, they both sat down before a small table. Theodosius looked around the hut, and perceiving nothing save a basket containing some bread, said, with a smile, 'Father, give thy blessing, that we may commence our meal.' The hermit brought some bread and salt, and filled a cup with water, and sought to entertain his guest to the best of his power. The emperor, who wished to enliven by conversation this his sumptuous repast, asked his host, 'What was the employment of his brethren the holy fathers in Egypt?' 'They pray,' he replied, 'for you who are in the midst of the world, and find no time for prayer.' The emperor then inquired, if he knew who he was? And upon the hermit answering, that he did not, Theodosius added, 'Know that I am Theodosius Cæsar Augustus, and that I have come here with good intentions. Happy are you who, free from the tumult of the world, enjoy a peaceful life, solicitous for nothing save the welfare of your souls. For, I assure you in sincerity, that never yet have I eaten my bread without care and trouble.' Having concluded these words, he bade his host farewell, and departed.

On the following night, the hermit entered into counsel with himself, and began to consider what might be the next event. 'What,' he thought, 'will be the consequence of this visit? Led on by the example of the emperor, many from the court and from the city will come to my hut to shew me honour. And what security have I that my heart will not be elated by their praises? How, then, can I dare to remain any longer here?' That same night he girt his loins, took his mantle and his staff, and leaving his cell, commenced his journey to return into Egypt. By this conduct did the good man evince full clearly that, neither in meat, nor in drink, nor in human honours, did he seek his pleasure, and that the little which he required was devoted solely to the Divine service. Thus did he secure the perfection of happiness. But in what strong contrast to him stood his guest, who, though monarch of the enormous empires of the East and of the West, was bowed down with countless cares and solicitudes!

Let us also place ourselves in spirit at the table of the holy hermit, and hold with him some short converse. 'Far be it from us, O holy father, to suppose that, because thou hast chosen for thyself solitude and prayer, thou art therefore to be numbered with the indolent and slothful; but yet must thou not accuse us of neglect of prayer, if the occupations and anxieties of our life allow but little time to think on God and divine things.' The hermit having heard our words, laments our lot, then asks, with a smile, whether, amidst so many cares, we yet can find a time for meals? 'Certainly,' we reply; 'for this, how could we possibly not find time? Is it not for our daily bread that all these labours are undergone?' Such was the reply expected by the holy man. 'As,' he rejoins, 'it is beyond doubt that you have time to eat, so is it equally evident that you have time to pray, since prayer and eating are so essentially united, that one without the other cannot exist.'

As the food of which we partake is our supersubstantial bread, as it will be converted into one substance with a being which belongs to God, and for Him is created, so is prayer, as well before as after meals, an indispensable duty, whereby, as St. Chrysostom remarks, we are distinguished from beasts, acknowledge God as the Giver of all good gifts; by it we return Him thanks, and implore His blessing on what He has bestowed. " All food," says the Apostle, " is made by God, to be received with thankfulness by the faithful, who know the truth; every creature of God is good, since it will be hallowed by prayer and the word of God." (1 Tim. iv.) That is, by the prayer of man and the Divine blessing, our earthly food becomes worthy to be converted into the organic life of the body, and to partake in its communication with our spiritual life.

Let us now rise a few degrees higher, and let us ask which is more important and salutary, the food itself, or the thanksgiving wherewith it is accompanied? They who have not ascended so high may perhaps ridicule such an inquiry, and jeeringly reply, ' By prayer nature is not satisfied; and we, for our parts, would give the preference to the substantiality of food.' But this superficial scoffing cannot decide the question. Corporeal food is doubtless indispensable for the support and invigoration of our animal life: on this subject there can be no contest between the sensualist and enlightened; for few are the truths more universally acknowledged. But we possess, moreover, a spiritual life, which cannot be nourished by corporeal and earthly food; and if it be not difficult to decide whether our spiritual life holds a rank superior to the animal, so is it no less evident to which we should give the preference, whether to our corporeal or our spiritual sustenance.

That the soul requires its support, who can for a moment doubt? "Come," exclaims Wisdom, "and eat my bread, and drink the wine which I have mingled for you." "For man lives not by bread alone, but by every word which proceedeth from the mouth of God," that is, which cometh to us by Divine revelation. "He who loves justice," says Ecclesiasticus, "him will she feed with the bread of life and of understanding, and give him to drink of the water of wholesome wisdom; and she shall be made strong in him, and he shall not be moved." (Ecclus. xv.) As there is a hunger and thirst of the body, occasioned by the necessity of continual renovation and refreshment, so is there a spiritual hunger and thirst for truth and for justice, for the knowledge of God and of His will, which, when the soul has discovered, she becomes spiritual, according to the promise of our Lord: "Blessed are they that hunger and thirst after justice, for they shall be filled." Who shall supply our wants? who shall replenish us with this bright, this healthful truth, if not the Divine wisdom in its sweet revelations? The Divine Word, proceeding from, and abiding in God, has visited man, and brought to him this food of positive truth; not solely for his instruction, but also to be his life and salvation; as we learn from the words of the Psalmist: "With Thee, O God, is the fountain of life, and in Thy light shall we behold the light."

To this most exalted of all sciences shall we be conducted, if, with St. Augustine, we consider more closely these words of the Psalmist. For what is signified by these words: "With Thee is the fountain of life, and in Thy light shall we behold the light?" This may we learn from the Gospel: "In the beginning was the Word, and the Word was with God, and the Word was God; in Him was life, and the life was the light of men;" that is, their spiritual life and their inmost wisdom by their intercourse with God. Who, then, is this Fountain of life, this Light in whom we behold the light? He is the Fountain of fountains, the Light of light, the eternal Word. Thus did He Himself instruct us when He said, "As the Father hath life in Himself, so hath He given to the Son to have life in Himself." And behold the Word, the Life, and the Light, the eternal Thought of the Father, has bowed Himself down to a created being, in order to assume human nature in His own Person; the Word became flesh, and has dwelt amongst us, in order to restore the whole man, in His spiritual no less than in His corporeal being, to an immortal life.

And what a work of unfathomable love has He not effected, in order, on His part, to accomplish in all men this exalted object! Doubtless by His incarnation He has espoused our nature, and belongs thereby to all mankind; but this union, this participation in His being and His sacrifice is perfected in each one by that mystery, which by St. Chrysostom is termed the expansion and extension of His incarnation, by that miraculous food, that truly supersubstantial bread, which, by the creative power of the Word, conceals the substance of His assumed and glorified body. This is that bread which came down from heaven to give life to all mankind; this also is our daily bread, since of it we are in daily need; and which, therefore, by the ministers of Christ, as the successors of their Master, and by the power of His omnipotence and last will, is daily produced on our altars.

Such is the interpretation of most of the holy Fathers; and thus in the liturgy received by Spain from the holy Isidore, the priest having pronounced the words, "Give us this day our daily bread," the choir, in the name of the people, replies, 'Which is Thyself, O Christ.' This bread is also truly *our* bread. 'For,' says St. Cyprian, 'the bread of life is Christ, not the bread of each one, but our bread; and as we say, "Our Father," since He is a father to the believing and the enlightened, so do we call this bread our bread; for Christ, with whom we are herein united, is ours. And as we say, "Our Father who art in heaven," so do we likewise pray for that bread which came down from heaven, and gives to mortal man a heavenly life; for in Him is the life, and the life is the light of men; and the light of the Divine brightness has entered into the darkness of our corporeal nature, to be to it the pledge of its future glory and immortality.' "And who," exclaims the Psalmist, "shall declare the power of the Lord? who shall make known all His wonders?"

As the holy Princess Elizabeth, accompanied by many nobles, was journeying from Hungary to Germany, to be espoused to Louis duke of Thuringia, much doubt was entertained by the knights and lords of the duke's court, whether he was sincerely attached to his bride; and, in confidence, they asked him to disclose to them his sentiments. Louis thus replied: 'Do you see yon neighbouring mountain, whose woody summit lords it over the surrounding country? Were it of pure gold, yet would Elizabeth, my future spouse, be to me more dear and lovely.' Walter of Wargeila then came forward, and said, 'I entreat you, my lord, to permit me to go and tell her these your words.' 'Go,' replied Louis; 'and as a memorial and pledge of my sincere affection, take her this small present.' He then entrusted to him a small mirror, on the reverse side of which was figured an image of our crucified Redeemer. Elizabeth expressed great joy on receiving this gift, and carefully preserved it; and can we doubt that oftener far her eyes were turned upon the image of her Saviour than upon the mirror?

If to this narration we give a symbolic and a higher application, we may truly say, that every human soul is espoused to a great and heavenly Bridegroom, to whom its earthly life is but a pilgrimage. He himself would thus be styled; and He has termed His incarnation and His sacrifice an espousal, which for ever will unite Him with the human race. Moreover, as He is the Holy One and the Lord, and we frail and sinful; as, too, He was despised and crucified by His creatures, and is yet daily contemned and scorned; we might truly feel a well-grounded fear lest we should lose His love and forbearance. And therefore, to banish every doubt, and to be a living memorial, He has sent us a heavenly gift, which, under the form of bread, is a lively representation of His redeeming sacrifice, as well as a shining mirror which collects all light within itself, and again reflects it back. For, as Eusebius of Madrid observes, the rays of the sun cannot inflame combustible matter, unless these rays be first collected in a focus; so are the countless effects of the Divine goodness as so many irradiations of the Divinity, spread ineffectually throughout the world, unless they be united in Christ, who has manifested the fulness of His impassible light, and the brilliancy of His eternal beauty, in His blessed state of mortality, that we might be inflamed to His most holy love. And this it is which He Himself has declared: "I am come to cast fire upon the earth." And where shall these rays of the Divine sun of love, where shall all the powers and exertions of entire nature be collected and united in the highest perfection, if not in the body of Christ concealed in the sacramental species? 'Love Him,' exclaims St. Austin, 'who, through love to you, has humbled Himself to this condition, and has converted the substance of bread into that of His Body, in order that by thus humbling Himself and exalting you, He might unite the light of His eternity with the clay of your frailty. For this He Himself has solemnly promised: "He that eateth of this bread hath eternal life, and I will raise him up at the last day."

And in what circumstances did He speak these words? On an occasion which called forth an instruction similar to that which we have followed. For after, by prayer and His word of blessing, He had in the wilderness of Bethsaida multiplied ordinary bread, and therewith replenished thousands, and the multitude now with more than wonted ardour had thronged around Him, He thus addressed them: "You seek Me not because you have seen miracles (the manifestations of My superhuman power), but because you have eaten bread and have been filled. Labour not for the meat which perisheth, but for that which endureth to everlasting life, which the Son of Man will give you." This food is truly our supersubstantial bread, since it far surpasses the substance of bread, and the human body, and even all created matter. For the substance of bread being the nourishment of man, is exalted above itself when converted into the higher order of the human body, and thereby united with our spiritual life. But in the eucharistic food, the same substance becomes the body of Christ, which is personally conjoined not only with His created spiritual life, but also with the divine being of the Word; here, therefore, is our corporeal substance raised above all created being, even to a union with the creating Word, that it may be to man a supernatural support. In this bread, therefore, the God-Man is immediately united with, and enters into, all who approach His table, to implant within them the life of the new and heavenly Adam. (John vi.)

That it was with this view that He chose the form of bread, how can we possibly doubt? for from this material bread we may so easily ascend to that which is supersubstantial. In no place is this reason more clearly declared than in that prayer which the Church employs on the Festival of the Mystery of our Altars: 'Grant us, O Lord, that we may be replenished by the perpetual enjoyment of Thy Godhead, of which we receive a temporal pledge in Thy precious body and blood.'[1] This prayer, addressed to the Lord, and consequently to

---

[1] Post-comm. in Miss. votiv. de S. Sacr.

Christ the God-Man, contains much instruction in the careful choice of its expressions.

For as, in ordinary discourse, the contemplation of a work of art, the hearing of the melody of music, or of a poetic or oratorical discourse, is called a spiritual enjoyment, so, in truth, is every sight and every knowledge a spiritual nourishment, which therefore heals and satiates the desire and hunger of a soul, as by corporeal food our natural life is refreshed. The eternal and perfect accomplishment of all spiritual desires, which is the contemplation of the Word in eternity, and is the end of our existence, can therefore be by nothing more strikingly symbolised, that is, figuratively represented, than by corporeal food and drink; as, on the other hand, these (food and drink) are generally signified by those two productions of nature and human industry, bread and wine, which represent all other kinds of nourishment.

This symbolical and figurative language, so consonant to the nature of man, in which the spiritual is represented by the corporeal, and consequently spiritual by corporeal food, leads us to the knowledge why, in the heathenish worship of so many nations, there have been offerings consisting of food and of drink; but we may not always conclude that in these usages there existed a foreshadowing or an imitation of our Christian mysteries. But that we must not stop at these symbols, and consider the eucharistic food as a mere figure of a future, spiritual, and divine fruition, is sufficiently evident; since in this banquet we possess Christ's body and blood, the reception of which in time is a pledge of the enjoyment of the Godhead of Christ for eternity.

But the ground of this reasoning is far deeper. For as the God-Man, in character of our second Adam, is the essential Founder and Preserver of the human race, which, without His mediation and sacrifice, was, with the first man, eternally ruined, so is He the Preserver of each one of the human race; and as through Him alone mankind enjoys an historical existence (whence He is called by the Apostle our Head), so is it likewise with each member of the human family. He is, therefore, both the source (the element) of life to the whole, and the nourishment (aliment) of each individual; and this not merely in a spiritual, but in a real and material manner, in the kingdom of our natural life.

Those to whom these views do not appear satisfactory can derive no pleasure from aught that would remind them of their interior destitution; for in their empty self-satisfaction they require no heavenly food, no supernal life and light. And doubtless there exist many who, after their own manner, esteem and acknowledge this mystery; but as the words of Christ and the doctrine of the ancient Church cannot accord with their views, they devise that rare hypothesis whereby they make it so clear and tangible, that, in their hands, it vanishes into a mere pantheistic emblem (since their God, who is one and all in every thing, exists in bread), they reduce it into a lifeless ceremonial, a religious memorial of Christ, and consequently a symbol of His presence, which must be considered as empty and yet real, lifeless and yet vivifying; as if we should consider the wooden eagle over the entrance of the imperial or royal palace, not only as representing the sovereign or imperial authority, but as that authority itself, and thus uniting at once the type and that which is typified. In one word, in their vain and thankless exertions, they imitate that effeminate emperor so well known under the name of Heliogabalus.

This weak and ridiculous man once invited the chief members of the Roman senate to a banquet, for which there appeared the most sumptuous preparations; the seats and couches were covered with the richest tapestry, and the tables laden with gold and crystal vessels. The numerous guests were already seated, and the first course was with great pomp served up; but what was their surprise when the contents of the dishes were discovered to be either wood ingeniously carved and coloured, or earth and sand, and other indigestible substances, kneaded and artfully arranged! The guests, basely and unworthily deceived, departed more hungry than when they came. And thus do they act who spread the cloud of their cold and extravagant views over the banquet of Christ, the feast of eternal love. They convert the table of the Lord into that of Heliogabalus, and debase existence and truth into an empty symbol.

But Rationalism, whether shallow or profound, is ineffectual when opposed to the evident declaration of the Divine Word. Christ did not say, 'My body is as, or like to, food; take, and eat, in remembrance of My life, My sufferings, and My presence on earth:' nor did He say, 'This bread shall be to you a substitute for My corporeal presence; as often as you do this, Christ, the eternal idea of Christianity, abides with you.' No; but He declared, "My body is truly food; take, and eat; this is My body: unless ye eat the flesh of the Son of Man, you shall not have life in you." And who has ever doubted as to the literal acceptation of these words? "The bread which we break," asks St. Paul, "is it not the participation of the body of the Lord?" In this inquiry does he not evidently appeal to a truth well known to the first Christians?

No; Christ has not thus coldly loved us, as some men would, in their subtlety, dream. Let him who would prescribe a measure to Divine love, first find a measure for the All-Infinite; for God is love. So ardent is His desire for our salvation, that He has invented this admirable manner of planting in each an immortal life, and of bestowing a pledge of future freedom and greatness; which, although a pledge, is no less excellent than this greatness itself. And justly so. For need we observe, that every pledge, if not more precious, must, at least, be of equal worth with the object for which it serves as a security?

But where shall we find that faith so living, that knowledge so elevated, as to esteem as it deserves this infinite treasure? An illustrious example is recorded in the annals of antiquity, in the person of St. Louis. In his unfortunate crusade to the Holy Land, being captured by the Sultan of Syria, negotiations were entered upon with the latter to obtain for the king leave to return to his country. The sultan, in conformity with general usage, demanded some security for the fulfilment of the conditions which had been stipulated. And what pledge did he require? Was it the deposit of some large amount of gold? Was it the surrender of the principal knights and lords of the French army? No; but, as we are informed by Gregory Mastrilli, that which is revered but little by many men, but which, nevertheless, is more costly than the entire world,—the pledge he required was a consecrated Host. And by what was the sultan induced to make such a demand? He had witnessed the indescribable love, the deep respect evinced by his royal captive towards the Sacrament of the altar; from which he justly concluded, that he could demand no greater or more certain security.

And if we wish to secure to ourselves the peace of God, and a participation in the eternal inheritance, what greater pledge could we desire than that which we specify in the petition, "Give us this day our supersubstantial bread?" 'In our earthly pilgrimage,' says St. Augustine, 'this pledge must be our sovereign consolation and support; for He who has bestowed upon us so great a pledge is prepared to give us all things: if the pledge be so great, what must be that for which it stands security! How will He replenish us in our heavenly home, who here below so bountifully feeds us! O mystery of Divine goodness! O band of holy charity! he who desires life knows well where to find it; he approaches this banquet, he believes, he unites himself with the body which gives him life to live for God and by God!'

CHAPTER XI.

And forgive us our Trespasses.

EXALTED and heavenly, sweet and joyful, honourable and elevating is all that we specify and request in the first four petitions of the Lord's Prayer. Therein do we express to our heavenly Father our heartfelt desire, that His name may be hallowed, that His kingdom may be established, that His will may be fulfilled; and, under the name of our daily bread, we pray that He would bestow upon us whatever is requisite for our soul or body. All these petitions and desires are well becoming faithful, zealous, and sinless children, who have in view nought save the honour and love of their Father.

But as in the petition for our daily bread we acknowledged our destitution and dependence, and consequently turned our reflections to ourselves and into our interior, so do we now perceive and acknowledge that we may not presume to utter with fullest confidence these exalted petitions, as if between the sanctity of our God and our sinfulness there were not yet much to remove, and as if we possessed that spiritual and corporeal health which would render the food we request immediately beneficial. We rather confess that we are sick; and as weak and crime-burdened children, fly to a Father of mercy inexhaustible. Such was the conduct of the prodigal of the Gospel, who, after he had proudly demanded and shamefully squandered his inheritance, and now sat amidst swine and their loathsome husks, resolved to fly to his father for clothing and for food. And in what manner? " I will arise, and say to my father, Father, I have sinned against Heaven and before thee; I am not worthy to be called thy son." But the father celebrated a feast of rejoicing; "for," said he, "this my son was dead, and is come to life; he was lost, and is found."

Well worthy is this 'and' of deep consideration, "I will arise, and will say to my father." We arise, we leave this earth and its husks of swine, so often as we elevate our hearts to our heavenly Father to implore His powerful assistance; but yet is there an 'and' still necessary, in order that our merciful Parent may say, "He was dead, and is come to life; he was lost, and is found." What is this powerful 'and?' "Our Father, who art in heaven, give us this day our daily bread, AND forgive us our trespasses;" or, as it is expressed in St. Luke, "and forgive us our sins," for we have sinned against Heaven and before Thee; against Thy love and in sight of Thy love, and we are no more worthy to be called Thy sons, nor even Thy servants, since we have not performed Thy work, unless Thou forgive us our transgressions; for Thou art still our Father.

This, then, is that necessary 'and' which connects the fifth with the preceding petitions, but which is so seldom considered in this its connecting quality. Of this did the holy hermit Sabbas once complain. Oppressed with hunger and with thirst, a troop of barbarians of the tribe of the Agareni prowled through the desert in which he lived; they discovered his cell, rushed wildly in, hoping to discover some refreshment, and finding their expectations deceived, they loaded the hoary recluse with opprobrious words and with every inhumanity. Sabbas, without opposing a word of remonstrance, spread out a sheep's skin, and laid before them the whole treasure of his poverty, consisting of some gourds and other fruits. They eat, and went joyfully on their way; but after a few days returned once more, and in a manner more courteous, bringing, in testimony of their gratitude, various provisions. 'Wo to us,' sighed the holy Sabbas; 'savage barbarians are thankful for so inconsiderable a favour, and repay it with all gratitude; but we daily receive gifts from our Creator, and return Him nought save unthankfulness!' And such is the acknowledgment which connects the fourth and fifth petitions. Give us this day our daily bread; grant us the gifts of which we stand in so great need, *and* forgive us our trespasses, wherewith, by ingratitude for Thy gifts and towards the Giver, we have burdened our souls.

And albeit we cannot repay Him for His beneficence, to which we are indebted for our being, for our honour, and for our happiness, and although by our fidelity we cannot augment His essential felicity, yet does He call for our gratitude, and demand that wise use of His gifts whereby we shall be rendered worthy to receive other and yet higher favours, and promote the hallowing of His sacred name, by evidences more resplendent of His pure love.

We employ our corporeal and spiritual life, and whatsoever else we receive from the world and from nature, in conformity with God's holy will, when we subject to this holy will, made known to us by conscience and by revelation, our entire freedom; acknowledging our dependence as finite beings upon Him who is infinite, and confessing that the Uncreated has the right of sovereignty over the creatures of His hands. As God alone is self-existent, He is necessarily the absolute Lord; whilst every created being, not existing of itself, cannot be its own lord, but must consider as its rule the will of God. Should the creature possessing freedom reject this rule, it revolts to become its own lord, it invades the right of God; and in this usurpation consisteth sin.

What, therefore, is sin? The word is very common; not so the interpretation. As to the definition, it is generally said, that sin is an offence of God; and this is not merely ingratitude, for ingratitude may denote only a want or delay of thankfulness. But here we enter upon a labyrinth similar to, if not more intricate than that which presented itself when we discussed the ideas entertained concerning the hallowing and profanation of the Divine name.

Let us suppose, what has often happened, that a sensualist and a Christian are journeying on the same road. The former, with many jeers, exhorts his pious companion to be encouraged by his example to perform such and such an action. 'I cannot,' replies the Christian. 'Wherefore?' rejoins the other. 'Because I dare not.' 'Dare not! What restrains thee? what canst thou fear?' 'It would be,' replies the servant of God, 'an offence against the Almighty; and by it I should grievously insult my Lord.' In the proud sense of his emancipation, the man of refinement utters a loud laugh, and begins to catechise his childlike friend. 'Where is God,' he demands, 'that you can approach Him with your offence? Who is God, that you can insult Him? Is He a man, irascible, sensitive, passionate, and ambitious, like to us? Do you form of Him so weak, so low and superstitious an idea, as to suppose that you, a frail mortal, can inflict pain on Him, the Almighty?' 'Certainly not,' rejoins the Christian; 'in this sense I cannot offend God.' 'Why, then, not act as I do?' 'Because it would be sinful.' 'What, then, is sin?' 'An offence against God,—an infinite offence, which He must necessarily punish.'

But we have not yet made any advance, but have returned again to our former position; so that the impious contemner of God and of sin, exulting in his success in having, although blind, conducted his blind disciple to so exalted a height, in triumph claps his hands. But a deep pit, a yawning abyss, lies not far beneath this dangerous elevation; for the child of man, when once confirmed in the splendid idea that God cannot be offended, is at once in harmony with sin and guilt, and confidently trusts that he shall pass over this dread abyss. Standing, then, on this so awful precipice, and seeing well the necessity of seeking some other path by which we may arrive at the comprehension of the guilt of sin, let us have recourse to a remarkable narrative, which, although it may appear fictitious, will yet lead us to farther objects.

Whilst atheism flourished under the protection of fashion, a noble youth of Toulouse had the misfortune to find himself among the advocates of this shallow infidelity; and, under his new preceptors, he made so rapid progress, that he was on the point of declaring his system of belief, or rather of unbelief; for the religion of these men, unlike that of the nineteenth century, consisted, not in the elevated and glittering formulas of pantheistic piety, but in the mere denial of a real and personal Divinity. Previous, however, to his ultimate determination, and in order to satisfy his many yet remaining scruples, he resolved to have recourse to an experiment of a peculiar character (a theognostic essay), that he might ascertain whether there dwelt on high a watchful and all-seeing God, who observed our every deed, and preserved a knowledge of them. With this intention the youthful Titan left the city in the dusk of eve, and stationed himself on a naked and solitary heath beneath the open heaven; he laid aside his Spanish mantle with his plumed hat, and drawing from his girdle the short dagger then worn by students, raised it towards heaven, and challenged, in these formal words, the Lord of the universe: 'If there be a God, either in the realms above or in the depths below, let Him come forward; let Him present Himself, and join with me in honourable combat; then shall I know that Thou dost really exist; then will I believe and acknowledge Thee.' As we should naturally expect, this audacity was ineffective,— all yet remained still and tranquil. Then, struggling between dread of spirits and heroic courage, this French Prometheus gave vent to his passion, stalked, like a second Roland, across the heath, and in words breathing more of madness than of sense, defied the omnipresence of the Almighty, scorned Him as a mere nonentity, and with haughty sneers renounced his service.

What, then, followed? Did the storm call up some thundercloud above his head? Did the whirlwind rise with its howling terrors, to dash his corpse against some rock? Did the lightning's dagger pierce his breast, or did the thunderbolt shatter his haughty head? No; even the heathen Jupiter, had he punished every blasphemy with a thunderbolt, would have been in constant occupation. But perhaps some hideous form, some frightful phantom, rose before the eyes of the dauntless hero, to bristle his hair in dread affright? Such, doubtless, would have clothed with new interest the narration, and would have excited anxious expectation; but such did not occur on this battle-field of Toulouse. What then? For surely something must have occurred to mark this scene. Let us hearken to the relation, as it was confirmed on oath by the hero himself, and from whom alone the preceding circumstances were obtained.

'There appeared,' he says, 'a resplendent brilliancy in the heavenly vault, and, as it were, a sheet of paper of transcendent whiteness, which, gradually descending, fell at last at his feet. He seized the sheet, and raised it from the ground to read the writing thereon inscribed in golden characters; and these were the commencement of the fiftieth Psalm: *Miserere mei, Deus*— "Have mercy on me, O God." Suddenly, as if changed into a new man, he fell upon his knees, struck his breast, and, bathed in tears, turned with pensive steps towards his home. The whole night he spent in sorrow and in penitent reflection; and, at the morning's earliest dawn, hastened to the house of God, to obtain, by dolorous confession, forgiveness from his Lord. His after-life was one of constant holiness.' Such is the narration of the learned James Lobbet, as it occurs in his *Inquiries and Researches on the Gospels*.

But here a question will arise, whether this apparition is to be considered as real and substantial, or as existing merely in the mind; and whether, in the latter supposition, it is to be viewed as an ordinary dream, or as a deception of the unslumbering physical life; or, in fine, as a warning mental figure of a higher order. Psychologists will undoubtedly contend that the conduct of the youth proved him to be rather a fanatic than a luxurious profligate; and that, as extremes are closely bordering, the departure from the wildest audacity would easily conduct to remorse the most dejected, which must soon end in a vision. Their view, they argue, is strengthened by this, that the young enthusiast did not bring home the golden illuminated paper which fell from heaven.

These objections, it is true, cannot be fully answered; yet may the history prove greatly useful and instructive. As to the presumption of standing on the naked heath, and, unaccompanied by other second save his own audacity, formally to challenge the Lord to combat, this is an undertaking too often repeated in every place and every time. "The dwellings of the unrighteous," says Job, "are full of abundance, and they provoke God boldly." (Job xii.) "They have provoked Me to wrath with the work of their hands." (Jer. xliv.) Those who are the most abandoned in impiety, continually springing up from the cursed race of the philosopher or fool of Ferney,[1] challenge God to shew Himself, protesting their willingness to believe in the Invisible so soon as they behold His countenance; and whilst they live and act in shameless wickedness, they pretend that God, who is so far removed from man, cannot be heedful of his deeds, much less can He be offended by them. Such were their words in the time of holy Job: "The clouds are his covert, and He does not consider our things; He walketh about the poles of the heavens." (Job xxii.) They, on the other hand, who glory in a higher and a nobler mind, and in themselves have found the All-absolute, speak of God and of divine things with religious elevation; yet they know no personal and super-earthly God, who, in loving omnipotence, and by nought constrained, created them and the entire world: that God can be offended is to them also incomprehensible, since they themselves, with all their deeds and passions, are but so many manifestations of the Deity. They too would call on God to shew His personality.

In the night of our mortal life, there floats from heaven's vault many a white and shining leaf inscribed with golden letters. These leaves, collected, form the whole Divine revelation contained in the books of the Old and New Testament, so often styled by the Fathers, 'God's proclamation unto men.' And what would it proclaim? "Seek the Lord whilst He may be found;

[1] Voltaire.

call upon Him whilst He is near. Let the wicked forsake his way, and the unjust man his thoughts; let him return to the Lord, and He will have mercy on him, and to our God, for He is bountiful to forgive. For My thoughts are not your thoughts, nor your ways My ways, saith the Lord. For as the heavens are exalted above the earth, so are My thoughts above your thoughts." (Isaias lv.) "I am the Lord, and there is no Saviour beside Me. From the beginning I am the same, and there is no one who can deliver out of My hands; I will work, and who shall turn it away? I am your Lord, the Holy One; I am your Creator and King." (Isaias xliii.)

What are we taught by these and a thousand similar passages in Scripture? That there is a true, living, personal, loving, and in the purity of His love, holy God; whose love-inspired will is our law, a contempt of which constitutes sin. Sin, therefore, cannot be known in its true character, unless by those who are acquainted with the living connexion which should subsist between God and His creature,—between the Divine and the created will. The destruction or interruption of this connexion is caused by the revolt of the created will against God, and God's conduct upon this revolt. How shall we style this revolt of the creature against the sanctity and the love of God? It is termed an offence of God. In what sense an offence? Behold before us the youth of Toulouse, his naked dagger raised towards heaven, challenging the Almighty to combat. Could this madness injure or afflict Him? Certainly not. Did he then, by his senseless audacity, offend his Creator? Without doubt. For when the created soul, in its personality and freedom, rebels against God, renounces its allegiance, opposes by action the reign of pure love, and robs the Creator of His sovereign right over the created will, he in reality offends God, and, as much as in him lies, deprives Him of His ruling power. For the true dominion of God, His dominion of love over His free creature, is relatively lessened or destroyed, so often as this creature refuses its obedience; and the soul by such conduct denies, and to its utmost destroys, the sovereign rule of God.

What, therefore, in its true sense, is an offence of God? Every offence consists in the discovery or perception of a violent and unnatural condition. As often as the creature rebels against the Divine will, or opposes the ideas, the providence of God in its regard, the discovery or perception of this unholy opposition enters into the Divine mind, to which opposition God, as He is the eternal truth, cannot be indifferent; neither, as He is essential felicity, can His happiness be thereby diminished. Such was the truth which led the prodigal to acknowledge, "I have sinned against heaven and before thee;" and which made the Psalmist exclaim, "To Thee only have I sinned," since all sin is an opposition to God; not that the hostile direction of the will can inflict any real injury or suffering on the Almighty, but it is the blasphemy of a rebel against heaven,—a lie against the providence of God; which to Him, to His omnipresence and wisdom, appears as a detestable lie, and necessarily calls forth the opposition of the Divine wisdom and truth.

But if an offence against God is not of such character as to inflict suffering (*passio*), yet does it still continue to be an offence, a violation of the Divine majesty.

As the invisible God, by His union with man in Christ, is personally incorporated and rendered visible in the human world, the opposition of men grew into such wickedness, that the offence of God became cruel enmity to the God-man, which brought on the sufferings, the passion of Christ. "He who hates Me," as He said, "hates likewise My Father." In the passion of our Saviour, whereby He sought to atone for all crime, all offences against God are united.

If, then, sin be on the part of the creature an offence of God, or an opposition to His truth, His honour, and His love, there follows, on the part of God, a declaration of His unchangeable holy will, and His opposition to the rebellious will of His creature; and from this opposition of God, which we call the Divine anger, proceeds the essential evil, the guilt of sin. What, then, do we understand by the Divine anger? We have seen that God cannot suffer in a human manner, nor can we conceive in the Deity human anger as a passion; the anger, therefore, of God is in reality one with His sanctity and His pure love. And how is this? Through pure love, which, by the creature, can neither gain nor lose, did God give to man the immeasurable gift of freedom, as also the law whereby this freedom might be fruitfully employed. If, then, the creature has abused this freedom and despised this law, God rises in opposition, declaring the immutability of His holy will, of His eternal wisdom; and it is this immutability, as opposed to the lie of the creature, which constitutes the Divine anger, which displays itself, as opposition to opposition, and is the thunder-like sentence to the faithless soul of condemnation and banishment.

Yet is this judgment, this punishment of sin, the work, not so much of God, as of the sinful creature upon whom his rebellion quickly recoils. Such was the acknowledgment of the penitent Psalmist, "I acknowledge my injustice, and my sin is always before me." He said not, Thou, O Lord, art against me; but, My sin, my rebellion is turned against me.

Though the sinful act may have passed away, its essential evil still remains; *the guilt*, and its inseparable companion, *punishment*, are yet to be removed, by submission to God and by sincere conversion. This was the conversion to which the golden words exhorted the youth of Toulouse: "Have mercy on me, O God, according to Thy great mercy; and in the fulness of Thy compassion blot out my iniquity" (my opposition to Thy holiness and Thy truth). These words did, in truth, descend originally from heaven, and were, by the spirit of Divine love, poured into a penitent heart, to ascend therefrom once more to God, and to prove that the Divine love, which, till now appeared as anger, was yet existing. This too should therefore be our daily petition: "Have mercy on me, O God; and in the fulness of Thy compassion forgive my sins."

And if to this petition we attend more closely, how far different shall we perceive is the sense in which we term sin *ours*, from that in which we prayed, "Give us this day *our* daily bread?" This bread is ours, as a gift and present bestowed by God; sin is ours, as its guilt is in us alone, proceeding from the opposition of our own free-will, from our inmost personality. We seek not, therefore, exculpation, nor would we, by a new lie and sin remove our guilt; but, acknowledging this guilt, we implore its remission through our participation in His merits, who for us has offered satisfaction more than needful. For the perfect sacrifice of deep submission, and the crimeless satisfaction offered by our Redeemer, has not only freed the human race from the ancient opposition, and with the Father wrought true friendship, but extends to the personal reconciliation of each individual, and abides amongst mankind so effectually, that even for each personal offence this fount of salvation is ever flowing.

As the teaching and the priestly office of Christ are, by the living Word and the daily offering, perpetuated amongst mankind, so does His kingly, His judicial dignity still abide in His Church, which, by the power entrusted to her, can free from the guilt and punishment of sin. It is not, therefore, sufficient that we should pray to God for the pardon of our sins, unless we at the same time remember our duty of obtaining our request by means of sacramental repentance. What believing Catholic can doubt of this? And yet, when repeating this divine prayer, does he always reflect on his sins, and on the duty of repentance and conversion?

There lived in heathen Rome an abandoned youth named Lucius Neratius, who made it his peculiar pleasure and delight to strike on the face the just and harmless men who met him in the streets. But this his wanton conduct proved to him somewhat expensive; for, by a law of the twelve tables, a heavy penalty was decreed in punishment of such insolence. Neratius was in consequence always accompanied by a slave bearing a purse to satisfy for his offences. As often as he experienced his wanton desire, he first struck the citizen whom he encountered, and then, to prevent all further complaint and suits, paid the sum appointed in the law. The prætors being informed of this shameless audacity, abrogated the ancient ordinance, and decreed that for all personal offences a penalty should be awarded proportioned to the circumstances of the deed and the quality of the injured.

And who amongst the children of the Church may justly claim the honour of resembling this Neratius? Such, doubtless, as deliberately offend, relying upon that means of reconciliation always at their disposal, flattering themselves that, by their repeated confessions, and the trifling satisfaction imposed, all will again be right. But who does not see how foolish is their confidence? Their crime may either violate their neighbour's right or not, yet is it always a transgression of the Divine law, and offence of God, an infinite enormity. God has indeed, in confession, appointed a means of reconciliation, of infinite, because of sacramental power; yet when this is misused to a constant repetition of offence, God, enraged at such mockery, revokes His determination, recalls this means, otherwise so availing. When we pray, "Forgive us our trespasses," we cannot pervert these words to such evil import, as though they meant, 'Liberate us from our criminality, free us from our duties to Thee, and to our neighbour.' As well might he who has despoiled his neighbour of his possessions, in place of thinking of restitution, rest satisfied with a pious sigh, and exclaim, "Forgive us our trespasses." Whilst this petition would encourage us to cherish a trustful confidence in God's mercy, it would remind us of His justice and His truth, with which alone we can properly be reconciled.

Towards the middle of the tenth century, it happened that Joseramnus, the eldest son of Lidericus, Count of Flanders, was, with his brother, indulging in childish sports beyond the drawbridge in the neighbourhood of the castle. A woman, poor, and weighed down with care and want, offered him a basket containing fruit, begging for some little money, that she might obtain food for her children in the then prevailing famine. Joseramnus purchased her little treasure, and, not having with him any money, he desired her to remain a few minutes, until he should return with the payment. He hastened back to the castle, and distributed the fruit amongst his mother's maids. In return, they entered with him into so many playful sports, that he quite forgot the destitute creature who stood without. In great anguish she awaited his coming, and constantly turned her eyes to the castle; with each quarter of an hour her anxiety increased, for she thought of the infants who languished for her assistance; often did she raise her foot to hasten to her hut, and then resolved to wait one quarter more; at length the night broke in, and the hopeless woman turned away. Weary and exhausted with hunger and her long and fruitless expectation, and yet more forlorn at the sorrowful thought that she brought no bread for her children, she tottered to her hovel, and, with palpitating heart, passed the threshold. On the floor, worn out by hunger, lay her lifeless infants. The night she passed in bitter tears, which soon gave way to loud complaints, which again were conquered by burning desires of revenge. The morning dawned; she seized her infants in her arms, bore her doleful burden to the castle, and demanded with such earnestness to see the Count, that she was admitted into his presence. With compassion he asked her request; when she laid her children on the ground, fell on her knees, and exclaimed, 'Wouldst thou, O mighty ruler of Flanders, prove thyself truly a prince, it behoves thee this day to pass severe judgment, to have no respect of persons, nor to yield to paternal love. Dost thou inquire the subject of my complaint? Behold these infants. Dost thou ask the cause of their death? Well can I tell thee. To name the culprit may to me prove dangerous. Yet, what have I to lose? He eats at thy table; he is one of thy own family; it is Joseramnus!' Lidericus, in consternation, caused her to narrate the whole event, and having heard his son's account, and made strict inquiry, he hastened privately to Tournay; and there, not mentioning persons, he laid the case before the Senate, and left with them the decision. They adjudged that the youth was guilty of the death of the children, and had therefore forfeited his life. Lidericus consented that his son should be beheaded.

This excessive, this untimely severity, would be little conformable to our present notions; for the youth had offended merely through want of consideration, not with evil design; no crime could be laid to his charge. But, independently of this, and considering the misfortune he had occasioned, who amongst us can tell with certainty, where and how he has injured his neighbour? How often do we view ourselves as guiltless, when, though perhaps without design, we have rent our neighbour's heart? If we consider how many human actions proceed from evil views, with what boldness injustice, usury, deceit, or violence crush the poor, the innocent, and helpless, well shall we understand those dreadful words: "Verily, I say unto you, You shall not depart hence until you have paid the last farthing."

The fifth petition would, therefore, remind us of the justice of God; not that we may challenge it forth, but render it satisfaction, and no longer abide in rebellion, which is the death of the soul. It would tell us too of the Divine mercy, since we address our words to a loving Father, who no sooner sees that we have renounced our opposition, than He gladly removes the guilt which we have drawn on our heads, and remits the chastisement deserved; not so much because we petition Him, but because our petition is based on a rightful confidence in that infinite merit which Christ has purchased. Who has ever returned to God in sorrow, unless awakened by his Redeemer speaking to his soul? How could the remission of his infinite guilt be attained, had not the Saviour offered for all mankind His mediating satisfaction?

Thus, then, we pray for the remission of that personal guilt which we have contracted after our baptism, and for our readmission into the favour of Christ; and as in the fourth petition we implored our daily bread, so in this do we beg for a daily forgiveness, since we daily fall into venial, or less grievous sins. We pray, moreover, in the name of all men, "Forgive our trespasses;" because fraternal charity obliges to this form of prayer; and because, through the humanity of Christ, we are all brethren, and members of one body. We also hereby acknowledge, that no one may claim, in his own person, an exemption from this petition; as though he addressed it, not for himself, but in the name of others. For where is the mortal who, like his Redeemer, can stand forth and demand, "Which of you can convince me of sin?"

It is related in the history of Alphonsus king of Arragon, that the council of Catalonia had determined, in consideration of the youthful age of their new sovereign, to select for him a certain number of advisers to assist him in the government of the kingdom. They accordingly went to the young monarch, and having acquainted him with their design, stated that they had chosen seven approved men, who were accustomed to have God always before their eyes, to observe justice with the greatest rigour, to hold their passions in the greatest restraint, and to remain immovable against praise, flattery, and all other allurements. Alphonsus extolled their wise proposal, and had but one remark to make. 'If, my friends,' he replied, 'you have discovered, I do not say seven, but even one such man, I not only desire to receive him as my counsellor, but am ready to give to him the entire government and the kingdom."

Was this declaration thoughtless or extravagant? Let the Scriptures reply: "There is no just man upon earth who does only good, and never fails." (Eccles. vii.) Who can declare, "My heart is pure and free from all sin?" (Prov. xx.) And thus teaches the Apostle: "If we say we have no sin, we deceive ourselves, and the truth is not in us." But he does not merely say this,

CH. XI.]   FORGIVE US OUR TRESPASSES.   177

but makes known to us a remedy for this universal evil: "If we acknowledge our sins, God is faithful and just, and will forgive them unto us." (1 John i.) Let, then, the Christian exclaim with joy, in the Psalmist's words, "Praise the Lord, O my soul, and let all that is within me (my interior existence, my personal being) extol His holy name. Praise the Lord, O my soul, and never forget all His benefits. Who mercifully forgiveth all thy trespasses, who healeth all thy diseases. Who redeemeth thy life from destruction, who crowneth thee with mercy and compassion. Praise the Lord, all His works; in every place of His dominion, O my soul, bless thou the Lord."

CHAPTER XII.

As we forgive them that trespass against us.

BETWEEN the rugged steeps of arrogance and presumption, and the abyss of dejection and despondency, we pilgrims of this earth, guided by the Divine grace, must preserve the only true, the narrow midway of holy humility. That we may never ascend the giddy heights of self-sufficiency, wherefrom the proud man will inevitably be precipitated into his lamentable nothingness, we are warned by our daily prayers: "Give us this day our daily bread, and forgive us our trespasses;" they lead us to the consideration of our constant dependence, and of our sinful unworthiness. Thus may we with truth ever acknowledge, O Lord, that all real good is from Thee, and all evil from us; the good that is ours is Thy own gift, the evil is our own work.

Yet this acknowledgment must not lead us into dejection and sad lowness of mind, so as to cause us to shrink into a corner, and there exclaim, 'I am nothing, do nothing, and am capable of nothing;' for from nothing, nothing will for ever be produced; and thus all active thought will be destroyed. This pretended self-annihilating humility was the assumed virtue of a certain class of Pharisees, who, with head cast down, and with eyes well-nigh closed, crept along the walls of the houses. No sooner, however, was their nothingness despised, than it instantly started up, and proved itself a very irritable and obstinate nothingness; similar to the yet existing sect of the Nihilists, who have always shewn themselves self-willed, selfish, and arrogant.[1]

The Apostle indeed teaches: "If any one believeth he is any thing, whereas he is nothing, the same deceiveth himself." But he here alludes only to the proud. 'Whosoever,' he would say, 'thinks he is something absolute, his own master, and has his power, his justice, and his virtue purely from himself, he is undoubtedly his own deceiver; since the true, the essential, the happy existence and life is above us all— God alone. But the something which we really are, is our created and limited being, in as far as we have been produced by God's power, and are destined to attain the highest excellence by the co-operation of our own will. That we may, therefore, neither grow arrogant in pride, nor be cast down by dejection, but that we may always be and continue—in humility and practical truth —the right and lawful something, we are here instructed in the way which leads from the abyss; we are placed before God as beings who may effect great good, but good which, when effected, will, as it is observed by St. Gregory of Nyssa, belong to God alone. And this

---

[1] These religionists are still found in some villages towards the south.

is what we express in the conditional petition: "Forgive us our trespasses, *as* we forgive them that trespass against us."

And in this prayer, which is the word which gives to it its tone? Doubtless the word 'as;' and observe, this word occurs twice in the Lord's Prayer, but in opposite significations. In the petition, "Thy will be done on earth *as* it is in heaven," the will of God is constituted the rule and standard of our will on earth; in this, however, where we pray, "Forgive us, *as* we forgive others," our conduct would appear to be placed as the rule for the conduct of God. And this is the observation of St. Gregory of Nyssa. 'The order of things,' says he, 'is in some measure here reversed; so that we presume to hope that God will imitate our mode of action; for we pray, 'What we, O Lord, have done, do Thou also; we have forgiven, do Thou also forgive.'' Or, as Theophylactus explains it: 'God takes us for His examples and models; so that He acts to us as we have acted to others.'

Yet this must not be so unconditionally received, as though the little word 'as' were truly the rule which we appoint for the Lord our God. His will is ever our law, but our will can never be a law for Him. Thus has Christ taught us: "Be perfect, as your heavenly Father is perfect." God will never imitate us; but imitation must ever be the study of the creature.

If, then, we reverse the order, and profess that we are willing to forgive our enemies, as God forgives us, our petition appears in the form of similitude or a proportion, where God stands in the same relation to us, as we to our neighbours. If, then, God's conduct towards us be the true 'rule of our conduct towards our neighbour,' we should ever keep the conduct of our God in view. Now, in every sin, we find, in the first place, an opposition against the will, the right, and the honour of God, which is called an offence; and also the opposition of God against this opposition, from which arises our guilt. For, as the Divine will, which is one with pure love, is ever constant, it manifests itself, in opposition to lies, as the Divine wrath, which again assumes its expression of love, as soon as the creature renounces his treason; and this is promised in the words, "Return to Me, and I will return to you." Yes, this is the ground of our fear, no less than of our hope, that the benevolent love and the just wrath of God are not two opposed properties, but only expressions of His one holy will, according to the conduct of the creature to Him.

Let us now turn to ourselves, and inquire what has befallen us, and what we are required to do, when we have been injured by our neighbour. The offence we have received is a contradiction to our will and to our right. This offence (differently from an offence against God) is committed when our neighbour has insulted or injured us, corporally or spiritually has invaded our right, has frustrated our designs,—all which against God is inconceivable. The result of this offence is our opposition to the injury suffered, and consequently our anger. But how shall this anger be regulated? It must exist only in our righteous and truth-loving will, without hatred, without passion; so that we may continue in that upright mind, which may be termed magnanimity, no less than humility, prepared for reconciliation the first moment our opponent perceives his injustice, which must be an injustice existing not merely in our imagination, but in reality.

But does this suffice for the perfection of our resemblance with God? By no means. If God had waited till rebellious man had acknowledged his injustice, when would the reconciliation have been accomplished? Adam did not acknowledge his wickedness, nor did Eve; for both considered themselves guiltless, and thus, with Cain, would all their posterity have acted; and none would have returned to God, had He not, in His infinite love, looked upon them to knit once more the broken band. For scarcely was the first man sunk in the dark night of sin, when the Divine Word placed Himself in a new alliance with the human race, to reconcile it to His Father. This He accomplished, first, by His revelations in the conscience; afterwards, by His law and the voice of the prophets; and finally, in perfect mediatorship in His advent in the flesh.

If, then, we would observe the rule of resemblance with God, it will not be sufficient that we are ready for reconciliation so soon as the offender knocks at our door to seek it by petition, but we must, on our side, go out and meet him; we must knock at his door, and present him our peace, unconcerned whether we shall receive a new insult; imitating the God-man, who lovingly approached those who, in return, prepared for Him the wood of the cross.

Were we thus minded, what a noble resemblance would subsist between us and the Son of God! "Blessed are the peacemakers, for they shall be called the children of God. Love your enemies, do good to them that hate you, that you may be the sons of your Father who is in heaven." "To whom of the angels," asks St. Paul, "did God ever say, Thou art My son?" 'What a virtue,' exclaims St. Chrysostom, 'is the love of our enemies, since it rewards us with so high a title.' When Jacob approached his hostile brother Esau, and when Esau, removing all bitterness from his soul, went forward in friendship to meet him, Jacob exclaimed, "I beheld thy countenance, as it were the countenance of God." Whence did this rude inhabitant of the deserts acquire such an appearance? 'The man,' replies St. Augustine, 'who forgives his enemies is like to God.' 'To restrain anger,' says St. Chrysostom, 'assimilates man to his Creator.'

If this, then, be true, and be moreover confirmed by the doctrine of Christ, who will feel any further surprise at the power which the peaceful exercise upon earth? In the city of Assisium there raged an implacable enmity between the bishop and the nobles. The bishop excluded his enemies from all communion with the faithful, and forbad them entrance into the church; whilst they forbad the people to hold further intercourse with him. Hereupon the seraphic Francis sent some of his brethren, who remonstrated mildly with the infuriated nobles, and conducted them to the bishop. Then in alternate choir they sang before both parties a hymn taught them by St. Francis. 'Be praised,' they sang, 'be praised and honoured by all who, through love for you, pardon injuries and endure impatience! Blessed are they who abide in peace; they shall receive from Thee a crown.' Scarcely had they entoned these words, when the bishop and the nobles fell into each other's embraces, and promised mutual forgiveness and harmony.

Truly, a beauteous hymn, this hymn of the Saint of Assisium; for, as forgiveness is the act of God, the man who pardons his neighbour performs upon earth the Almighty's work; and thus the fifth petition rises from the depth of self-knowledge and repentance to the height of Divine glory, to the height of the first petition, "Hallowed be Thy name," by the resemblance with God, and especially with Christ, who offered His life for friends and for enemies.

Such was the thought which animated a youth of Lisbon. According to the account of his contemporary, Benedict Fernandez, he was wandering on the shore of the sea, when he perceived a man, who, helpless and alone, without rudder or anchor, lay upon a boat, cast to and fro by the roaring billows. He looked steadfastly, and recognised in the unfortunate man an old opponent, who had injured him most grievously, and against whom he had vowed destruction, but which he had not as yet been able to accomplish. He paused for a moment; one stone on the boat, and his enemy was destroyed: with sudden resolution he sprang into the sea, swam to him, and rescued him from certain death. All thoughts of revenge were now banished from his soul; he had offered his life for his enemy.

Are the like heroism and magnanimity required of us? Are not such circumstances extremely rare? Let us hearken to the Abbot Piminius, and he will give us a fitting reply: 'When any one is addressed by his neighbour in injurious words and unseemly terms, and, although able to reply in like language, struggles in his heart, and restrains himself from answering in bitterness, lest he should afflict his aggressor, such a one has laid down his soul for his neighbour.' As this solution undoubtedly is true, it evidently shews what is the resemblance expressed in the fifth petition. We offer our souls for our neighbour when we grant him forgiveness, as Christ, to obtain for us reconciliation with His Father, sacrificed His life. Is this resemblance a proportion similar to what is announced when we say, one is to ten as one thousand to ten thousand? This we cannot pretend. For if, in the parable of the Gospel, the servant was obliged to remit ten pence to his fellow-servant, since his master had freed him from a debt of ten thousand talents, yet is this similitude far beyond any arithmetical ratio. How, then, is any proportion possible between human and divine things, for God is unlimited, man finite?

A certain individual had written against the sainted Pius V. a pasquinade, breathing the most bitter invective. The Pope summoned the ruthless calumniator into his presence, not indeed to punish him, but to lead him to better sentiments. With as great condescension as goodness, he himself shewed him the way whereby to escape from the penalty of his grievous offence. 'I have cause to believe,' said the Saint, 'that you have written all this, not so much against the Pope, the representative of Christ, as against your brother Michael Ghislieri. (Such was Pius's name previous to his election.) Is it not so?' The culprit, who stood trembling before him, affirmed that it was; and Pius dismissed him with the fatherly advice, to renounce for ever an evil tongue and a malicious pen.

How, then, did he raise the offender from his difficulties, in order to grant him pardon? By distinguishing his person from his dignity, and viewing the insult as directed against himself as a mere man, and not as the representative of Christ; for as such he would have been compelled to punish. The injury which we suffer is in itself, and in relation to us, but finite, since we ourselves are nothing more. Its enormity and infinitude can proceed only from its being a violation and contempt of the Divine law, and consequently an offence of God. This last offence, and its necessary guilt, are infinite, since God is infinite; now, between what is finite and what is infinite there exists no comparison which may be reduced to an arithmetical proportion.

If, independent of the greatness of the guilt, we consider the manner in which it is forgiven, we shall find that God forgives with an infinite love: "I am He that blots out thy sins for My own sake" (Isaias xliii.); whereas the forgiveness which we grant to our neighbour is one of a limited love. God, moreover, pardons with an instantaneous willingness, consoling His enemy with the joy of the Holy Spirit; we do so only gradually and with delay, and not without repugnance and opposition. God, in fine, forgives so perfectly, that He wipes away not only the guilt, but even all the remembrance thereof: "He will," says the prophet, "bury all our sins in the depths of the sea" (Malach. vii.); but we forgive with such imperfection and so superficially, that the endured offence for ever floats in the stream of our thoughts, and is scarcely ever entirely forgotten; for who, in such things, has not an unfailing memory?

When, therefore, we pray, "Forgive us our trespasses, as we forgive," what is signified by this 'as?' Certainly no rule of proportion in the strict sense, but merely a condition, as the words imply, in which this same petition is expressed in St. Luke: " Forgive us our sins, *for* we also forgive every one that is indebted to us." (Luke xi.) And such is the meaning contained in the important words of Christ: " If you forgive men their offences, your heavenly Father will also forgive you also your offences; but if you will forgive not men, neither will your heavenly Father forgive you." (Matt. vi.) And who does not perceive the reason? He who refuses to forgive his neighbour abides in opposition to the Divine will, which is always willing to pardon; and upon him who opposes the Divine love there rests the wrath of God; that is, he remains in sin.

How beautifully is this expounded in St. Augustine: ' The judge pronounces death, and the executioner goes forth and kills; but you, so often as you call to God, ' Slay my enemy,' raise yourself to the office of judge, and make God your executioner. And what does God reply ? ' It shall not be so; I will not the death of the sinner, but his redemption; I wish not his death, but that he be converted, and live; had I your sentiments I should long ago have destroyed you; for has not your wickedness often called for My justice? Have you never despised Me, either in My commands or My servants? Had I then destroyed you as My enemy, how could I now make you My friend? Why, then, do you require Me to do that to your neighbour which I have not done to you?''

In the year 1165, a celebrated duel took place in the presence of the Emperor Frederick Barbarossa. On the one side was an Italian noble, named Aldobrandini, of Padua, and on the other a German. After many brave assaults, the latter was brought to the ground; and as he refused to surrender, and the emperor commanded that the combat should be terminated, Aldobrandini presented his opponent to the emperor, who immediately raised the conqueror to the dignity of count. Whatever contest we carry on with our neighbour, it is with the displeasure of God. But suppose that we have convicted him of injustice, and he yet refuses to acknowledge his offence; yet, even in this case, God desires not the contest. Let us entrust the cause to Him; let us in our hearts pardon our opponent, and we shall have presented him to God; who, in consequence, will raise us to a noble elevation, will free us from our slavery, into which by sin we have fallen, and will exalt us to the rank of His children.

If, on the contrary, we refuse to forgive, and still bear bitterness and revenge in our hearts, what profit will there be to us from his unrighteousness and our justice? 'What does it avail thee,' inquires Francisco Petrarca, 'whether thou be the first or the last to offend?' 'What difference,' asks Tertullian, 'is there between the injurer and the injured who seeks revenge? That the first has fallen earlier into guilt, the second later. Both are guilty, both have offended God. What does it avail man, if he offer his life or his goods for the noblest object, and have not love? He who hates a single man upon earth, gains nought from the fulness of his good works; and what will the excuse avail him, that it was impossible for him to observe the command of his Lord?'

In one of the bloody feuds between the Lombards and the Gessidi (a German tribe, which, in the sixth century, inhabited the east of Hungary), Thorismund, son of the king of the Gessidi, was forcibly seized and murdered by Alboin, a son of the king of the Lombards, who was afterwards conqueror of Italy. The Lombards now maintained the superiority, and the mutual animosity of the two nations was greatly increased, until, through the mediation of the Emperor Justinian, peace was restored. The Lombards requested of their sovereign that Alboin should be allowed the favour of sitting at the royal table, as a reward for his heroism and chivalry; but the king refused this honour, although the boon was asked for his own son. 'You know well,' he replied, 'that, with us, no prince can sit at the table of his father, until he shall have been presented with arms and armour by a foreign sovereign.' Alboin listened, and was silent. The night had begun to darken; he took with him four brave youths, and bent his way to Thorisind, the king of the Gessidi, to whom he opened his desire to receive from him his warrior's suit. Peace had now been concluded, and the inviolable rights of hospitality amongst those nations compelled Thorisind to embrace the murderer of his son, and to entertain him and his companions in all sumptuousness. At the banquet, Alboin was seated on the very place formerly occupied by Thorismund. The aged father, sensibly reminded by this sight of his bitter loss, overpowered with anguish, exclaimed to some of his knights, 'Ah, how dear to my heart is this place, and how detested he who now sits there!' Cunimund, his second son, heard these words, and broke out into invectives against the Lombards, who made no reply. At length all started up and laid their hands upon their swords; but Thorisind commanded peace, took the Lombards under his protection, and forbade further hostility. After the banquet, he caused the arms of his deceased son to be brought, and presented them, but not without many tears, to the Lombard prince, and bade him depart in peace. In triumph Alboin returned home, where the magnanimity of the hostile king was no less admired than the boldness of the youth.

And what induced this heathen prince, not only to subdue his grief for the loss of his son, but to repress his wrath, already bursting into flames? Solely the laws of hospitality, to him so sacred, and on the observance of which so much honour depended. And if such human and earthly motives were so powerful, what may we not expect from the Divine law, from the dread of the eternal justice, and from the living example of Christ? "Be mindful," warns the son of Sirach, "of the last things, and refrain from enmities; be mindful of the fear of God, and be not angry with thy neighbour; be mindful of the covenant of the Most High, and regard not the ignorance of thy neighbour." (Ecclus. xxviii.) This also is the command of our divine Master: "When you shall stand to pray, forgive, if you have ought against any man, that your Father who is in heaven may forgive you your sins." (Mark xi.)

As often, therefore, as we repeat the Lord's Prayer, we must attend to the warning, Be mindful of the words which you utter in the fifth petition. For here but two cases are possible, either that we are willing or unwilling to forgive our opponents. In the former supposition, the significant 'as' will be to us as an encouragement, since it reminds us of the reward of our forgiving love, of our resemblance with God. But if we find not this disposition in our souls, this 'as' will be an admonition to tell us that, without self-subjection, we pray in vain for pardon.

But would it be well, if we cannot pronounce the petition in spirit and in truth, to utter it without consideration? Assuredly not. The Eternal Truth cannot be deceived by pharisaical falsehoods. It would therefore be wiser to pronounce it with magnanimity and reflection, and to view it in its threefold signification. For if we have really been injured by our neighbour, the offence against God, incurred by the injustice done to our right, must, in the first place, be considered; secondly, the offence against ourselves; and lastly, the real injury we have suffered. As to the offence against God, it is the Almighty, not we, who pardons it; in this regard, the offender is more worthy of compassion than the offended. As is implied by that injunction of Christ, "Pray for them who injure you;" that is, that God may forgive them. Neither should we hesitate to pardon the injury so far as it concerns ourselves, lest otherwise, by our hatred and animosity, we ourselves be guilty before God.

The last considered is the real injury we have sustained. And here we must distinguish the nature of this injury. When we pray, " Forgive us our debts," it is evident that we allude not to pecuniary debts, but to the spiritual debts we have incurred by disobedience and contempt of the Divine honour and truth. And when we add the comparison, "As we forgive our debtors," this is not to be understood in the ordinary, but in a spiritual sense; since no one would suppose that a faithful Christian is obliged to remit all his debts out of pure love. Our Lord merely enjoins us to forgive those injuries done to our well-being and honour, the forgiveness of which is essential to love; but it is by no means inconsistent with fraternal charity, that one man should be debtor to another, unless when extreme necessity, or oppressive circumstances, would even here raise an exception. When, however, there is no debt which really calls for restitution, but merely some other injury, such as of honour, here the important 'as' steps forward, and prescribes to the Christian a peaceful magnanimity, where, in common and earthly views, revenge would be inculcated.

In the history of St. Christopher it is related, that when brought before the Prætor to give an account of his faith, one of the attendants struck him on the face. St. Christopher, possessed of no less courage than strength of body, cast a significant look at the cowardly man, and said threateningly, 'Were I not a Christian.' These words need no comment. Were I not a Christian, were I not bound by the commands of Christ, well would I teach you, miserable creature, to strike me again. And, truly, how is it possible that anger and a desire of retaliation should not be excited by an injury? This is a natural feeling. And who can despise a Christian for not seeking revenge? Were I not a Christian, I would be revenged. And if I were not a Christian, what should I be? A child of wrath, a slave of darkness. "He who says he is in the light, and hates his brother, is in darkness even till now." Were I not a

Christian, I should be without an atonement, without joy, without a hope of light or life, without counsel, without grace, without a way to God. But I AM A CHRISTIAN, and therefore belong to Christ, and follow His holy precepts, His living example, in order that, by forgiving, I may enter into His merit, and find eternal forgiveness.

CHAPTER XIII.

And lead us not into Temptation.

BETWEEN the promises of Scripture which are affirmative, and those which are negative, there exists this great and essential difference, that the latter are universal; whereas the former are limited, and are to be understood in a restricted and conditional sense. Thus there is the promise, "He who believeth and is baptised shall be saved," and this is affirmative. It is also written, "He that believeth not shall be condemned," which sentence is negative. Is it, then, without exceptions? He who is truly a Christian can here raise no objection; for without faith salvation is impossible. Yet we cannot presume to decide whether Divine love does not avail itself of many means whereby to call him who is, without fault, an unbeliever, in the last moments of his life, into the bright region of faith, into the bosom of His Church, and unto happiness; and therefore it is not here said, 'He who believeth not, and is not baptised,' but only, 'He who believeth not;' for besides the ordinary baptism, there is also one in desire. But in the affirmative promise it is very different: "He who believeth and is baptised" shall be saved. An essential condition is here implied—the condition of perseverance in the life-giving faith, and of compliance with all the duties to which man is bound by faith and baptism.

And thus it is with regard to the important truth contained in the fifth petition. When announced negatively it is universal. "If you forgive not men their offences, neither will your heavenly Father forgive you your offences." But in an affirmative form it is different: 'If you forgive men their offences, your heavenly Father will forgive you also your offences.' For this condition is by no means the only one, the fulfilment of which will secure to us eternal forgiveness. There are also other conditions which must necessarily be observed. In vain shall we pardon our enemies, unless we persevere in holiness of faith, of morals, and of action.

The more we consider the greatness of our manifold duties, the more sensibly do we feel the difficulty of their fulfilment, and the numerous occasions of transgression or neglect, and consequently of new offences, which present themselves. Hence to the 'and' of the fifth petition—"and forgive us our trespasses"—we add another 'and;' and assist us that we fall not into sin: "and lead us not into temptation."

And what is that which will particularly strike us in this petition? The preceding petitions are all affirmative: "Hallowed be Thy name," &c., as is also the last, "Deliver us from evil." This alone is in the negative form; as though we here petitioned for something which God should not perform, or as if we wished to avert something which He was about to perform. Does not the Apostle declare, " God is true; in Him there is not yes and no, but all His promises are yes." (2 Cor. i.) We do not indeed pray, 'Lead us not into error;' for God is truth, and cannot lead into error. Neither do we pray, 'Lead us not into darkness—lead us not into misery;' for how can we ascribe this to the Light and Blessedness itself? But we petition that we be not led into temptation. Thus we arrive at the inquiry, what is temptation? especially in as far as it concerns man; and secondly, why does God lead us into temptation, and in what sense do we pray that He would not lead us?

As it would be a vain and unbecoming endeavour to seek the answer to these inquiries, and the signification of the entire petition, without some previous reflection, we will first ask, what is it to tempt a person? It is to place him in such circumstances, that, by their influence upon him, and his corresponding influence upon them, we may discover his dispositions and mind. Thus the chemist tries or tempts minerals and stones by submitting them to the fire, to acids, or to other dissolving powers, to discover what metal is contained in them, and also its proportion. One man is also tried by another, when he is placed in circumstances and difficulties whereby his prudence, his uprightness, and his whole mind are discovered.

Does God, then, apply to the human soul these means of discernment? To this the Scriptures bear evidence, when, in their figurative language, they so often declare, that the Lord conducts His chosen through fire and water; that He tries them in the furnace of tribulation, in order to separate the silver from the dross. "The Lord," said Moses to the Jews, "tries you, that it may be evident whether you love Him or not." (Deut. xiii.) "Try me," exclaims the Psalmist, "prove me, and see if there be in me any wickedness." (Ps. xxv.) But is this proving, this trial on the part of God, the same as human exertions, which arrive with difficulty at the desired knowledge? Does God require such means to discover the properties of His creatures? "All," says the Apostle, "is naked and open to His eyes;" and, as the son of Sirach, in the same figurative language, has declared, "The eyes of the Lord are brighter than the sun, searching the ways of men, seeing into the depths of the abyss, and into the most hidden parts of the heart of man; for to the Lord are all things known, even before they are made." (Ecclus. xv.) And how can they be unknown to Him, since the entire creation is but His own idea realised by omnipotence?

The solution of this mystery lies, however, far deeper, and in a principle with which we are already acquainted. Opposed to the Divine love, we have seen the freedom of the creature, which, on one side, should find and acknowledge its law in the Divine will, and, on the other, is free to oppose or submit to this will; for in this is the essence of freedom, that it be free from compulsion. And such is the doctrine of Ecclesiasticus: "God made man from the beginning, and left him in the hand of his own counsel. He added His commandments and precepts. If thou wilt keep the commandments, and perform acceptable fidelity, they shall preserve thee. He hath set water and fire before thee;

stretch forth thy hand to which thou wilt. Before man is life and death, good and evil; that which he shall choose shall be given him." (Ecclus. xv.)

If these words portray the dignity of man, as a creature to whom God has entrusted the highest and most noble gift—freedom of action—so that he may acquire virtue, merit, and eternal happiness; they also represent the danger necessarily connected with such a dignity, the danger of a deeper fall, if he abuse his freedom. Has God, then, raised him to so precipitous, so dangerous a height, without granting him the support of light and grace? "The eyes of the Lord are towards them that fear Him, and He knoweth all the works of man; He hath commanded no man to do wickedly; and He hath given no man license to sin; for He desireth not a multitude of faithless and unprofitable children." (Ecclus. xv.) Or, as Christ has said, "My Father loves those who pray to Him in spirit and in truth."

As man, therefore, by his spiritual life, is left to his own choice, wherein the Divine commands, or the revelation of the Divine will, cannot compulsively determine, but only incline him; it is evident that he must sometimes be so circumstanced, that he is required absolutely to choose and to decide; thus manifesting the essence of his being. These circumstances, whether internal or external, are a temptation; and the activity of the spirit, thereby aroused, is the struggle, or exertion, to correspond with the Divine will, and to resist the impulse of self-love; and thus to be steadfast and happy in God. "Let us strive manfully," exclaims St. Peter, "in expectation of an unfading crown of victory."

"Happy the man," says St. James, "who resisteth temptation; for when he shall be tried, he shall receive a crown of glory, which God has promised to those who love Him"

If such, then, be the truth, wherefore do we petition, "Lead us not into temptation?" Does the warrior pray to his general, 'Lead us not into battle?' Does the sailor implore the pilot, 'Lead us not on the deep?' A hermit once visited the Abbot Pastor, and said: 'I have prayed to God, and behold, He has freed me from every temptation.' Pastor replied: 'Go, beseech God to grant you again your temptations, lest you become negligent and slothful!' Yes, let us—the Apostle exhorts us—"Let us consider it as the perfection of happiness, to be tried by many temptations, knowing that the proof of our fidelity worketh patience; and that patience hath a perfect work." But how is this doctrine reconcilable with this sixth petition?

The warrior may exclaim to his general, 'Lead us on to war,' but only when he has a confidence of victory; the sailor may desire to launch out upon the deep, when he does not apprehend that he shall be engulfed in the waves. And, in like manner, do we petition, "Lead us not into temptation;" that is, lead us not into the midst of temptations, so that their darkness should on all sides surround us; lead us not into the depths of the pit, so that light and deliverance be taken away; but deliver us from temptation; or, as the Scripture says, "Deliver my soul from trouble and the pit; deliver me from the snare that is secretly laid for me; we have been led through fire and water (through trials and sufferings of every kind), and Thou hast conducted us into the freshness of life." (Ps. xxx., lxv.)

But is every human heart so fully sensitive, that it can feel the necessity of this petition in all its depth?

A noble youth in Peru, named Espina, had so abandoned himself to revelling and profligacy, that he had brought his entire family to shame. His uncle, an aged man, greatly respected, and of much prudence, invited him to his dwelling; he represented, in the most lively colours, the beauty and honour of Christian virtue and morality, the disgrace of sin and wickedness, and earnestly exhorted him to reform his life. After he had exhausted all his powers of persuasion, what answer did he receive from the shameless youth? 'You have spoken beautifully and pathetically; but I have heard the same words more than a hundred times before, and others even more beautiful; and they have always failed to produce any effect upon me, and it will be the same now!' It is also related in an ancient reading-book, that a youth who was addicted to drunkenness, was conducted by his father to behold an inveterate drunkard, who was lying in the streets, and rolling in the mire. The young man contemplated the miserable wretch; then, turning to his father, he said: 'Where do they obtain that sweet and noble wine, which has such power over man? Would that I could procure some!' To what class of men did this brutish creature belong? To that class which, if they made use of prayer, would pray, 'Lead us into temptation;' but who need not such a petition, since of their own accord they seek the occasions of sin; and to them nothing is more delightful than opportunities of contentions, of quarrels, of revelry, and injustice. But it is their lamentable example which must move us to this petition, 'Lead us not into those temptations, which will cause us to ensnare ourselves; lead us not into those temptations, in which Thou seest that we should perish.'

But is this the language that we should hold with God? Can God be so unloving as to place us in circumstances of inevitable ruin? Is not this supposition irreconcilable with the essential goodness of God? The Scripture here speaks in a language conformable to human usage. For thus Isaias exclaims: "Thou hast hardened our hearts, that we may not honour Thee;" and again, "Wherefore, O Lord, hast Thou caused us to err from Thy ways?" (Isa. lxiii.) In the same manner is it said of God, that He blinds the eyes of men, that they may not see; that He closes their ears, that they may not hear. And what is the true meaning of such expressions? God hardens the heart of man when He foresees that, without His assisting grace, it will become hardened, and yet permits this hardness; He blinds the heart of man when He suffers this blindness to come upon him, that is, when He does not prevent it by graces known to His wisdom, because He cannot, and will not, frustrate other and higher designs of His wisdom.

When, therefore, we read in the Psalms, "Thou hast led us into snares," it can only imply, 'Thou hast permitted that we should fall into snares;' and when we petition, "Lead us not into temptation," we can only mean, 'Permit not that we be abandoned to temptation.' But how shall we complain if He permit, and do not avert, these dangers? for we know that "as far as the heavens are above the earth, so far are His ways exalted above ours."

In praying, then, not to be led into temptation, we petition for two favours; first, that we may not fall into temptation, that is, into opposition to the Divine law, whereunto we are tempted; that we may not abandon God and our fidelity to Him, but that we may oppose the spirit of lies, and may be assisted thereto by light and the power of God, which is His grace. The second favour for which we ask is, that we may not be exposed to those temptations which act powerfully or secretly, before which the Divine wisdom foresees that we should fall. So that the sixth petition expresses an act of humility in our infirmity and littleness, and the determination of our will to persevere in our fidelity and obedience to God.

It was in this sense that Christ bade His disciples to watch and pray, lest they should enter into temptation. Such also, according to John Moschus, is the interpretation of the Fathers. We pray not, say they, never to be tempted, but that we may never be overcome by temptation. The martyrs were tempted by bitter tortures; but they were not overcome, they did not enter into temptation; they did not yield, as if assailed by the fury of some wild beast.

In the letters of the holy Cardinal Peter Damian, we read the history of an event which occurred in his days, not less remarkable than lamentable. A fisherman had placed his little son in the fore part of his boat, and had gone to a considerable distance from the shore, when suddenly a fish of enormous size darted into his net. Delighted with the possession of so rich a prize, the fisherman drew in his net, and cast the fish into the middle of the boat, so that its head was turned towards the child, who sat at one end. The man was now busy with the rudder, and, in his joy, thought of nothing but happiness, when his son, terrified by the look of the fish, raised a piteous cry, 'Father, the fish is staring at me; it will swallow me!' 'Foolish child,' replied the parent, 'thou wilt swallow it, not it thee!' Again the boy cried out. Hereupon the father turned again to reprove his folly, when, behold, the fish sprung forward, darted on the youth, dragged him into the sea, and vanished, leaving not a track behind.

But what has this history to do with our present purpose? It may be considered as a picture of our own times. Traversing the sea of empiricism, our fathers of the eighteenth century—the fathers of the present generation—have made a great capture; they have taken that leviathan,—that monster before which, in former times, children, old and young, trembled, and have endeavoured to teach their children the fabulous nothingness of former times. The poor little ones, when left to themselves, shuddered at the appearance of the monster, and dreading his threatening eyes, they trembled at the sight of sin; the fresh and sinless life still dwelling in the breasts of these young citizens of the world of men has yet a stirring sentiment of what is above the senses, it recoils from the vapour of death and the odious aspect of lying and unclean perversity, and shudders at the sight of him who is called the liar and the deceiver from the beginning. But the old fishermen and new apostles, who cast not their nets in the name of Jesus, despise the simplicity of these innocent children, and seek to open their eyes, that they may scorn the phantom of superstition, and may not suffer themselves to be troubled by anxious prejudices in the enjoyments and pleasures of rational life. The result is, that this supposed phantom seizes these youths almost before they have passed the limits of childhood, and hurries them into the abyss of shameless immorality, from which only few are ever delivered. They are surrounded and overcome by temptations.

There are three powers which assail the human will, and which labour to withdraw it from the will and law of God. These are, the senses, the spirit, and Satan. 'The senses,' writes St. Bernard, 'allure us with their enticements of gratification, the world with its vanities, and Satan with his violent and harsh temptations. But the Strength, the Truth, and the Fidelity, which came to destroy the works of the devil, for that end, and to offer as the high-priest of mankind the sacrifice of obedience, became in all things like unto us, excepting sin (Heb. ii., iv.), and desired therefore to overcome these three temptations;—the senses, when He was required to change a stone into bread; the spirit, when allured to vanity by the offer of the kingdoms of this world; and the devil, when He was required, through pride, to defy the omnipotence of God.'

And how did the heavenly Adam vanquish these temptations? By adhering to the Divine law, as it is declared in the holy Scriptures. And how may we, with the assistance of His grace, overcome temptations that may assail us? By the same means,—by directing our will and our exertions that we may not depart from the law of God. Therefore does the Psalmist exclaim,

"Enlighten, O Lord, my eyes, that I may not sleep in death; that the enemy may not glory that he has conquered me. In the depth of my heart I have observed Thy commandments, that I may not sin." (Ps. cviii.)

CHAPTER XIV.

And lead us not into Temptation; but deliver us from Evil.

IF, according to the ancient definition of St. John Damascene, prayer be an elevation of the soul to God, in what prayer is this more true than in that which the Orient from above, the Son of the Most High, has taught us? Here, even in the commencing words, we rise to the Uncreated and Eternal, that we may invoke Him as our Father, acknowledge Him in His threefold essence, holiness, and love, and pray for the hallowing of His name, the propagation of His kingdom, and grace to fulfil His will. What can be more exalted? Can the human soul aspire to greater elevation?

But even this soul, breathing such noble wishes, is not so free as to persevere in its elevation; it is bound to an earthly element, perhaps deeply weighed down by the chains of sin. "Who," exclaims the Psalmist, "will give me the wings of the dove, that I may fly away, and rest in Thee?" As the lark, with rapid wing soaring on high and floating in the pure air, scatters around it sounds of sweetest song, must yet again descend to the cold earth to seek its food, and at last to die; so the soul of man in its flight sees itself still borne downwards by the wants and dependence of corporeal life which it feels, and must confess its cry for daily bread, if not oppressed by crimes which render it poorer than poor, and compel it to pray for forgiveness.

But even in these petitions we ascend to some elevation; for when we pray to our Father for our supersubstantial bread, we acknowledge in thanksgiving to the Eternal Love the superiority of our natural or corporeal existence over the rest of creation, and aspire after the heavenly bread which unites us with the Author of all life; and we are assured, that if we forgive our enemies sincerely and with good heart, we shall be raised from the depths of sin unto a likeness with God.

But it is evident that, even when thus elevated, we have still far higher to ascend. When the lark floats amidst its song in the heights of air, it is not yet out of the reach of the fowler's shot, or it may even yet be ensnared into the treacherous net, and its joy give place to mourning. The state of the soul of man is not far dissimilar. When raised by religious, fervent, heartfelt thought above all that is earthly, and joyful in the region of light, then, when least thoughtful of his danger, he may fall into the snare of the hunters, he may be struck by the arrow which flieth in the day, or by the thing that walketh in the dark. Thus, in the depth of our misery, and in the full consciousness of our weakness, we send up our prayer to God: "And lead us not into temptation."

Temptation, according to Richard Victor, is sevenfold in its mode of attack. It may fall upon us inopportunely, as when any thing occurs contrary to our wishes, endeavours, and expectations, and which, therefore, may move us to repining, to ill-will, and to impatience. It may fall upon us in the form of doubt and despondency, as when our free-will is placed between two different resolutions and actions, not seeing clearly which is the better, or perhaps too weak to follow it when discovered; and hence arise a distraction and division of the mind, the expression of which is similar to the tone of a chord too finely stretched. Sudden and unexpected is the temptation which assails us unprepared for its attack, and it wounds us the more easily as we are the less able to offer opposition : it is concealed when, from want of vigilance, we are not aware of its approach; so that we are struck with blindness, not being able to enter into our interior, to discover what our mind may be. It may fall upon us by deceit, by assuming the appearance of virtue and honour, and thus delude us from our better thoughts. The last two are in the Scriptures likened to the snare and the serpent. It may fall upon us powerfully, as when, although its form be too evident to mislead us, its impetuosity is nevertheless so great, that without the assistance of an extraordinary grace, man's moral strength would fail. Temptation, in fine, may be complicated, when, presenting to our view many apparent goods and evils, it causes us to apprehend that, whilst we fly from one evil, we may fall into another, and that in obtaining one good, we shall lose a greater; so that, whatever be our decision, we must inevitably forfeit some advantage. Such temptations are amongst the most dangerous; they tear and lacerate the soul. As these trials must continue through all time, how must earth's pilgrim sigh on his long, long way, through so many dangers! 'A man,' says St. John Chrysostom, 'goes into the public square, and sees his rival, and is inflamed with anger; he sees a fellow-citizen who is honoured by the state, and he is filled with envy; he is accosted by a poor man, and replies with contempt; he meets a woman, and is seized by concupiscence. Behold, what multiplied snares! A friend is a snare, a relative is a snare, and oftener still is man a snare to himself.' What more frequent than this last!

Many have probably read of the awful deed of a German prince, who allowed himself to be carried so violently away by blind rage, that he fell into the deepest darkness of temptation, from which only the horror of his own act awakened him. Lewis, surnamed the Strong, was in a country on the banks of the Rhine, when his wife, who had remained at Donauwert, wrote two letters, one to him, and one to Henry Rucho, his general. By accident, the letters were changed, so that the latter fell into the hands of the duke. Some expressions of friendship contained in the letter at once aroused his jealousy. Instantaneously he mounted his horse, and hastened, in company with a few attendants, without once resting day or night, to Donauwert. At his arrival, he struck down the watch at the gate, killed one of his wife's maids, cast another over the battlements of the castle, and next morning caused his wife, notwithstanding her tears and protestations, to be beheaded. The next night he was seized with such horror at his deed, that his hair became blanched.

What was the cause of all these deeds of violence? A single temptation, to which the duke blindly yielded. Perhaps it will be said, that this is a history of a brutal, uncultivated age. But later centuries are not to be herein distinguished from former times; for let age after age roll on, temptations and the tempests of the passions remain always essentially the same. And who can pride himself on being free from their attacks? Shall the man who has risen to exalted science, or he who has performed much good upon earth, glory in his merit, or exult in self-confidence? "Verily I say unto you," exclaims our Saviour, "I beheld Satan falling as lightning from heaven. Watch and pray, lest you enter into temptation." And in the same spirit He taught us to petition, "Lead us not into temptation."

It may probably be asked, whether we can remain content with a sentence or petition purely negative. 'Not,' is in itself no ground whereon we can rest, without advancing onwards towards an affirmation. Thus St. Paul exhorts us "not to be overcome by evil." But does he conclude here? By no means; but proceeds to the affirmation, "but overcome evil with good." In like manner do we pray to the Almighty, "Lead us not into temptation,"—permit not that we be deceived or ensnared,—"*but* deliver us from evil."

One of the last prayers which our Lord, previously to His departure from the world, presented to His Father for His disciples was: "I pray not that You would take them from the world" (that they may be exposed to no temptation), "but that You would preserve them from evil." (John xvii.) This petition is also the last, as well as the most comprehensive, in the Lord's Prayer, expressing and comprising every thing; so that, as St. Cyprian remarks, if this be heard, nothing further remains to be desired. For it is evil that compels us to pray: "From the depths I have cried to thee, O Lord; Lord, hear my voice." It is evil that, in a thousand forms, attacks and proves us; and as its removal or defeat is the last and inmost supplication in the Lord's Prayer, so does this constitute the first step by which we rise to positive religion, to holy truth.

The full import of this, no one perhaps has better expressed than St. John Damascene in his account of Prince Josaphat. Avennir, he relates, the governor of a kingdom in the East Indies, had no sooner been gladdened by the birth of a son, than he received from his augurs and astrologers the mournful assurance, that his son, according to all presages, would one day be a Christian. The loving and too provident father would not delay one moment in taking precautions against this sad event; and for this purpose he adopted measures which we cannot but admire, and which would do honour even to the mind of an encyclopedist. He caused the child to be brought up in the abundance of every gratification and luxury, watched with the greatest care, that his least desire might not be contradicted, and, in order that nothing mournful or troublesome might offend his sight, he gave an irrevocable order that he should never be taken beyond the courts and gardens of the palace.

But when the little Josaphat began to advance in years, he beheld from the windows and over the garden-walls the surrounding hills and plains; and so bitterly did he feel his imprisonment, that his health began visibly to decline. This caused the father to perceive that his plan was as yet defective, that it could not preserve this fondling of earthly happiness from all trouble, nor ward off the approach of discontent and uneasiness. He was therefore compelled to allow his son to ride or walk beyond the bounds of the palace, under the shade of palanquins, and attended always by the officers of the court. The greatest caution was, however, taken, that nothing but what was pleasant and cheering should meet his view. The woods and groves resounded with joyful music, and on the flowery meadows were seen men mingling in cheerful dances; none but healthy, joyful, and well-clad men were suffered to pass on the road; in fine, the new Arcadia was to breathe forth nothing but pleasure and peace.

But in proportion as these theatrical adornments were more studiously arranged, the more striking and revolting were the contrasts which here and there, as so many forms from hell, crept upon the fairy scene. For as the evils of this world are so multiplied, that we can no more be free from them than from the weeds of the earth, so, in spite of all the solicitude of the attendants of the prince, objects of an unpleasing or disgusting character would ever and anon cross his path. Once, as they were journeying forward, a blind man presented himself, and soon after a leper. The prince was much amazed at these objects, and overwhelmed his attendants with inquiries as to the nature of these calamities, and whether they were equally the lot of all men. Upon his courtiers informing him that they were, he became thoughtful, and a stranger to his former joy. A few days afterwards, an aged bald-headed man, with wrinkled countenance and doubled back, passed before him; Josaphat asked with earnestness, what was that extraordinary creature; and was greatly astonished to hear that it was a man advanced in years and fast approaching to the grave; and when they added, that death was an event which awaited all men, the thought became so deeply fixed in his attention, that he could not for one moment dispel it, and tortured his mind with continual researches, until he met with a Christian named Barlaam, who instructed him in holy truth.

The subsequent life of our hero is narrated by the author of this history, who has endeavoured to represent by examples all the practical truths of Christianity. We shall not proceed further, but remain and contemplate the wise device of Avennir; a device which was well planned, although, like so many other devices, it had that one small failing—it did not attain its object.

In truth, he who knows not, and will not be instructed in evil, has no further problem to solve; he is not tempted or desirous to search into the darkness of the future, and, like the child in the cradle, he slumbers on in his seeming happiness. But where shall we look for the man who can pass so trancelike a life? Even the babe in the cradle is visited with pains and sorrows, which serve to develope its consciousness. Is not life itself, in its thousand necessities, a succession of evils? We need but name a mortal man, and we have named the whole train of human evils.

This, however, is a reflection not acceptable to the young, the vigorous, and the thoughtless, for whom sin has still many enticements. He who is yet in the buoyancy of health thinks seldom of the short hour of death; and if the necessities of eating and drinking, of clothing and repose, are numbered amongst the evils of life, they are to the gormandizer and the lover of ease, evils that are most welcome and beloved. And if even the undeniable evils of the body are insufficient to awaken man to reflection, how shall it be with those, incomparably greater, of the soul? Death will be viewed as a mere metamorphosis of organic nature; or if the commonplace idea of a passage into a better life be admitted, they prefer to this better life their present miserable state. The faults and wanderings of man will be considered as consequences of his passions, and of his very nature, and as inevitable as this nature itself. Sin will be declared nothing more than an attempt in man to raise himself in freedom and independence; and provided he does not violate the laws of the state or of society, no one need lose his breath in reproving him for his acts. In fine, it will be said, that eternal guilt and the punishments of a future life are the mere monster offsprings of senile minds and trembling superstition.

And as they affirm that there are no moral evils to unfold the germ of such as are eternal, so they pretend that there needs no Physician or Saviour, no Mediator or Redeemer, and consequently no Christianity. Thus does our little European Josaphat of the nineteenth century grow up without hope and without Christianity, ignorant of all real evils. What immeasurable evils are in ignorance of God, in arrogance, and in sensuality, he knows not, until the evils that he has sown within himself burst upon him. His body is becoming enfeebled, his soul comfortless and miserable, his mind bitter and implacable; he is lost to all sense of honour, and is constantly invading the rights of his fellows. The void in his heart seeks for some consolation, his soul sighs for repose; and, after taking refuge in some wild romance, various forms present themselves in high elevation before his mind, and on these he endeavours to build his hopes of repose.

Thus one advocates ancient fate, and leaves all things to come as they must; another takes some notice of a supreme God, but yet is impious in his notions of Him; he denies Him justice and wisdom, and considers Him as some Demiurgos, who beholds many evils and disorders, for which he has no remedy; a third deprives Him of all personality, but allows Him to exist in the universe as its great Spirit, and seeks his own felicity in gross Pantheism; a fourth deserts Pantheism for Dualism, and as he sees good and evil, in imitation of the Manichees, divides his deity into a good and bad principle; a fifth has clung to the ancient Mephisto, and contents himself with a malicious wit, and superiority over every thing; a sixth despises all such inquiries, drinks his wine, and lives in stupid indifference. And what do we think or say to all this? We sigh, and exclaim: "Lead us not into temptation, but deliver us from evil."

Truly, then, it is not without reason that the Church has prescribed that, on different occasions—and particularly in the Sacrifice of the Mass—these two petitions should be pronounced aloud. The minister at the altar says, "Lead us not into temptation;" and the choir replies, "But deliver us from evil." For temptation and evil are closely related, and each is dependent upon the other. The numerous evils of this world surround us with many and bitter temptations; and these temptations, if not properly resisted, produce new and greater evils, by which man is constantly assailed and besieged.

Hence, if we endeavour to find the beginning of this entangled thread, the great question arises,—whether originally evil be the cause of temptation, or temptation the cause of evil. This question is important, for on its decision rests the solution of all doubts; nor is this decision difficult, as we can have no doubt of the holiness and love of God. We have already seen that temptation is nothing more than an occasion in which man is required to make a free election between his own will and that of God; and that in this self-determination and free choice consists the proof of freedom, of which privilege no created intelligent spirit can be deprived. Since every free creature must perfect itself, and God cannot perform for it that, for the free accomplishment of which it was created. "What can he know who has not been tempted?" inquires the son of Sirach. (Ecclus. xxxiv.) He has not yet established himself in his perfect self-consciousness; he has not yet perfected his true relationship to God.

If, on one side, we perceive that temptation and trial are essential to every free creature; on the other, what must we say of the occasions which lead to temptation? If we allow that these occasions are themselves evil, the evil itself must have had prior existence; but in what can this original evil consist? Shall we say, In Satan, and place in him the first cause of all the evils and temptations of the earth? But he himself was originally guiltless; and temptation was to him the occasion of his fall. If, then, temptation itself were an evil, or if evil were its first source, God must have been its creator and mover; but what is this, if it be not blasphemy? "Think of God in goodness, and seek Him in the simplicity of your heart. Great is the Lord, and praiseworthy; above all, immeasurable is His goodness. One generation after another shall praise His works, and proclaim His might. They shall declare the power and glory of His holiness, and narrate His wonders. They shall renew the remembrance of His abundant sweetness, and rejoice in His justice. Good is the Lord to all, and His mercy reaches above all His works." (Ps. cxliv.) Think, therefore, of God in goodness; for "God is love; and he who abides in love, abides in God."

And what can we say of God, but that "God is love?" Shall we call His very being mercy, or justice, or severity, or all-directing Providence? Amongst the three eternal and infinite Persons, into which the one self-knowing and self-loving divine Being unfolds itself, there can be no reciprocal justice, or mercy, or guidance; amongst them there can be nothing but holy love; and when we fear the justice of God, implore His mercy, or commit ourselves to His guidance, these divine properties (as they are called) are but the different expressions or manifestations of the one divine and holy love to its free creatures, according to the conduct of these creatures, and their conformity or opposition to the holy will of God.

When, therefore, we inquire concerning the origin of evil, it cannot be doubted that we must look for it in creatures; and as we are now speaking of such as are free or spiritual, who bear a relation of morality and justice to their Creator, it must be a violation of this relation which brings their guilt upon them.

Thus do we arrive at the knowledge and understanding of the great event, upon the reception or rejection of which Christianity stands or falls. We stand under the tree of the knowledge of good or evil, which, as sacred Scripture informs us, gave occasion to the decision on the weal or woe of the human race. And here, under the shade of this tree, — so full of destiny, which to one appears to veil mysteries impenetrable and incomprehensive, whilst another can find in this mystic gloom only the origin of fabulous story — we must linger awhile, and see whether this true account of man's misery and man's salvation, of evil and of redemption, be clearly fixed upon our minds, and then, with the Psalmist, we may exclaim, "In heaven, O Lord, is Thy mercy; Thy truth reaches to the clouds. Thy justice is like to the eternal mountains; Thy judgments are an unfathomable abyss. But the sons of men shall hope with confidence under the shadow of Thy wings. Extend Thy mercy over all who know Thee. Give Thy justification to all who are of a right heart." (Ps. xxxv.)

CHAPTER XV.

But deliber us from Ebil.

IN the ancient chronicles of France we read of one of its kings, that he made it his custom and his rule to eat every day at dessert a pealed apple. Once, when his three sons were standing around him, it occurred to him to make upon them a physical experiment, or, as the Germans would express it, to prove clearly the dispositions and sentiments of his children. They were taken so much by surprise, and the circumstance appeared to them so insignificant, that they could not possibly divine their father's real intention. The chemist may indeed say to a mineral whose contents are to him a problem, 'In such an hour I will employ against you my acids, my waters, and my alkalies, or place you between my galvanic poles, that you may be compelled to unfold your constituent parts;' but the master would not say to his pupil, 'To-morrow at this hour I will do this or that to try you; collect yourself, and acquit yourself as I desire you, for this is the probation to which I will subject you.' Would not such a master destroy at once the desired effect; like to the lion in the Midsummer Night's Dream, which kindly and providently informed the public of his harmless nature, lest they should give themselves up to anxieties about him?

This was the prudent view taken by the French monarch, who, presenting on his knife a piece of apple, already pealed, to his eldest son, Goband, or Gobandus, said, 'Come and take this morsel from thy father's hand.' Goband refused with great politeness, objecting, with courtier-like fastidiousness, that he was wholly unworthy that his king and his father should condescend to serve him with his own hand. The king did not allow him time to complete his well-arranged reply, but called his second son, who answered, 'Any thing, my father, which you command. I am indebted for all things to your goodness and wisdom.' He thought it needless to say more, and without further delay received the morsel with open mouth; and for his ready obedience was declared the next heir to the French crown. Lothaire, the third son, instructed by his brother's example, came and did in like manner, and received for his reward the reversion of the throne of Lorrain. Hereupon Goband began to bewail his too artful conduct, and hoping to recover the favour of his father, said, 'Father, I pray you give me a portion of the apple. But the king, Charles, replied, 'There is now nothing remaining for thee of the apple or of the kingdom.' And hence arose the ancient French proverb, 'Goband, thou hast opened thy mouth too late.'

But what could the king mean by this singular

conduct? He wished to make a chemical experiment in the region of the soul,—a kind of spiritual analysis and separation, which led to a determination. And to what? To evil or to good? Certainly to the latter. He gave his sons the opportunity of proving their obedience, their alacrity, and their reverence, and tried them in these virtues. That he should have selected an apple in preference to any thing else, no one will be much surprised. And because the first man's probation was also connected with the fruit of a tree, who will consider that this fruit is to be viewed as any thing essential in this event?

For let us now pass from this history to another and more holy one, and inquire how the obedience of the first man, as a filial obedience towards his heavenly Father and the Lord of the world, was proved; whether by a command to do, or a command not to do something, consequently by a prohibition. The sacred Scripture informs us that it was the latter. And if we advance a step farther (not through any presumptuous curiosity, but through a desire of information) and ask, wherefore was the probation constituted in a prohibition and not in a command; the answer, on one side, will be founded upon the relation of a free creature to its God,—a relation of subordination, by virtue of which the creature has nothing more to do than to desire the will of God, and to submit its own will. And, on the other side, the answer will be founded upon the nature of a probation, which must lead to the determination of the object proved. For this determination cannot take place without some division in the interior; and this division, between the desire and accomplishment of the Divine will and our own, is necessarily produced by the prohibition ; for our own will manifests itself in its inclination and exertions to prevail and to continue in its superiority. But this prohibition insisted upon the contrary, and thus it was calculated to divide the spirit of man ; that is, to decide it to some object, to make it select between God and itself.

Thus this law which was given to our first parent was in itself a temptation, or the occasion of his self-determination, to which Satan's additions and allurements might be joined or not. Before his probation man was guiltless, for he was still in his original holiness, that is, in that control over all his spiritual faculties with which God had created him. But that which man was by the immediate creation and ordinance of God, that he was to continue, as a free creature, by his own act and determination, although he could be directed in this free action solely by the guiding will of God. For it was by the ordinance of God, and by his own immediate and active correspondence, that man was gifted with the capacity for free action, and with self-consciousness ; but this self-consciousness (the very flower of the life of the soul) was not yet thoroughly established or unfolded, as long as it was merely separated from external things, and had not yet learned its inmost character, its freedom. This knowledge was to be preceded by some deed, some free action, which alone could develope this self-consciousness in its full bloom, and perfect the life of the soul. And thus does this probation of freedom, so often and so variously misunderstood, become the chief point in the self-perfection of man.

In whatever light, therefore, we consider this probation, the eventful tree must ever be confessed to have been the tree of knowledge of good and evil. For as God alone is good and the essential good, so is good in the created being the union of the will with the essential good; whilst, on the other hand, evil can be nothing more than the opposition of the creature to that which is truly good. Man falls into this direful opposition by his free and premeditated disobedience; and as in him both nature and soul rule in personal union, so must this disobedience be punished in both; the correct knowledge of this necessary consequence is essential, if we would know the true source of all human evils.

How the soul of man has been punished for its opposition to its Creator, we have already seen in the fifth petition. The daring presumption whereby the creature denies or renounces its subjection or subordination to the Divine will is an injury against God, a high treason against His holiness, against the will and dignity of His pure love. And as this holy will must declare itself against every opposition, so there must arise from this offence a destruction of the mutual intercourse between the Divine will and that of the created soul, which destruction we denominate guilt. Thus guilt has two points of origin: the one, the holiness of God, which, in its love, has bestowed on man his freedom, and in its absolute dignity has imposed upon him law; the other, the free choice of the creature, which has despised this love and this dignity. Hence a twofold knowledge must arise: first, of the greatness of sin and of its consequences; secondly, of the real author of these consequences.

But as, without God, no guilt can be imagined, according to the words of the Psalmist, "To *Thee* only have I sinned, and done evil before *Thee*;" and as God is infinite, so must the offence of God, although proceeding from a created being, be also infinite; so are the consequences, the separation of the creature from God, and the death of the soul. As, moreover, it is the sinner alone who burdens himself with sin, so it is in no manner God who strikes the sinner, but the sinner who strikes himself. An example, although perhaps of a strange character, shall place this truth in a clearer light.

Towards the close of the sixteenth century, the wild hordes of the Tartars rushed into the territory of the Poles, burnt and plundered all that they met with, and drove away whole herds of cattle which they had seized in their depredations. The Polish general at length advanced with his forces in array to meet them, when the Tartars resolved to oppose them in a manner as unexpected as it was barbarous. They drove the cattle before the van of the army, and goaded them forward against the Polish soldiers, to throw them into disorder. But the Poles immediately fired upon the beasts, whereupon, in pain and fury, they rushed back upon the Tartars, and caused such confusion and discomfiture amongst them, that the Poles speedily, and without great labour, obtained a complete victory; and the robbers found their destruction in their own robbery.

Thus does the sinner, when he opposes the Divine will, and consequently rises in enmity against the Divine love, send his offending words, or thoughts, or deeds, like to so many horned beasts, against God; according to the words of Ecclesiasticus, "Raise not thyself as a heifer in thy thoughts, lest thy strength be broken by thy folly." (Ecclus. vi.) Sin cannot inflict any injury on the Creator; but it recoils back upon the sinner, as the royal penitent acknowledged when he exclaimed, "I acknowledge my iniquity, and my sin is always before me." Thus also, when man commits a robbery against God, by assuming to himself his superiority, his injustice rebounds back upon him; and the love and holy will of God, which must ever be active and all-subduing, becomes to the sinner justice, or, to use the expression of the holy Scripture, Divine wrath.

And what must be the life which the soul lives when under the seal of this wrath, separated from God, the foundation and end of its life? Most certainly this life, if we may still term it by that name, is a constant misery—an opposition to itself—an ever-enduring monstrous lie—an incurable blindness and malice on the part of the creature—a self-seeking, as hostile to God as it is comfortless in itself, and which must manifest itself in pride, discord, ambition, treachery, and inconstancy, in every man who knows not how to petition God in all earnestness, "Deliver us from evil."

Yet this misery of man's fallen soul can no more be considered as affecting the soul alone, than we can contemplate man alone, separated from the body and from the life of nature. The fall of the soul from God includes, as a necessary consequence, the dissolution of man himself, or the fall of his nature from his spirit. Nature, no longer free, was by personal union in man subjected to his free spirit, and by it restrained and made steadfast; but by sin it was again restored to its own activity, it rose against the spirit, began to manifest itself by its passions and desires,—strangers to the spirit, —and became a victim to the change, the being, and the wasting, which are the ruling law in common nature.

Inasmuch as man is subject to death in his human existence, which is the union of spirit and nature, his dissolution and destruction commenced when his organic body fell once more under the dominion of universal nature; and this nature, the entire object and activity of which is concentrated in man, must thenceforth manifest itself against man in opposition and passions, and fall into disorder and opposition within itself; so that whatever now meets the eye and senses on earth —contests and dangers, labours and necessities, sorrows and troubles—all is one opposition to man, an immeasurable raging sea of evil.

And where shall we seek for the source of all these calamities? The whole problem, the entire exertion of nature, is that exalted personal life which she can find only in man in union with the human soul. In man she attains her end, is raised and received to the freedom and immortality of the spirit; but only when man's soul remains true to its object, and perfects itself by its union with God. But if the soul does not perfect itself by this union, whereunto God has destined it, but falls into separation from its Creator, and thus disowns the idea of God,—that is, the end for which it was created,— the two elements of man fall into opposition and disunion; the spirit struggles against nature, and nature against the spirit; the free spirit loses its dominion; nature, the slave, prevails, and cares not for the spirit; the lord of created nature sinks into the subject, and the powers and creatures, before submissive, turn as enemies upon him; the storms, the clouds, and the waters roar against him; the plants and the trees prepare for him mortal poison in their sap; the beasts pursue him with thousands of weapons on all sides; necessities and dangers and death lurk around his path.

And has nature, then, been changed? Have powers of death arisen within it which existed not before? This supposition is unnecessary; for as the life of nature is one constant state of existing and perishing, death is one of its properties as well as existence: but these powers of death and destruction could not assail man, so long as he was without sin. The hound which fawns upon its master, but immediately attacks a stranger with fury, has not changed its nature because it acts differently towards its master and one whom it does not know. In the same manner did nature begin to be hostile to man, so soon as he ceased to be its lord and became its enemy.

And thus by one man sin, and with it death, which before sin could have found no place, entered into the world.

This entrance of sin and of death into the world and into the human race is that deep wound, that overwhelming evil, which, affecting both the soul and the nature of man, transplants itself inevitably from one generation to another, and is therefore termed original sin. What, then, is original sin? Is it death itself, the dissolution of organic nature? or is it the rebellion of the passions against our better understanding, the blindness of the intellect, the incapacity of the will? All these are but consequences of a weighty fault,—not original sin, but its punishment. But no one, as Divine justice cannot be impeached, suffers without guilt; and as on all men the same punishment falls, they must all be comprised in the same guilt. But how can we have incurred a guilt in which we had no share? Were we present when the first parent of mankind sinned, by acting according to the dictates of his self-will?

Let us explain. Adam, as the head of the human race, was also the representative of his entire posterity, in the same manner as the will of the prince is considered as the will of his subjects; he was appointed to preserve righteousness for himself and for all, so that when he lost it for himself, he forfeited it also for us. But this reply may not suffice, and it even suggests another great inquiry: Wherefore should we suffer for the infidelity of a representative whom we ourselves have not elected? Wherefore should we so severely atone for that of which we ourselves are not knowingly and personally guilty?

Before we institute any further inquiry on this subject, let us contemplate a vision, to which we are invited on the authority of Venerable Bede, the awful flashing of which, like the lightning in a dark forest, will enable us to behold much in the obscurity of this world. The Abbot Furseus, one of the most holy men of ancient Britain, who, although sprung from a high family, had from his earliest years devoted himself to an austere life in the service of Christ, was once lying in severe illness, surrounded by his parents and relations. After some time he fell into a deep slumber, which all around supposed to be the sleep of death. In this state, so full of mystery, and which in later times has been an object of many and various researches, he beheld a great army of angels, of brilliant beauty, arrayed like a warrior host prepared for battle. Opposed to them appeared many frightful spectres of darkness, who cried out, with hideous voices, 'Where is the justice of God? If God be just, this man can never behold the glory of heaven. For it is written, "Unless you humble yourselves, and become as little children, you shall not enter into the kingdom of heaven." When has this man ever been truly humble? It is written, that man must render an account for every idle word. How many idle words have been on the lips of this youth!' Furseus hereupon began to fear and to tremble, when an angel came to his support, and directed him to look down upon the world. The youth obeyed, and saw a barren and gloomy vale, over which were waving four glaring flames, which destroyed and laid waste every thing on the four quarters of the world. Then the angel said, 'Do you understand the mystery of this vision?' Furseus replied, that he did not. The angel then continued: ' These are the flames which consume the human world; and which, notwithstanding the Divine redemption, bring destruction upon mankind. They are lies, covetousness, impiety, and disunion. For after man's ancient guilt is remitted to him in baptism, after he has renounced the spirit of wickedness and his deceits, the flame of lies still consumes him, since he does not observe what, in baptism and subsequently, he had solemnly vowed to observe; then comes the flame of covetousness, for he prefers the goods and pleasures of this world to the love of God; then the flame of impiety, for, as far as his power and circumstances enable him, he oppresses and deceives his fellow-man; and lastly, the flame of disunion, for men heed not for what trifling and useless things they provoke enmity.' As Furseus was wondering at the rage of these flames, they ascended higher and higher, and began to curl even around him, so that he was seized with dread; but the angel said, 'Be comforted, and fear not. What thou hast not enkindled shall not burn in thee.' Then he took him and led him through the flames without injury, until a man met them who was known to Furseus. This man sprang from the flames and burnt the shoulders of Furseus. But the angel cast the enemy back, and then said to his companion, 'What thou hast enkindled, that has burnt in thee; for this man, who died in his sins, left thee an ill-gotten mantle, which thou hast kept, instead of giving it to the poor.' At these words, Furseus awoke from his death-like sleep, and, excepting an acute pain on his shoulders, he was perfectly recovered. Soon after he entered the pulpit, and recounted what he had seen and heard.

Such was the vision of the holy Abbot Furseus. It casts a brilliant light upon the idle dreams of a thoughtless and sinful life. But what is it that is here most conspicuous? It is the truth, that no punishment is inflicted upon us from on high which we have not deserved. 'What thou hast not enkindled shall not burn in thee.' When, therefore, we behold so enormous evils raging upon the earth, amongst which, those that are spiritual are more violent than the flames themselves, whence, we ask, arise these evils, if not from some universal guilt? Whence spring these tumults and devastations of lies, of enmities, of wild desires, but from a deep disorder and wound in the inmost being of man? But it is difficult (and our language would be obscure) to speak of original guilt, without at the same time thinking of the mystery of redemption; and as this work of Divine love cannot be duly comprehended unless the truth of original sin be first explained, so does this latter remain dark and fearful, if not illumined by the light of redemption. These two mysteries are closely enchained. Man alone was capable of the redemption, for he alone was capable of original sin. And the foundation of universal guilt contained within itself the foundation of universal redemption.

To obtain a full view of these great truths, it will not be useless to look back upon the evils of the human world, and upon the predominance of evil represented to the holy Furseus by the raging flames. By whom, then, were these flames enkindled? By God? Certainly not. For the prophet of former days has cried out, "Behold, all you who light a fire, encompassed with flames, walk in the light of your fire, and in the flames which you have kindled! Which of you will dwell in consuming fire? Which of you will dwell in eternal flames?" (Isa. 1. 33.) This fire, therefore, is not lit up by God, but by created beings. And what is the fire that is here signified? It is the fire of lust, of covetousness, of anger, of envy, of pride. But wherefore are these termed a fire? All life, as an existence ever active, and always displaying its inmost qualities, may be compared to a fire; the divine, creating, animating, enlightening love often calls itself a heavenly fire; every trial of freedom of a created spirit is a fire-proof of Divine love; every being which abandons God, and seeks itself as the object of its existence, is an unhappy, self-destroying fire. The fire of God is light and gladness; the fire of pride and hatred is darkness and rage.

Thus do we suddenly come in view of the fearful forms and darkened side of the universe, of those fallen spirits, which, by the abuse of their freedom, have for eternity severed themselves from the Divine love, and prepared for themselves a hell,—unhappy spirits, for which there is no delivery or redemption. For as the free spirit, by virtue of the Divine ordinance according to which it was created, had the privilege to declare itself, by its own choice, for or against the highest will of God, and thereby to perfect its being, so, after this free determination, it remains irrevocably in the condition which it has chosen. For what it was originally through God, it was by its creation; what it is through itself, it became by this act of self-perfection. And what further can now be accomplished in its regard? It is impossible that God should dispose and compel His fallen creature to return, for God cannot contradict His own ordinances, which are Himself; it is likewise equally impossible that the spirit which has deserted God should, of its own free determination, return to Him; since it has once declared itself against God, and will and must remain in the condition in which it has placed itself, in its haughty weakness, in its powerless pride.

Thus the spirit, having abandoned God, continues what it was at its origin, a creature gifted with freedom. For, as St. Augustine with beautiful simplicity observes, even a bad will is still a will. But this spirit is now without comfort in its self-seeking and self-destruction; it is robbed of light and of happiness, and is in perpetual opposition with God and with itself. For by its spiritual life it bears witness of the almighty Power which created it out of pure love, to which it did not correspond, so that it is not now that whereunto God had destined it; and in the same manner as, in its self-determination, it opposed itself to the loving will of God, so does it now struggle to deny the love and truth which, however, are the first authors of its existence. And as every purely spiritual being is perfected and interiorly enclosed within itself, or, in other words, forms for itself an entire whole, so, in the spiritual world, we may suppose the seduction of many through the imitation of the example of one; but we cannot suppose a substitution and satisfaction by which the merit of one may be extended to the advantage of all others.

But that which is inconceivable in the spiritual world was, in its full extent, possible for the human world. For although man be a spirit, and therefore an individual person, he is also a being of nature; and as his natural life is no less essential to his existence than his life of the spirit, it necessarily follows, as all must perceive, that an individual man cannot be considered otherwise than in his humanity; that is, not as a single being enclosed within himself, but as a member of a great whole, — of the human race, from which individuals, in the series of generations, are developed, through their generic life, or the natural life of the species. The life of nature, as we see throughout the world of animals and plants, unfolds itself in the species, whilst the spiritual life is shewn in the individual personality. Thence it is, as we have already shewn, that every man, as he consists of a twofold substance, has also a twofold origin; since his spiritual life is an immediate creation of God, whilst his corporeal life is so only mediately, being a work of nature. As, however, the spiritual and corporeal life are united into one life and into one individual, so there must be relations entirely peculiar to man, and which declare his nature.

All these relations are expressed in the term *communication of idioms*[1]—the properties of the spirit and the nature of man. By virtue of this, the spirit of man takes part in the properties of nature, and nature appropriates to itself those attributes which are, and would for ever be, unknown to it, were it not for its union with the spirit in man. It is only by means of this exposition that we can understand how nature can inherit that which, in the region of pure spirits, could not be inherited; and how that can be restored in man which, in the region of pure spirits, when once effected, must, as we have seen, remain for ever.

The consequences of this power of inheritance through nature are therefore evident. As man in his corporeal existence, as a being of nature, necessarily proceeds from a species, the personal guilt of his first parent must descend upon him, and this inherited guilt must enter into his person. By his opposition to God, Adam incurred a twofold misery,—that of guilt and that of punishment. This punishment, as a consequence of guilt, must again be twofold,—temporal and eternal.

[1] Communicatio idiomatum.

The temporal punishment shews itself in the self-seeking struggles of the spirit and of nature, in pride and sensuality, in mortality or death. But as this misery, which we acknowledge to be a consequence or punishment of guilt, transplants itself from man to man throughout all the human race, which, according to the necessary law of nature, must descend from Adam, so it follows that, with the punishment, its cause also, that is, guilt, must continue to be inherited.

Now as this misery of man is one of his spirit, and as every spirit of man is a new creation of God, might we not be led into the error of imagining that this spirit was created by God in its depravity and propensity to evil? But so blasphemous an error can arise only in one who reflects but by halves. For the human spirit, the immortal soul, is, by the Divine ordinance, not a being existing for, and enclosed in, itself, like wholly pure spirits, but it is created for nature, for an organic body, as nature also has been created for *it;* and both together, by their mutual union and penetration, like the two factors of a product, form the one individual of man. Thus the spirit is dependent upon the body, and the body upon the spirit; and the spirit, at the moment of its union with the body, partakes of the destinies of the species into the living whole of which it enters.

It might now be asked, if, after the fall of Adam, God still desires that man should continue, wherefore does He place him in a path which leads to all the miseries incurred by our first parent? Could He not remove the separation made by Adam, and renew, for the souls which He creates, their proper union with their Creator? The answer is found in what we have already said; it is found in the ordinance of God Himself, whereby He decreed that man should be a creature of spirit and nature, and consequently a species. And as God cannot contradict Himself, He beholds each individual solely in the entireness of all mankind, and this entireness in each individual. And thus is original sin the participation of all men in the guilt and punishment of their common first parent, on the very principle, that from him they all descend; or, what amounts to the same, that they, by their natural life, compose an exalted whole, a single species, in whose destinies they must share, since their personality is the living union of the life of nature and spirit.

Should now any mortal dare to contend with God, and urge, that by such an ordinance He gives occasion to the multiplication of guilt and of misery, he need but turn his eyes to the enlightened side of the great divine work, and he will see his folly, and say with the Psalmist, "That Thou mayest be justified in Thy judgments, and mayest overcome when Thou art judged." For truly, by the side of this very woe there lies blessing; and under this evil, sown by man, we find salvation.[1]

---

[1] For if an inheritance, which in itself is uninheritable, namely, an inheritance of guilt and of merit, be possible only in man, we cannot speak of it in general terms, but only in a certain manner, and in a constantly mutual relation. For we have on earth, since the fall of Adam, in a peculiar manner, an inheritance of guilt, as we have also an inheritance of merit which we derive from the second Adam, which God foresaw, and through which man possesses existence and continuance. This important consideration, which throws the brightest light over the principles of Christianity, is well and fully explained in A. Günther's *Sud- und Nordlichtern*, letter xi.

Since spirits, as purely spiritual beings, exist for themselves, one not being dependent upon another, so that each one incurs guilt and obtains merit solely for itself, there can be no salvation for those that have been once separated from God. But, on the contrary, for men, being men, that is, part of a whole, individuals of a species, so that each is included in the destiny and properties of the whole, salvation is possible, and grounded on this, that as one could destroy all things for all, so another can repair all things for all.

And this was the noble work of love, which, in its manifestation to guilty man, is indeed the greatest mercy. For what does love desire? It desires to remove the opposition of the creature, and, as far as it can do so without contradiction with itself, to render it happy. This was indeed possible in regard to man, since there is a Father and representative for the spiritual part of man no less than for the corporeal. This new representative, who, in spirit, was likewise Adam's Father and restorer, had the office of cancelling, by His own free obedience, the free disobedience of the first Adam, and thus to liberate the whole race from the guilt of opposition. "When the Son," He declared, "shall free you, then shall you be truly free." (John viii.) On one side, therefore, it was necessary that He should proceed from a sinful race, and yet Himself be free from all guilt and stain of this race; and thus proceed, not by generation, but as a new creation of God, from a virgin daughter of Sion; and, on the other side, it was necessary that, as the creating restorer of the dissolved union, He should come from God, bearing in Himself, in living union, divinity and humanity, so that His human soul was created in original union with the Logos, in order to pour into humanity a new merit, destructive of eternal guilt,—an infinite inheritance pertaining to the whole race.

And this is that great and glorious mystery, the accomplishment of which the Church celebrates on holy Saturday. 'O happy fault,' she exclaims with exultation, 'which has deserved so great a Redeemer!' This too is that joyful mystery, to a grateful remembrance of which the Psalmist exhorts all men and nations. "Praise the Lord, all ye nations; praise Him, all ye people; for His mercy is confirmed upon us, and His truth endureth for ever." (Ps. cxvi.)

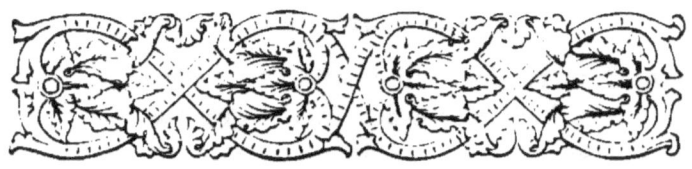

CHAPTER XVI.

But deliver us from Evil.

WHATEVER we wish to distinguish as least in importance and signification we generally name last, and place in the lowest rank. But as our Lord has in some respect taught us the contrary, that "the last shall be first," we also make many exceptions to this rule; as, when presenting a number of petitions, we reserve those for the end which, although they may be less pleasing, and even disagreeable to our patron, are nevertheless more important to us, and more conducive to our welfare. In this order are arranged the seven petitions of the Lord's Prayer; of which the first is, "Hallowed be Thy name," and the last, "Deliver us from evil." That the first is the greatest and the most exalted is evident; but because the last is in the last place, shall we conclude that it is therefore the least and most insignificant? By no means. For, besides that it expresses that which is of well-nigh the greatest moment to us, it embraces in its full import an elevation that soars even to the height of the first, as by its accomplishment we attain also to the fulfilment of the first. For in a proper understanding of the words of the seventh petition is contained the entire doctrines of positive Christianity—the doctrine of evil, or of the guilt and punishment of sin, and the doctrine of salvation, or the removal of both through justification and salvation.

For as the essence of sin is guilt, and its necessary consequence punishment, or separation from God, so must the redemption be perfected in a twofold manner: first, by a redemption or liberation from guilt, or the justification of man through the merits of Christ,—that is, through His all-satisfying sacrifice; and secondly, by redemption from punishment through Him whom He has inherited or merited for us, namely, the Holy Ghost, who deserted the first man, but has now "been poured out upon all flesh,"—upon the posterity of Adam,—to remove their separation from God. We have seen, that in very woe there was blessing, and that from evil salvation arose. On the very principle, that each individual of mankind must partake in the lot of his race, so that the fall of the first man brought demerit upon his entire posterity, it is possible that a new representative and father of men, according to the spirit, should enter amongst men, to restore salvation to all, and to cause the eternal love, now displaying itself as mercy, to remove and to destroy ancient opposition. "God was in Christ," says the Apostle, "reconciling the world to Himself." For from God alone can proceed the commencement of redemption; which, however, must be accomplished and perfected for the entire race by one Man, since this Man Himself, free from all original or personal guilt, repaired, by infinite obedience to God, the injury which the disobedience of our first parent brought upon all. His merit, therefore, became the merit of inheritance to mankind, as Adam's sin is also the sin of inheritance to all.

And in these exalted ways of Providence, do we not acknowledge the truth of the words of the Psalmist, "The judgments of the Lord are true, justified in themselves?" (Psalm xviii.) For assuredly God, when He created mankind, foresaw the destruction which the offence of one would bring upon the whole race. But as this did not deter Him from creating man, in whom all the rest of creation was to see its completion, by the union of spirit and nature, so had He prepared a remedy and salvation, wherein the greatness of His love would display itself in a far richer degree. And it was this Providence which, in the moment when man fell, looking on the redeeming obedience of the second Adam, ran towards man with helpful mercy, in order that, with the entrance of guilt and ruin, redemption might also take its commencement. For if the first man, as far as in him lay, turned himself from God, and found eternal separation and darkness for his lot, the second Adam, by His influence upon all mankind, has healed this otherwise incurable evil.

And thus it is that the Word of God, Divine Logos, long before His union with the man Jesus, and as if in pledge of His approaching incarnation, again formed a bond of union with man, not by a voice of love, but by that of conscience; a voice of superiority and rightful power; a voice sounding unto every self-conscious man, whether he will or not; a truth which sheds over every soul, however much in darkness, some light; "a light which enlightens all that come into this world."

In regard to many, it would indeed seem that this voice were wholly silent, this light entirely extinguished; and that we might say of these, as it is customary to say of those who are compared to Satan, 'that they have no conscience.' Of this class of men might have been that general who, in the reign of Henry the Second, when France was devastated by the people of the Netherlands, caused a church to be burnt wherein several hundreds had taken refuge. A sergeant of the army, who had been born in this neighbourhood, not enduring to see the misery of his countrymen, assisted by some companions, broke open the doors of the church against the will of his general. The first that met him was his own mother, who, although seriously injured by the flames, at the sight of her son sprang towards him and embraced him. All around were filled with emotion; the commander alone was unmoved at such a scene of woe, and gave orders that both the mother and the son should be thrust back into the flames, and the doors again closed.

What conscience could this man have possessed? Assuredly such as appears already consumed with the flames of hell, and which is termed by St. Paul a "branded conscience." But even a branded conscience is still a conscience; and so long as man journeys on in this earthly life, he is not irreconcilably separated from God; for whilst by the life of nature man claims part with the life of the whole human race, he has a share in the inherited merit of the Redeemer; and so long as he retains this, so long must conscience still live within him. 'God,' says St. Chrysostom, 'has implanted in us conscience; and by this He acts in a more loving manner than our natural father; for this latter, after he has warned his son ten and a hundred times, expels him from his house, but God ceases not to warn us by conscience even to our latest breath.'

For what is conscience, in its proper signification? Certainly nothing less than an immediate Divine revelation to the soul of man. In place of Divine love, or of the Holy Ghost, whose communications the first man lost by sin, the creating Logos has entered in, commanding faithless man, and threatening as the inmost law : " In Him was the life, and the life is the light of men ; He is the true Light, which enlighteneth every man." This light, manifested in conscience, man can and must follow, subduing for this end his inclination to evil, as it was said to Cain, " Thy desire is under thee, and thou must rule over it." But as man was faithless even to this interior law-giving voice of his Creator, and by his criminal course and abuse of freedom so increased the darkness of his interior sense, that his free spirit, in the grossest ignorance of itself, fell down in homage to unfree nature, or, in one word, that it sunk into the depravity of heathenism ; then exterior revelation succeeded, by the Law of Sinai, to that of the interior, until, the fulness of time having arrived, the same Logos, the Son of the eternal Father, entered into the midst of the human race as Son also of man, in order, in His character of God and man, to accomplish the work of redemption; which, as it consists in a new divine revelation, and in a representative satisfaction, could be perfected only by a God-Man.

And since by His merit the guilt which weighed upon the human race has been removed, and man is placed in most intimate friendship with God, and raised from the lot of eternal death unto life (Ecclus. xlviii.); so can each individual man now freely partake of the merits of his Saviour, and thus secure redemption to himself. It is related of a great Saint, who was the glory of the thirteenth century, that when a child of four years, he was sinking, beyond all hope, under a violent illness, until his mother implored with earnest supplication the prayers of the seraphic St. Francis. He consoled the weeping parent, and prayed for her child; and so great was his favour with God, that the child suddenly arose in perfect health. St. Francis was much rejoiced, thanked the Divine goodness, and exclaimed in his joy, 'O bonaventura!' (O happy event!) From that time the child, whose real name was John, retained that which, through him, has become so well known, Bonaventure. By the Greeks he is called Eutyches, that is, the Fortunate. Every Christian who perseveres in the grace of God is raised from death unto light and life, and is, therefore, a Bonaventure; his mortal wound is healed, his soul is freed from guilt and blindness; the Gospel—that is, the good tidings, the great joyful intelligence—announces to him the cancelling of guilt through the satisfaction of the Mediator; the abolition of punishment—that is, the removal of his separation from God through the coming of the Holy Ghost—and, consequently, the redemption from all evil.

But if this redemption be already perfected in superabounding fulness, wherefore must we still petition, " And lead us not into temptation ; but deliver us from evil?" How is it that all those evils still encompass us which before reigned upon the earth? How is it that errors and passions are no less predominant now than before the time of grace? How is it that men still entangle themselves in fresh guilt by new and personal sins? He who can make such inquiries has neither a proper idea of the work of redemption, nor does he comprehend the truth that, without the co-operation of man (self-conscious man, of course), his happiness is unattainable. For by the Redeemer's entering amongst men as the new and heavenly Adam, the old Adam was not annihilated; but rather there was opposed to him, as the father of guilt, a father of justification and of grace, by whom we are born again to a spiritual life.

And thus do all men bear within them two opposite elements: that of original sin, through their corporeal descent from the first Adam; and that of justification, through the spiritual new birth, by the inherited merits of the second Adam, implanted in the Sacraments of the Church. Personal participation in these merits is in the Church, and by her offered to the free choice of each one. Yet even those who accept this invitation, and become the children of God, must, whilst here on earth, continue as children of Adam to bear the lot of their race, and seek daily, by the grace of Christ, to subdue the propensity of nature to evil.

And on this account there are, for all who are called to a participation in the redeeming merits of Christ, two great by-ways especially to be avoided. In the first, those are walking who think to conquer evil by their own exertions; and in the second, such as, laying aside all their own endeavours, wish to leave every thing to the power and grace of God. The first are either those modern Pelagians and moral Titans, who would reach to heaven by their own power; but, not knowing Christ, they contend in vacuity, without any resting-point whereon to place their ladder; or they are those members of positive Christianity who desire to attain a higher point than is given to mortal man; they therefore represent a species of Titans, who seek to gain heaven, not so much by storm as by undermining.

Thus did it happen to a certain religious, who, in his zeal, went so far as to endeavour to attain the perfect innocence and purity of man when in Paradise. To reach to this exalted point, he sought above all things to subject the life of the senses; and by excessive fasts, watchings, and other corporeal austerities, to obtain the superiority of the spirit. When he took any food, he strove to repress every feeling of sensual delight; and in all things he endeavoured to destroy within himself the slightest traces of sloth, of curiosity, or other vices, that thus he might lead a life of heavenly purity, free from imperfection or venial sin. But finding himself disappointed after all his exertions, and, despite all his mortifications, seeing himself not yet arrived at the perfection to which he aspired, he fell into such bitter and melancholy dejection, that he began to consider the smallest failing as a mortal offence; and at length concluded that it is impossible, in the present state of human misery, to secure to ourselves a happy life. He was at length undeceived of this error by a holy virgin, who was endowed with exalted spiritual gifts, the holy Mary of Oigniez.

His error consisted in this: he forgot his descent from Adam, which, so long as our natural life subsists, will ever make itself known, and which causes, even in the just, the prudent, and the faithful, many passing and small failings and imperfections, which are speedily and without difficulty pardoned. 'For these small daily faults,' says St. Augustine, 'which, in this present life, must always continue, satisfaction is given by our daily prayers.'

Although, therefore, the words of Christ, declaring that "the kingdom of heaven suffereth violence, and the violent alone bear it away," are to be taken in their full import, we are not to understand by them either the heathenish or the self-sufficient, too spiritual Titans; but such men as, by the power of the grace of Christ, subdue self-love, and grow strong by mortification. Those, therefore, are involved in still greater error who, wandering in the latter of the above-mentioned by-ways, desire, without any co-operation, to claim part in the merits of Christ.

A traveller, as Ambrosiaster relates, had once sunk in a marsh up to his neck, when, seeing from the edge of his prison a man passing by, he stretched forth his hand, and exclaimed: 'Take pity on me, and draw me hence.' His deliverer approached and extended his hand, that the man might grasp it; but the unhappy one drew back his hand, sunk it into the marsh, and began again to implore assistance. Afterwards he again stretched forth his hand, and again buried it in the marsh. He who had come to his assistance then asked,

'Wherefore do you ask for delivery, and still remain so obstinately in the depth of your misery? If you prefer destruction, take what you have chosen.' This parable represents those Christians who day after day repeat their 'Our Father,' always closing it with the words, 'Deliver us from evil,' but who by no means hate and avoid evil as far as in them lies; but assiduously persevere in their revellings, their brutal lusts, their hostile and deceitful feelings and actions, and seem to be expecting a kind of pulley, with heavenly wheels and cords, which, when all earthly cords are broken, may transport them, by a supernatural mechanism, from their much-loved evils to the possession of eternal but as yet not desired goods. Until this time shall come, they rest in almost undisturbed peace of mind, as the ancient prophet has described them: "They sleep, and love their dreams."

Does not their conscience, then, arouse them? Does it not keep them awake? No, they are but little disturbed by their conscience; and thus we say that they sleep. They have so exalted an idea of the death-sleep of Christ upon the Cross, that they believe that His merit, being one of inheritance, and belonging to the human race, must be shared by each one, whether willing or unwilling, provided he receive in faith this inherited merit, and preserve it in remembrance, even without thought of it, or personal appropriation. These men may justly be compared to those well-known marmots found on the Alps, which, being discovered by the people during their winter sleep, are taken asleep, sold at the market asleep, brought into the kitchen asleep, and do not awake until the very moment when the knife is put to their throat.

This is the freely-chosen lot of those who, exchanging the name of Bonaventure for Malaventure, are, in the sleep of a deceived and darkened conscience, sold to sin. (Romans vii.) They are ensnared by that lying spirit who is called, by excellence, the wicked one; and whose wickedness is so active that, in the seventh petition, *Libera nos a malo* (Deliver us from the Evil One), we implore the Divine assistance for delivery from his destructive craft and power.

For what is Satan's work and labour? To spread over the entire spiritual creation that same opposition to God, those same lies, which are his very existence and origin—as he himself is the living lie—living through God, lying through himself. In his complete perversion and abandonment of God, in his perfected, unholy desires, he is totally deprived of conscience: for the voice of conscience, as a revelation of God, can find no response in him, as he is entirely separated from God; in him there is only a wretched consciousness of guilt, a haughty obstinacy in unrighteousness, and an eternal enmity towards his Creator. Consequently every creature devoted to the Divine love, either by innocence or by repentance, is to him no less hateful than the Divine love itself; and therefore his rage seeks to sever and destroy every tie between this love and the creature. Thus did he withdraw the first man, by insidious questions, from his guiltless innocence; thus did he seek, by lying representations, to excite his self-love, and determine upon a woeful choice. And although the Divine love did not suffer man to fall entirely, but imparted to him new revelations by conscience, yet was it less difficult to the tempter to avail himself of the fettered natural powers, and the darkness of the spirit, in order to entangle man, in spite of the dictates of conscience, in fresh opposition, even than when the Divine love revealed itself more powerfully than before in the Law, and finally, in the fulness of its majesty, in the Church.

It must not, however, be concluded that he who, in his entire separation from God, in his constant opposition to God, is termed the Evil One, is the essential original cause of sin. For if this cause were not founded in the freedom of the creature, and in his own choice, or self-determination, we must seek for another and more ancient Lucifer, who deceived that archangel, and buried him in sin. Yes, it must necessarily lie in the very essence of guilt, that it is not produced by any foreign extrinsic will, but by our own free will: and this we acknowledge in the triple repetition of the '*Mea culpa.*' And it would seem that the Evil One for once, perhaps in an ebullition of its ancient pride, had become so enraged at the accusations cast upon him, as to forget his depravity, and from very fury to speak the truth. For, as we learn from St. Athanasius, who assures us that he received the account from the holy hermit himself, Anthony was one day surprised by a violent knocking at the door of his hut. He went out, and beheld before him a man of gigantic stature, of awful and strange appearance. 'Who art thou?' inquired Anthony. 'He,' replied the stranger, 'whom you call Satan.' 'What is thy desire?' continued the fearless inhabitant of the desert. 'I wish,' said Satan, 'to know the reason why thy monks, and so many others upon earth, defame and curse me, and wish me all that is evil, whenever any adversity befalls them?' 'No wonder,' replied St. Anthony, 'that they curse thee, since thou art the origin and sower of all evil.' 'Thou liest,' exclaimed the demon; 'it is not I who cause the sins of men; for I can do nothing against those who are unwilling: it is they themselves who are their own destruction, since they give ear to my suggestions, seduce each other, and cast themselves into crimes and occasions of evil, and therefore they must blame themselves, and not me, for their sins.' With these words he disappeared from the hermit's view.

Albeit for this once the spirit of lies spake the truth, still he did not allude to the great share he has in all the evils into which human perversity suffers itself to be led. For, in proportion as man turns from his obedience to God, and abandons himself to his own depravity, he soon forfeits the high dignity of his spiritual freedom, and falls a prey to the powers of darkness; so that we have always cause to pray— "And lead us not into temptation; but deliver us from evil." For the more we enter into temptation, the more we follow the impulse of the life of nature freed from the spirit and its sovereignty, the more deeply does darkness begin to shroud our interior, and the more multiplied are the weak points and the breaches whereby the spirit of lies may enter in and ruin us; for he employs different weapons, and attacks men according to their temperaments and their favourite inclinations and constitutions, and occasionally will appear upon the scene as an angel of light and a creature of pure reason.

Thus the legend of the holy hermit Abraham relates, that once at midnight, whilst standing in his cell in prayer, suddenly a light as brilliant as the sun shone around him, and a voice was heard, saying, 'Happy art thou, O Abraham, and no one is like unto thee; for thou hast fulfilled all the ordinances of my will.' But the Saint was one of those solid critics who are not dazzled by false light, or blinded by false darkness, by rationalism, or by mysticism. He answered with dogmatic certainty: 'May thy darkness be with thee to thy destruction!' A similar midnight deceitful light was thrown by the ancient master-sophists over the present life, when they praised men for their intelligence, their humanity, their liberality, and their extraordinary civilisation.

It is indeed true, that many branches of human science have been greatly advanced, that the circle of natural knowledge is widely enlarged, and that imagination and research are more energetic than ever; but whether the powers of darkness are not more prevalent, we may easily learn if we look at the infidelity of many, who despise all positive Christianity, and at the vague belief of others, who for the most part build upon Pantheistic principles, and consider, finally, the multiplied decided fallings-off from Christ and from His Church. Spectres and apparitions are now rare; every thing is undisturbed, and we know of demons and ghosts only as we read of them in ancient chronicles, and in the newly discovered regions of entranced and ecstatic beings; but in truth there is, throughout the world, so much delusion and disorder, that Satan has no need to assume any special form, for he is every where heard and followed.

St. Gregory the Great relates, that this evil spirit once occasioned so frequent and such dreadful disturbance in a house at Corinth, that no one could venture to dwell therein. Datius, Bishop of Milan, being on his way to a Council that was to be held at Constantinople, came to Corinth, and found no lodging sufficient for himself and his numerous attendants excepting this uninhabited house. The citizens cautioned him to be heedful, and related to him what reception he might expect. Datius replied, that on that very account he wished to lodge there. The house was speedily prepared, and Datius had already sent his attendants to rest, and was himself watching in prayer, when suddenly an extraordinary noise was heard. The roaring of lions, the bleating of sheep, the neighing of horses, the howling of wolves, and the hissing of serpents, now singly, and now in chorus, were heard with painful distinctness. Datius arose, and exclaimed in a voice strengthened by anger, ' Justly hast thou been punished, O wretched one; thou didst say, I will raise my throne above the stars, and be like the Most High; behold, thou art cast down by thy pride, and instead of being like to God, thou art like to the beasts!' And by these sarcastic words, as St. Gregory relates, peace was restored to the house.

The pantheistic sophist, in like manner, who bears within himself the God of the universe; the highminded man, who invests his weak reason with absolute dignity; and he who thinks but little, if at all, and who, in pretended absolute freedom, disregards every Divine law : all these would make themselves like to God, and imitate the several corporeal forms and impulses which exist in the enslaved natural life of the brute creation; for all these forms and impulses are united in the corporeal man, who is the highest creature of nature. And thus do the passions, with their hundred dreadful cries, rise in rebellious tumult within man, disordered by his fall, whenever the old serpent is aroused. But the Psalmist seizes his harp, and exclaims, "Arise, O Lord, and scatter Thy enemies, and drive from Thy face all who hate Thee!" And not only so, but it is also written: "Arise, O spirit of man, and by the strength of the heavenly Adam, fight against all evil. Call to Him, that He may free thee from evil; but do thou also strive, that thou mayst overcome evil by good."

"Fight the good fight of faith and fidelity; lay hold on eternal life." (1 Tim. vi.)

CHAPTER XVII.

But deliver us from Evil.

AS those only can be reckoned amongst real goods which bring us nearer to the end of our spiritual existence; and consequently, as those only can be called real evils which threaten us with eternal separation from God, it follows, that temporal evils, those which pass with time, if we profit by them as we ought, prepare the way to eternal goods; and cannot, therefore, be compared with the evils of sin and of eternal punishment. If temporal evils alone were the object of this petition, it would with full propriety be placed the last of the seven. For if the impulse be implanted in the heart of man, that in want and danger he should call to God for help, and if God Himself command him so to do, saying, "Call upon Me in the day of trouble, and I will deliver thee" (Ps. xlix.); so has He also said, "Seek before all things the kingdom of God and His justice;" and has, moreover, so arranged the order of the prayer

He would have us to say, that we always think, in the first place, of the highest object of life, and implore temporal favours only inasmuch as they tend to the glory of God. Let us hear the prayer of the penitent king: "Chastise me not, O Lord, in Thy wrath;" and he gives the reason: "for," says he, "there is no one in death who is mindful of Thee; and who shall confess to Thee in hell?"

We pray, therefore, for deliverance from temporal evils; but as we commence our prayer with the words, "Hallowed be Thy name," we acknowledge that we do not place the granting of this petition as a condition of our future service, but that we will, in all events, be faithful. Such was the sentiment of the three children at Babylon, when they were left to the alternative of adoring the statue, or of entering the fiery furnace. "Who is your God," said the Asiatic despot, "that He should be able to save you from my hands?" Whereunto they replied: "It is not necessary that we answer to you concerning these things; for behold, that God to whom we pray has assuredly the power to free us from the furnace and from your hands; but if He be unwilling, yet know, O king, that we will not adore your statue." As they knew that the only real evil was the abandonment of God, the noble trial of their free-will was truly a fire-proof; and as the spiritual death of sin could not come nigh unto them, the powers of nature were to them no subject of dread. And even had they been deprived of temporal life, they would not have considered this as any real evil, since they were strengthened and enlivened by faith in the promised Redeemer. And how must this faith have strengthened the first Christians, to whom the Redeemer had already come!

It is related by John Moschus, that on one occasion, amidst a dense crowd of men who were accompanying a murderer to the place of execution, there was a hermit who walked close by the culprit, and endeavoured to follow in his steps. The criminal, on looking around him, beheld the hermit, and said, 'What have you to do here, my father? Have you no cell, or no employment?' 'Pardon me, my brother,' replied the other; 'I have both.' 'Wherefore, then,' inquired the malefactor, 'do you not rather remain in your cell, and pray, and work, and bewail your sins?' 'You are right,' replied the man of the desert; 'I am but too negligent of myself: my heart is obdurate, and without contrition; and therefore it is that I am come to behold your death, that I may at last be in some degree moved to repentance.' Whereupon the poor sinner replied, 'Go, father, and remain in your cell, and thank our divine Redeemer; for since He has become man, and died for us, man dies no more.'

And in truth, to him who, in so awful an hour, could speak with such recollection and joy, death was no real evil. To this man death had lost all its terrors, because its near approach was certain; for it was impending over him as a temporal punishment, it excited him to repentance, and restored him to salvation. Positive Christianity may be designated, by many of its enemies, by the honourable title of the 'Theory of poor sinners:' and there is no reason why we should defend it from the intended scorn. The judgment of poor sinners, passed upon us all, has sentenced us to walk in the way of death. We are *sinners* by our opposition and rebellion against God; and we are *poor*, weak sinners, since our will is despoiled of the full power of execution, and seeks either to free itself from the sovereignty of God, or to rank itself among the free lords of the universe, or again to be reconciled, and return to the love and peace of its Creator.

But what we ourselves could neither wish nor execute, the Divine love has wished and executed for us. "Wisdom," says the holy Scripture, "led the first man from his sin." (Wisdom x.) The Divine wisdom entered by conscience into a new intercourse with man; but in order that he may hearken to this voice of conscience, the numerous evils which encompass him, and death, which is ever impending over him, must serve as warnings, as they also excite him to implore the Divine aid, and to turn the eyes of his soul to God. And this returning path, as it was prepared for the first father of men, so is it for all his posterity; and the miseries and necessities which sin has engendered upon earth urge them to walk therein. "Call upon Me in the day of trouble, and I will deliver thee; and thou shalt give Me honour." This paternal admonition, contained in the 49th Psalm, is thus paraphrased by St. Augustine: 'Therefore have I sent the day of trouble upon you, lest, in freedom from misfortune, you might neglect to call upon Me. But when calamity befals you, you invoke Me; when you invoke Me, I will deliver you; when I deliver you, you will honour Me, in order that you may never more fall away from Me.'

And thus does the last petition return into living connexion with the first: 'Deliver us from evil; and thereby will Thy name be hallowed.' And such likewise is the acknowledgment of the Psalmist: "It is good for me that Thou hast humbled me, that I may learn Thy justifications! I have found calamity and sorrow, and I have called upon the name of the Lord." Calamity and sorrow are considered by him as a happy discovery, because they incited him to renewed zeal in prayer and watchfulness over himself.

And, indeed, what would become of the great as well as the little children of Adam in this education on earth, were not their loving Father also a strict parent, who visits them with many severe chastisements? In one of the few hospitals of the kingdom of Mogor, wherein, from some superstition, beasts, and not men, were the objects of attention, a Christian missioner beheld a vulture which had been severely wounded. So long as the sharp-clawed bird was sick and weak, it remained wonderfully quiet and peaceful; but no sooner was it healed, than it immediately, with renewed vulture-like rage, pounced upon the other patients, wounded and killed them, so that it was necessary to expel without delay this furious convalescent from the house. How many such vultures and hawks do we not find amidst those featherless creatures, which do not, as once was the case at Athens, first require to be plucked, to be unfeathered!

Some such creature was that notorious tyrant in the Hussite wars, who, on account of his cruelty, was at length confined in a prison at Prague. When the senators were sent to him to inquire how he was, he replied: 'Never better than at present. For so long as I was surrounded by all that could pamper my haughty ambition, as long as I was drowned in revelling and tumult, I had but little time to think on God. But here, where I am deprived of every thing, I can do it without interruption.' These sentiments continued with him only so long as he remained in his narrow, damp confinement; scarcely was he released, when he plunged into greater excesses than ever, until at length, in a paroxysm of rage, he died of apoplexy.

But is not this the common course of human depravity? "Thou hast shewn to the people patience and forbearance, O Lord; and hast Thou been honoured for it? All nations of the land have removed themselves far from Thee." (Is. xxvi.) Such was the exclamation of the sorrowing prophet, when he observed the ingratitude of his country to the Divine goodness, and how little it was moved by it to holiness; and such too are the complaints of the holy Fathers, even in the first ages of the Christian Church.

Thus, during the long rest and security which the Christians enjoyed under the Roman emperor Philip, their zeal and discipline fell into decay in proportion to their repose. But how they were again reanimated to fervour may be seen in the letters of St. Cyprian. A Christian was favoured with a vision, wherein it appeared to him that the father of the family was placed on an elevated seat; near to him, on the right, was a young man weeping, covering his face with his hands; and on the left was another, who stood erect, and, with outspread net, was waiting to seize the numerous people collected around him. As the pious man to whom the vision appeared was labouring to discover its import, he was thus instructed. The youth on the right laments, in the name of Christianity, that the Divine commands are neglected; the man on the left is awaiting the permission of the father to rage among faithless men. And truly, adds St. Cyprian, we already see the accomplishment of what was then prefigured; for the dreadful persecution which soon after broke out under the Emperor Decius shook the Christians as in a sieve, and aroused them from slumber to watchfulness in the Christian warfare.

The life of man upon earth is twofold: a life of slumber, which is devoted to sensual knowledge and enjoyment, and exists in the region of nature, and the world of deception in earthly space and time; and a life of watchfulness, which manifests itself as a striving, a seeking after an infinite, exalted, spiritual object. He who restored this true life—He who is the resuscitator and conductor of this existence—has shewn Himself in a threefold capacity, as the way, the truth, and the life. For man had indeed lost the true, the Divine life, since he had separated himself from God, the fountain of life; he had wandered from the way leading to happiness, as, by his abuse of freedom, he had turned aside from God; and as he had endeavoured to remove his subjection, his subordination to God, and had affected a similarity with God, and hence fallen into the lie of pride and self-seeking, the light of truth had also abandoned him. Thus, instead of the way, he had only mazy by-paths and tedious labyrinths, conducting to still more dreadful spiritual precipices; instead of life, only filthy sensualities, leaving the soul unsatisfied; instead of truth, error in all its sophistic and fantastic shapes.

As, then, the divine Logos appeared upon earth as life and truth, He smoothed for men the only way which can lead them out of error, and the night of death; and this way is the Way of the Cross. For, in order that man may desert self-seeking, the lie of pride, and abandonment to the sensual life, and return again to truth, to humility, to spiritual exertion, he must tread the road of self-denial; and therefore the Logos Himself walked before him in this path, in external lowliness, in free submission of His entire will to that of God.

The more rebellious the insubjection of the old man, the more deep and dreadful his moral decay, the more unlimited was the obedience of the heavenly Man, ending only with the death of the cross; and this freely chosen slave-like death, whereunto the heavenly Man resigned Himself, was the ample, and more than ample atonement for the false sovereignty assumed by the earthly man. With Him, on the same way of the most exalted self-denial, proceeded His virgin Mother, willingly taking part in His poverty, degradation, and suffering, that, in the communion of Saints, she might merit to be a mother and guide to mortal men. And who that looks upon these high models can cast aside the precepts of self-renunciation, and shun those salutary evils which find in the cross of Christ their true emblem and expression? The sword which pierced the soul of Mary should also wound every thoughtless Christian; the weight of the cross which lay on the Redeemer should also press upon all the vain and haughty, and cause them to bow cheerfully to the Divine sovereignty.

This latter, as we learn from the testimony of Sachino, occurred once in a very peculiar and, at first, mechanical way, on the fishing coasts in the East Indies. In the year 1564, when St. Francis Xavier had already preached the Gospel in every quarter, and erected crosses in most of the streets, a heathen was proceeding in quiet thoughtlessness along a road, on the side of which was one of these crosses. He had scarcely arrived at this cross, when it suddenly fell down, and struck him so violently on the shoulder, that he was seriously wounded. This occurrence was not indeed very extraordinary, for, owing to the constant rains which had lately prevailed, the cross stood so loosely in the ground as to be overturned by the first wind. The Indian, however, viewed this accident, and the wound which he had received, as a warning to embrace Christianity; and this he did as soon as he had recovered from his wound. And, in like manner, does some sudden misfortune frequently befall many a tepid or spiritually dead Christian; and happy is he if he consider it a call to a more perfect life. For, as every evil is a chastisement, a warning, or an occasion for self-denial, resignation, confidence, and victory in temptation, so does all that which the world terms evil stand in inmost connexion with living Christianity or the Christian life.

But if this be true, why, then, do we pray, "Deliver us from evil?" that is, from those sufferings which are the portion of this mortal life. Why do we petition for freedom from those seeming discords, without which our life could never be in unison with the Divine life? But, in truth, we do not pray, 'Deliver us from sickness, from sorrow, human opposition, and other calamities;'

but only, "Deliver us from evil." For when, through the mercy of God, one is freed from danger of death, another from oppressive want, a third from some great responsibility, is this a freedom from all troubles and burdens? Is it without meaning that it is written in Scripture, "One evil is past, another cometh?" Do the rude attacks of the weather, the insatiable desires of the body, the snares of enemies, the anxieties, dejection, and troubles of the heart, and all those other sufferings to which human life, by the sad decay of nature, is subject,—do these ever cease?

"Every creature," says the Apostle, "is subject to vanity in hope; for the creature also shall be freed from the servitude of corruption to the freedom of the glory of the children of God. But we know that every creature groans, and is in labour even until now." (Rom. viii.) Nature also being a life unfree, created by God, and opposed to the spirit, is striving incessantly for a personal, immortal existence; and, as it cannot attain to this object, it seeks to preserve itself by the constant propagation of its species, the individuals of which must all successively fall away and perish. Thus does created nature groan in constant labour with new forms; and shall then only rest when man, being again restored and arisen, she also shall receive immortality and freedom, being raised to a participation in the glory of the spirit, which was accomplished in Christ, as the First-born amongst His brethren, in His resurrection and ascension; but yet not before He had consummated His sacrifice on the cross.

If, then, in the petition, "Deliver us from evil," we refer to the collected sufferings which encounter us on the side of our spiritual as well as of our natural life, it is as if we desired to be transported, with sanctified spirits, with glorified bodies, into the delightful land of Paradise, where evil is found no more. And who will not be pardoned for so exalted a wish, reaching over all mountains and depths? Is not this the happiness of infants, guiltless, and purified from the ancient sin? By baptism the merits of Christ become theirs, so that they are received into the freedom and honour of children of God; and, departing this life before the development of the consciousness of death, they are entirely removed from all trial of freedom, and, consequently, from all danger of personal guilt.

But the exception which the Divine power and love here reserves to itself (without shewing, as it has been said, unmerited favouritism) *is* an exception, and therefore no rule.[1] The duty imposed upon us is, to combat, and to persevere in fidelity and obedience. This duty continues with life; that is, so long as there exists within us the opposition between the nature of the earthly and the grace of the heavenly Adam. Nor does this duty cease even at the gate or on the threshold of death; for it is then that our greatest care and watchfulness is re-

[1] To the thoughtful wanderer through life it must cause heartfelt pain, when he sees so many tender life-buds destroyed by the storms of the life of nature; but, as a Christian, he cannot imagine favouritism in God, if he consider that the Omniscient, for higher ends known only to Himself, can, in His providence, take the will for the deed. Let us hear the Wise Man: " The just man, if he be prevented by death, shall be in rest. For venerable old age is not that of long time, nor counted by the number of years, but the understanding of man is grey hairs, and a spotless life is old age. He pleased God, and was beloved; and

quired. This was beautifully illustrated in a very extraordinary circumstance by the holy Anselm, Archbishop of Canterbury.

Riding with some attendants to his manor at Herse, a hare pursued by the dogs sprung from a thicket, and ran under his horse for refuge. Anselm stopped; the animal remained trembling between the feet of the horse, and the hounds stood at bay. The servants laughed; but Anselm saw in the occurrence subject for serious thought. 'You,' he said, 'may laugh; but for this unfortunate creature there is no joy: it is pursued and surrounded by its enemies; and, to preserve its life, it flies to us, and implores protection. And, indeed, thus will it be with our souls when on the point of leaving the body and this earth. Their invisible foes, who, so long as they were united with the life of the senses, pursued them on the crooked ways of vice, will then encompass them, in order, by their impetuous attacks, to plunge them into eternal death. How will the poor unfortunate soul then cry for help; and with what trouble will it look for a deliverer to free it from danger!' Thus spoke the Saint. He then bad the hounds be still, and suffered the hare to depart.

Where is the frivolous or self-sufficient sophist, who

living among sinners, he was translated. He was taken away, lest wickedness should alter his understanding, or deceit beguile his soul. For the bewitching of vanity obscureth good things, and the wandering of concupiscence overturneth the innocent mind. Being made perfect in a short space, he fulfilled a long time; for his soul pleased God, therefore He hastened to bring him out of the midst of iniquities: but the people see this, and understand not, nor lay up such things in their hearts." (Wisdom iv. 7-14.)

will not acknowledge that this occurrence, with its exquisite allegory, is deeply calculated to impress with terror any unholy soul? Very many high-boasting natures have discoursed most magnanimously on death, who, at last, when the little hour struck, comported themselves far differently; and who, if in their last moments they had had the power, would have spoken far otherwise. Death, on the side of the natural life, is, in and for itself, no evil; for decay is the lot of nature, which it seeks to escape by constant new forms. But at present, even for nature, it is an evil; for, through the sin of man, it is not merely a decay and a change, but also a real destruction; and hence it appears in terrors, whereat nature herself must shudder.

But the destruction by death must appear to us still more terrible, when we reflect that it annihilates, at least for the present, the whole being of man as such; that it tears asunder the union of the natural and spiritual life, of which the essence, man, consists. What an awful stroke is this upon the entire being and life of man, whose spirit must await until, on the day of resurrection, the voice of the Almighty shall go forth to nature, to bring together the old and mouldering limbs, in order that the spirit of man may be again united with the other active part of its personality, and again come forward in its perfect human being! And if we seriously consider that "it is appointed for all men once to die, and then the judgment," how can death appear devoid of dread, which in one moment puts an end to all existence and merit, to all trial and temptation, to all vice and virtue, and which decides our doom for eternity?

For as a predominant class of men in our time may comfort themselves with the imagination of a hell, or rather of an intermediate region, wherein the souls of the departed are gifted with a gradual moral improvement, and a gradual beatification, exposed, however, according to their wanderings and depravity, to many trials and temptations, and purified by sufferings, and thus led to a knowledge of the light, and to saving repentance; this imagination may appeal to certain plausibilities which abound in the broad land of fantastic dreams; but the Catholic Christian and philosopher must ever reject such fables, as they are opposed to faith,—that is, to Christian truth,—even although their folly were not evident from the fundamental view of life, and of the exertion and end of a spiritual being.

For as the happiness or misery of a pure spirit must depend upon the moment when it decides for or against God, so must the eternal lot of the human soul rest upon the chain of trials to which it is exposed on earth, and upon the last moment of its mortal life, which is the threshold of eternity. It is indeed true, that the justified, who at their death are found still tepid and imperfect, dwell in an abode (the Church suffering) where they supply for those sacrifices which, during life, they have not offered, and undergo those pains which before they were unwilling to endure; they are purified by means of their ardent aspirations towards God, yet for them the time of merit is past; that time of which the Lord spoke, when He said: "Work whilst you have the day; the night approaches wherein no man can work;" neither can they any more be subject to personal probation, which belongs only to the day,—to the time of life on this earth.

Herein lies the terror of death, that it is the hour of birth to happiness, or to misery eternal. Although we may truly say with the prisoner mentioned by John Moschus, 'Since Christ has died, man dies no more;' yet this consoling truth must be understood with the condition revealed to St. John: "He who has conquered will not be injured by the second death." By his descent from the earthly Adam he must be subject to the first death, not, however, to the second; for he will go forth anew in the resurrection of life. O happy death, which may be called a victory,—a victory over all the powers of lies and darkness! But before this victory is gained, we must sustain the combat, and who is so presumptuous as to behold its approach without dismay?

Alphonsus, King of Arragon, was accustomed, as we learn from Æneas Sylvius, to entertain daily a number of indigent people. Amongst these there was a blind man who particularly attracted his attention. One day the king asked him, whether he did not find his privation of sight very afflicting? The man replied, 'Without the assistance of the grace of God, no blind man could desire life, so great and so devoid of comfort would his misery be, especially if he had once enjoyed the light.' The king inquired, 'Would you desire to leave this life?' 'No,' answered he. 'But as you are so miserable,' rejoined the king, 'should it not be your wish to be freed from such calamity?' 'Without doubt,' replied the blind man, 'were I but certain which way I should take, and that a greater misery did not await me.' 'But do you not know that the kingdom of bliss lies open to the virtuous?' 'This I have often heard, and I know well that all good will be mine, if I die happily; but who is secure that he will die a happy death?' Alphonsus answered, 'You have spoken well, and profoundly as a theologian.'

Thus we see that it appeared more desirable to this blind man to grope along for many years in his earthly blindness, than to hasten to that place where the Church prays, 'that eternal rest may be his portion, and that perpetual light may shine upon him.' And if we wish to follow up the important meaning of the blind man, we may say, that a happy death is morally certain to him who can bear testimony to himself, that he has considered and received the temporal evils of this life as a remedy against those which are eternal.

If, therefore, we consider temporal evils as essential constituents of this earthly life of probation, and under the petition, "Deliver us from evil," include also these passing evils, we pray for deliverance from them only so far as the divine Providence shall have ordained for our salvation. For, instead of freeing us entirely from all burdens, which, since the destruction entailed by sin, is neither conceivable nor necessary to the state of man, Providence has three other far more exalted ways to impart to us succour.

The first is by those mild consolations whereby we are strengthened to support all future evils with resignation, and even with joy. Thus St. Paul, when encompassed by dangers of every description, persecuted by deadly foes, and straitened by hunger, by sickness, by tempests, and a hundred other calamities, was enabled to exclaim, " I overbound with joy in all my troubles!" A second and third kind of succour is, when the Divine goodness repays our evils by other favours, and, as we see in the person of Joseph in prison, converts our present evils into greater goods.

When, therefore, we pray to God, "Deliver us from evil," our intention is not, as it were, to bind His hands, by desiring Him to keep from us all calamity; but we implore Him not to allow any of those evils to befal us which might prevent the sanctification of His name. The Church, in truth, does pray, ' From all evils deliver us, O Lord!' but the continuation soon manifests her meaning: 'From all sin deliver us, O Lord! From Thy wrath, from sudden and unprovided death, from the snares of the devil, from anger, from hatred and all ill-will, from the spirit of uncleanness, from eternal death, deliver us, O Lord!' These are the evils from which we beg the Almighty entirely to preserve us; whereas temporal sufferings and the calamities of this life we commit wholly to His wisdom and goodness. "I have raised my eyes to the mountains, whence my help cometh. My help is from the Lord, who made heaven and earth. Behold, He will not slumber, nor will He sleep who preserves Israel. The Lord preserve thee from all evil; the Lord preserve thy soul. The Lord preserve thy entering in and thy going out, now and for ever." (Ps. cxx.)

CHAPTER XVIII.

Amen.

"BETTER," says Solomon, "is the end than the beginning of a discourse;" or, as we may likewise explain it, better is the end than the beginning of any prayer or occupation. But how is the end of a discourse better than the beginning? He who commences to speak knows not how far and whither he may go, or in what labyrinths he may be entangled; but as he approaches the conclusion, he beholds his labours about to terminate, and the desired object of his labours within his grasp. And in our occupations, the end is better than the beginning, since a good beginning cannot always secure a happy termination, whereas a happy termination justifies a confidence of the goodness of the beginning. In prayer also the end is better than the beginning; for, as Cardinal Hugo remarks, he alone can derive profit from his prayer who perseveres therein to the end.

But may this truth be equally applied to the Lord's

Prayer? It commences with the address to our heavenly Father; it concludes with the little word 'amen.' In some Greek versions of the Gospels there is, indeed, the termination, "For Thine is the kingdom, the power, and glory, for ever and ever;" but this, like the close of the Psalms, "Glory be to the Father, and to the Son, and to the Holy Ghost," appears to be an addition placed by the hand of man; for St. Cyprian, Tertullian, St. Jerome, St. Augustine, St. Ambrose, and others, make no mention of this conclusion; but, on the contrary, St. Jerome terms the word 'amen' the seal of the Lord's Prayer. Can we, then, say that here the end is better than the beginning? What is there great in the simple little 'amen?'

We might, moreover, inquire, as all the prayers of the Church which are addressed to the Father end with the words, "Through Jesus Christ our Lord"—words which manifest and acknowledge that our admission to the Father, and the granting of our requests, are obtained solely through the merits of Christ—we might inquire, wherefore this highest and universal prayer is not terminated in the same manner? It may be replied, that Christ in person pronounced this prayer with His Apostles; for as Man amongst men, and as Head of the Church, He prayed not for Himself, but for His brethren, and in their name; and therefore He did not add, "through Jesus Christ our Lord," but only the word 'amen.' But this explanation is not sufficient; for, to speak truly, if, in human discourse, a good end is better than a good beginning, in this divine discourse also the end is by no means inferior to the beginning; and in the word 'amen' there is no less power and elevation than in the words, "Our Father, who art in heaven."

For if we consider this 'amen' more closely, and examine the meaning of this word, we shall find that it admits of many explanations. Sometimes it is interpreted, *let it be, so be it;* at other times, *indeed, verily;* and frequently in the holy Scriptures it signifies *truth, wisdom,* and *reality.* Thus Isaias foretells a time when the heathens shall no more swear by their gods and goddesses, but by the God AMEN; that is, by the God of truth,—by the true God. And still more expressly do we read in the Book of Revelations, "Thus speaks He, who is the Amen; the true and faithful witness, the beginning (that is, the author) of all the creatures of God;" where we say that the word 'amen' implies the Eternal Word. No less evident is the meaning of St. Paul in his Epistle to the Corinthians: "The Son of God, Jesus Christ, who through me is made known to you, is not Yes and No, but Yes; for all the promises of God are in Him, Yes;" that is, all strengthened and fulfilled in His reality and truth; "by Him, therefore, we cry to God Amen, to the glory of God through us." In other words, we confess that whatever God has promised us in and through Christ is Amen or truth.

Thus the "amen" wherewith the Lord's Prayer concludes is no less important than the invocation, "Our Father." The commencement is the raising of the soul to the Eternal Father; the termination is the sealing of the whole through the Eternal Son; consequently the commencement and the termination are bound in essential unity, and the simple 'amen' has no less signification than the words, "through Jesus Christ our Lord," wherewith the prayers of the Church are concluded.

Thus far as to the highest and most absolute meaning of the word. Now let us examine the manifold senses in which it is applied. It is of great consequence to observe what situation this word occupies in our discourse—whether it be placed at the beginning or the end. Every one conversant with the Gospel is aware who it is that ordinarily commences his discourse with the word 'amen;' it is He who is Himself the absolute truth, the real 'Amen.' "Amen, I say unto you; Amen, amen, I say unto you," were His common, His peculiar mode of speaking; signifying nothing less than, 'Thus speaks to you the eternal truth.' When the Apostle desired, in like manner, to prefix to his words the seal of truth, he did not commence with 'amen,' as he spoke not in his own name, but in that of Christ; and therefore he contented himself with the assurance, "I speak the truth in Christ, I lie not; a faithful word, and worthy of all acceptation."

The word 'amen,' whenever employed by us, is placed at the end. And what would we hereby signify? Principally our confidence and the firm assurance of our faith, and also our inmost desire of the accomplishment of our wishes and petitions. Thus it is written in the 105th Psalm: "Blessed be the Lord our God, from eternity to eternity; and let all the people reply, Amen, amen." This inmost and unconditional desire was the spirit which called forth that great and noble exclamation from the holy doctor and martyr Cyprian, when, in presence of a numerous assembly, his condemnation for being a Christian was publicly pronounced. And what was this exclamation? The sentence of the Proconsul was read to him, decreeing that Thascius Cyprianus should be put to death by the sword. The Saint, raising his voice, replied, 'Amen.' And was not this a noble 'amen?' With it he sealed his cheerful acceptance of his condemnation, for the greater glory of the Divine name, for his entrance into the kingdom of light, for the joyful fulfilment of the will of God, and for the atonement of all his past sins. And when we, in a far less difficult situation, pronounce 'amen' at the close of our prayer, what do we wish to signify? Our confidence in God, that He will fulfil our petitions (Psalm xix.), and our confidence that we shall observe what we have promised; "For with God it is not yes and no, but always yes."

And is there with us also a constant 'Yes?' "Alas," sighs the Apostle, "the good which I would, I do not; and the evil which I would not, that I do; I rejoice according to the interior man in the law of God; but I see another law in my members in opposition with the law of the spirit, which holds me captive." (Rom. vii.) Is not this the history of the life of man—the constant opposition of lies with truth—the unhappy impediment to every human 'amen?'

On this subject we will find space for an example, which may suffice for a thousand others. Edgar, one of the ancient Saxon kings, had been deprived by death of his wife, and had now determined to enter upon a second marriage. He had heard extolled the beauty and virtue of Elfrida, daughter of the Earl of Devonshire; and he resolved to commission Ethelwold, his favourite minister, to visit the far-famed lady; and, if he should think her worthy, to demand her for the king. Ethelwold came and saw, and not only found that fame had spoken truly, but was himself so captivated, that, forgetful of his fidelity to his sovereign, he resolved to make no mention of his commission, but to seek the hand of Elfrida for himself. Having obtained her consent, he returned to his master, and by his assurance that Elfrida was not worthy of the hand of so powerful a king, removed from Edgar's mind all intention of the marriage. After some time, he solicited permission to espouse Elfrida himself. The king granted his prayer, and dismissed him; and Ethelwold departed, and conducted Elfrida to one of his hunting-castles, hoping that there she would be concealed from the king.

Notwithstanding all his precautions, his wife's beauty could not remain concealed, and at length it was reported even to the king. The curiosity no less than the anger of Edgar was now excited; and, to learn what was really the truth, he ordered a chase, and by taking a wide circuit arrived at the castle of Ethelwold. The nobleman had no sooner, to his great alarm, heard of the approach of the king, than he hastened to reveal to his wife the whole history of the transaction, and entreated her to pardon the deception his too great love had caused him to be guilty of towards herself and the king, and implored her with tears that she would, as far as possible, conceal her beauty, and appear in her simplest dress.

But how did Elfrida act in an affair so perilous to her husband? Did she disfigure her face with false colouring, and clothe herself in plain attire, and seek by every means to conceal her charms? Far from it. The temptation was too strong for this daughter of Eve. Forgetful alike of her husband and of her little son, she arrayed herself with her choicest ornaments, and displayed her beauty in all its brilliancy. Her own infidelity, and the death of her husband, were the consequences. Here we behold a threefold struggle of human passion against truth and fidelity. Ethelwold violated his plighted word to his sovereign, and forgot his 'amen' by a temptation of envy; Elfrida forgot the 'amen' she had sworn to God and to her husband, being led away by the suggestions of vanity; Edgar, in fine, despised the 'amen' of a state sanctified by God when to the passion which had already taken possession of his heart he associated revenge.

Other events similar to this, wherewith the history of man so lamentably abounds, evidently shew, however great and noble a word 'amen' may be with respect to the sanctity and omnipotence of God, it is in the mouth of man a dangerous and insidious word. Its import and application in the Lord's Prayer is sevenfold, as it is a seal to each petition. Thus, if we expressed ourselves fully, we might say, 'Thy will be done. Amen. Forgive us, as we forgive others. Amen. Lead us not into temptation. Amen. But deliver us from evil. Amen.' But what testimony does not this 'amen' give against us, if we do not seek a knowledge of the Divine will, or follow up its dictates; if we do not pardon our enemies, if we freely expose ourselves to temptations, and if we ourselves sow evil?

This melancholy difference between the divine and the human 'amen' was in the mind of St. Paul when he declared, "that God alone is true, and all men deceitful." For if even the holy and sincere are encompassed by many deceptions which darken their understanding and weaken their will, what will become of those who deliberately oppose the 'amen' of God, His person, His power, and His fruitful love, as well as His positive revelation, in order thus to throw off all subjection to their Creator? "Who say to the prophets, See not what is right; speak what is pleasing to us; prophesy for us deceits." (Isaias xxx.) Will their 'no,' their negation, destroy the 'yes,' the affirmation, of God?

Of this we behold a remarkable example in Rodolph, king of the Heruleans. He was about to engage in a decisive battle with the Lombards; but as he imagined himself secure of victory at the very commencement of the contest, he remained in his tent playing at chess. However, that he might not be ignorant of the progress of the battle, and that he might be informed of the defeat of the enemy, he ordered one of his shield-bearers to ascend a high tree which stood before the tent, and to watch both armies; but added this extraordinary warning, 'Take care not to tell me that my Heruleans fly; for otherwise thy head shall be struck off!' The man in the tree observed his instructions to the letter; whenever he was asked how affairs proceeded, he always replied, 'Very well! very well!' At length he burst out into a cry which he had long restrained. 'What is it?' exclaimed the king; 'are my Heruleans slain?' 'Sire,' replied the other from his watch-place, 'my head is at stake; I have not said it, but yourself!' Thereupon the king sprang forward to arm himself for the contest; but it was too late: the Lombards rushed impetuously on, and Rodolph, with his attendants, fell beneath their swords.

Not very differently from this hero do the great host of those behave who will not hear the positive truth: "Speak to us what is pleasing; see for us errors; turn aside out of the path; let the Holy One of Israel cease from before us." Speak not to us of the holiness of God, which will display itself as justice to the disobedient; picture not to us those awful views of the misery of a soul separated from God, of the darkness of hell, of the fire which never dies; as if by this "Say not," by this unwillingness to hear, their cause would be improved, and their danger would cease to exist.

Thus it happened with a native of Holland mentioned by Erasmus. He was seated at a splendid banquet, but somewhat too near the fire, for the end of his robe of state began to burn. His neighbour remarked it, and whispering to him, said, 'I have something to tell you.' The magnanimous reveller, who here, in the midst of his elysium, desired not the intrusion of any care, considered these words thoughtfully, and replied, 'If it be any thing sad or unpleasant, defer it for the present, for at table all should be joyful.' 'It is not, indeed,' answered the other, 'very pleasant.' 'If so, tell it me after the banquet.' True to his practical wisdom, he persevered through the entire feast, and then, turning to his neighbour, inquired, 'What is it you would say to me?' His friend stood not in need of any preface, but pointed to his robe, which was very much burnt. The man was enraged, and exclaimed, 'Why did you not warn me in due time?' The other replied, 'I did intend; but you did not wish it.'

How many in this mortal life continue at the banquet of luxury, and dream on in vain security, without any serious consideration! But they have placed themselves too near the fire. Is not the robe of every one who gives way to his natural lusts already on fire? Are not unrighteousness and impurity termed in Scripture a fire, which burns into the inmost marrow, and prevails over every good seed of life? Yet the thoughtless sinner, so long as it is granted to him to partake of the banquet of nature, rejects admonition, and then at length, when the table is removed, when his life is decayed, and his soul must take her leave from this visible world, he is willing to pray to his eternal Father : 'As I can no longer enjoy the goods of this world, deliver me from evil,' that thus his prayer may be sealed with the Divine 'amen.' But this last unchangeable 'amen,' to be pronounced to salvation, presupposes the human 'amen' to be a word of true, earnest, and righteous desire.

It is not, therefore, without meaning, that in all other public prayers, as in the collects of the Mass, the 'Amen' is always pronounced by those who minister at the altar, or by the choir, in the name of the people, whereas in the Lord's Prayer, they pronounce the words, "Deliver us from evil," and the priest answers, "Amen." For in these prayers, which are concluded by the people's 'amen,' this 'amen' signifies their desire that their petition may be hearkened to and granted; but in the Lord's Prayer, the priest replies, 'Amen;' for here, standing between Christ and the people, he announces the fulfilment of the Divine promises, which is necessarily connected with a high and indispensable condition—the correspondence of man. As, therefore, the 'amen' of God expresses His unchangeable truth and absolute holiness of will, so also should the human 'amen' be an expression and seal of firm resolution and fixedness, which can be manifested and crowned only by perseverance unto the end.

Thus, even in this respect is the proverb of Solomon well founded, "Better is the end than the beginning of a discourse;" better is the end than the beginning of a Christian life. For albeit by baptism we enter in a heavenly manner into a participation of the merits and co-membership of Christ, still is fidelity in the combat of great importance; and if the commencement be often renewed by revivifying penance, the same condition still remains, "He who perseveres unto the end, he shall be saved." He, however, who awakens within us the good will, gives also the accomplishing, that the redeemed and the blessed may all unite in the praises of the Divine name, which, as St. John is witness, begin and close with 'Amen.' 'Amen. Benediction, and glory, and wisdom, and thanksgiving, and honour, and power, and strength to our God, for ever and ever. Amen.'

'AMEN.'

Ave Maria.

WELL known in ancient and in modern times has been the fable contained in Greek mythology, of the heavenly messenger, Pandora, who, despite her beautiful and much-promising name, brought nothing but evil upon the earth. For thus the fable speaks: "When Prometheus had stolen the sacred fire from heaven, and had infused it into mortal man, Jupiter, to revenge the crime, sent this virgin, the first woman, to the earth. He entrusted to her a casket, which was outwardly adorned with many a dazzling and precious gem, but which contained within evils that could not be numbered, and that, like a spiral snake, awaited only the opening of the casket, instantly to burst forth." But, as all the fables of mythology are rich in variations, so this also is sometimes differently narrated. To justify old Jupiter, it has been said, that the casket of Pandora was filled with the best gifts that could be conferred on man; that when this imprudent virgin opened it, the inconstant goods flew out, and that when the covering of the casket closed, only hope remained within. The traces of allegory which are contained in this fabulous narration gave occasion to the earliest teachers of the Christian Church of many beautiful reflections and of many motives of instruction. If ever there existed a true Pandora, remark Tertullian, St. Irenæus, and St. Fulgentius, it was indeed that illustrious Virgin who gave birth to the God-Man, and who therefore conveyed to mankind the fulness of all good gifts; for this is the signification of the name Pandora. As there was one father of all men in the order of nature, the ancient or earthly Adam, and one father of mankind, in the order of grace and of the spirit, the new and heavenly Adam; so there is one mother of the human race, whom we may liken to Pandora, for by her rashness she caused all the evil that has since existed on the earth, and the loss of all celestial goods, save the hope of again receiving salvation by the Saviour who was promised to her. To her there stands opposed the new Pandora, " the mother of beautiful love, of knowledge, and of holy hope," who, as she is the mother of Him who raised mankind from its fall, may be called the mother of all men in the order of grace.

To her, therefore, for two reasons, the highest reverence is due,—a reverence which is ever given to her in living gratitude through the communion of Saints by the Church militant. For she was not only chosen and made worthy to become the virgin mother of the new, the heavenly Adam, for although descended from the old Adam, she partook not of his guilt, but, as a spiritual and free creature, she was deeply instructed in this mystery. The free consent of her will was required, which was not given without the sacrifice of the most perfect obedience.

But the words of the celestial ambassador, by which he announced the glad tidings of man's redemption, and that salutation of joy and veneration with which the holy Elizabeth met the royal Virgin, are the same with which the Catholic Church daily honours the mother of its Founder. It generally repeats them immediately after the Lord's Prayer, as they are intimately connected with it—"Hail, full of grace; the Lord is with thee: blessed art thou among women, and blessed is the fruit of thy womb!"

The greeting of the archangel is read in three different ways. By the Orientals it is said, "PEACE BE TO THEE."[1] In the Greek text we find, "REJOICE; BE OF GOOD COURAGE;"[2] and in Latin, "HAIL."[3] These three expressions of peace, joy, and benevolence, have all the same signification; they all denote the blessings that were lost by sin, and that were restored by our redemption.

For when the first man tore away the bond of peace which united him with his God, and placed himself in opposition to Him, his Creator,—when he stood in enmity with himself and all nature, he lost, together with the pure light of the knowledge of God, all joy that could beatify him; he forfeited the friendship and benevolence of God, for God beheld within him nothing but contradiction and lies, so that grace departed from him, and a curse fell upon him; for what else is a curse, if a departure, an estrangement from God be not? But that all these infinite blessings that were lost to man by the rash disobedience of Eve, are restored by the humble obedience of the Virgin (in as far as she consented to become the mother of the Redeemer), is expressed in its triple form by the word of salutation spoken to her by the angelical herald of peace.

The ancient Romans were accustomed, when they announced a declaration of war to a neighbouring state, to send a messenger bearing a lance pointed with iron and stained with blood, which he brandished over the confines of the hostile territory; but when peace was proclaimed, he bore in his hand, as an emblem thereof, a green branch of the olive-tree. Thus the generations of Pagan antiquity could imagine only enmity and fierce hostility between themselves

---

[1] Salem. [2] Χαιρε. [3] Ave.

and God; they considered Him as an offended Lord seeking dire revenge, who for ever wielded his blood-red javelin, and who would be appeased only by sacrifices of propitiation, until the heavenly messenger came and bore to the holy Virgin of the house of David, and through her to all mankind, the olive-branch of peace, when he saluted her with this word, "Salem"—Peace be to thee.

This is the first signification that is conveyed to our mind, as often as we repeat these words, "Hail Mary:" Peace be to thee, and peace be to us, through the Prince of Peace, our Saviour and our Redeemer, who was born to us from thee. But by these same words we express also a second gift, which flows immediately from the first,—the return of true joy; for as soon as the blessed Mary appeared upon this earth as the bright aurora of a new and heavenly day, when she had conceived Him who is the true light and life of men, the path that lay before him again became gloriously bright; the Divine will was again made manifest to us, and the strength and grace to obey it were imparted to us; we can now walk with exultation amid the sorrows and transient evils of this our earthly life, for we know that the love which God bears to us will conduct us to our destiny. With reason, then, does the Church salute the holy Virgin as the "Cause of our joy."

But the most ordinary and almost universal signification given to the angel's greeting is this: "Ave," "Hail." By this we express our grateful and reverential benevolence to her who is the pure lily of the human race,—the first, the most excellent amongst mortals; on whom, on account of her spiritual purity and loveliness, the plenitude of Divine benevolence reposes. And in truth, what an exalted signification does this salutation—"Ave"—bear! According to the custom of this world, we do not greatly embarrass ourselves with forms of salutation and courtesy; for, however earnestly we may seem to utter them, we give only a superficial signification to them. But if this greeting be considered in the full depth of its import as a testimony of friendship, of heartfelt benevolence, and as a sign of communion in feeling and desire, let us hearken to the Apostle of Divine love, the blessed St. John: " Whosoever continueth not in the doctine of Christ, hath not God. If any man come to you, and bring not this doctrine, receive him not into your house, nor say to him, Ave: for he that saith to him, Ave, communicateth with his wicked works." (2 John i. 9.)

If these words sound harshly on the ears of some, as twice strange in the mouth of that Apostle who for ever exhorteth us to love, let such persons examine their real signification, and they will find that these words inculcate not hatred of our neighbours, but that they admonish us to enter into no intercourse with the enemies and blasphemers of Christ; for this would lead us to associate ourselves in their wicked thoughts and opinions. But what we have at present to conñider in these words is, that St. John esteems this form of salutation—" Ave"—as the symbol and expression of the most intimate friendship and affectionate unanimity.

Now, to whom amongst mortals has such a form of salutation—" Ave"—been addressed by the Omnipotent? When He speaks to those who have burdened themselves and offended Him by their crimes, thus His words of thunder peal: " Adam, where art thou?" " Cain, what hast thou done?" And, on the contrary, when He speaks to his friends, to the patriarchs and holy seers of days bygone, we hear sweet words of consolation and joy that are spoken in reference to the approaching mystery of redemption. When the time of its completion came, the blessed Mary (and all mankind) was greeted with this word of friendship, " Ave." She was greeted as full of grace, as one in whom the choicest graces of God resided. If the grace of God be the infusion of the Holy Ghost, that is, a revealing and bestowing of Divine love to men, which incites them to a return of love for love, which imparts to their actions a spiritual dignity, beauty, and worth, upon whom should the abundance of this spiritual dignity and beauty flow down from the treasures of Heaven, if not upon her of whom Jesus Christ our Lord, who is grace and truth itself, was born; upon her who, by her own free choice, and in the most humble obedience, took part in all the bitter sufferings of her 'divine Son, nor sought for a moment her own happiness or joy? Phidias, the most famed of the sculptors of antiquity, completed a statue, the master-work of his art, in which magnitude and beauty vied with each other in extorting the admiration of the beholders; for the Pallas or Juno that was represented by this statue was seated upon a throne, and with the crown of its head almost touched the roof of the hall in which it was placed. Among the numbers of those, wise and unwise, who crowded to contemplate this wondrous work, to condemn and to praise, there came one more observant, as he thought, than others, who was not content to form his judgment by their remarks or opinions. "In this work which you behold before you," he exclaimed, "the sculptor has sinned against the first principles of art; for when the statue shall wish to raise itself from its feet, it must either fracture its head, or make its way through the roof of this hall!" When the artist had heard this wise sentence, he came forward and said: "Thou hast judged well, my friend; but I have provided against the evil of which you complain, as, for the formation of this statue, I prudently selected marble of such a nature, that the statue shall never be able to arise into a standing posture."

That to which the critic objected in ridiculous earnestness, and which the artist, with serious sportiveness, refuted, finds its full force and signification in the world of spiritual creatures. For what can be more perilous to man, before continued and repeated trial, than complacency in himself, than the attempt to raise and exalt himself in his pride, and, in an affected comparison of himself with God, to exclaim with that foolish one of whom Isaias speaks, "I will ascend to the Heavens (by piercing through the atmospheric canopy), and I will be like to the Most High."

But as no one of created beings was ever endowed with qualities equal to those enjoyed by the Holy Virgin, or raised to the excellence eminent as that to which she was exalted who saw herself high above all mortals in the sublime dignity of Mother of God, so she becomes more venerable to us by that profound humility, which taught her to give the glory to the Divine Omnipotence, and not only to name herself, but always to act as the lowly handmaid of the Lord. But the more humble, and the more concealed from human gaze, the more noble in the sight of God, and the more rich in grace was this royal Virgin. Thus bloomed this wondrous and lovely flower, turned ever to the Sun of Heaven, without the faintest tinge of complacency in herself. The angel, therefore, bowed himself in reverence before her, and said, "Hail, full of grace; the Lord is with thee; blessed art thou amongst women!"

There are many ways in which the Lord may be with men,—by His omnipotence, by His protection in danger, by His consolation in sorrow and mourning, by His friendship and grace. Thus, when He commissioned Moses to go to Pharaoh and to the children of Israel, He says, "Fear not; for I am with thee." To the patriarch Isaac he addresses the same words: "Fear not; for I am with thee." And in the Psalm we read: "With him (the just man) I am in his tribulation; I will deliver him, and I will glorify him." And again: "If I should walk in the midst of the shades of death, I will not fear; for thou, O Lord, art with me." In all and in every one of these ways the Lord was with Mary. In her He manifested His omnipotence, when in her person He united the highest dignity of mother of his divine Son with the glory of virginity, which she herself declared, when, addressing her holy cousin, she sang, " He that is mighty hath done great things to me, and holy is His name." He was with her by His especial protection, guidance, and consolation in many afflictions, troubles, and dangers, and in that alliance which is formed between the creature and the Creator by Divine grace ; more wonderfully still was the Lord with her when she became the living ark of the new covenant, the temple of the eternal " Word made flesh," and thereby the most exalted of all creatures, and by preeminence " blessed amongst women ;" for she conceived in her womb, and gave birth to Him who destroyed the curse brought with Him, and, as mother of the spiritual Father and of all men, she was and is our mother in the spiritual order of grace.

And this we gratefully confess and repeat as often as we speak to her with this salutation, " Hail !" and with a holy and more firm confidence we supplicate her protection, as to her, the " mother of God," there is given a power in heaven greater than to all the blessed ; for as He, the " fruit of her womb," is true God and true Man, she gave birth to the person of the Son of God, according to His human nature ; she is, therefore, although not mother of the Godhead, mother of God ; for Christ, the God-Man, is her Son, and as the divine word, Christ, is now eternally God and Man in one person, so shall she eternally possess the dignity of mother of God.

As mother of the Redeemer of the world she feels a deep compassion for all sinners ; she can desire nothing more earnestly than that His merits should be applied to all ; and as she, the mother of the heavenly Adam, brought forth Him who is the true life of the world, we cry to her, in the conclusion of the *Ave Maria*, according to a most ancient practice of the Church, that she would exert her powerful intercession for us mortals and for us sinners now, and more powerfully at the hour of our death, and in that great and awful hour that shall separate us from nature and from the world, and which shall determine our doom for ever; that, being freed from all evil, we may arrive at that happy destiny which is promised to us in that word, *Amen.*

www.ingramcontent.com/pod-product-compliance
Lightning Source LLC
Chambersburg PA
CBHW031333230426
43670CB00006B/330